You Can Do It!

Presented to

_____

_____

By

_____

_____

Date

_____

You Can Do It!

Lives of great men all remind us
We can make our lives sublime
And, departing, leave behind us
Footprints on the sands of time.
—Henry Wadsworth Longfellow

Published and distributed by Executive Books, Mechanicsburg, Pennsylvania

Library of Congress Catalog Card Number 92-60702
ISBN 0-937539-19-8

Printed in the United States of America
1 2 3 4 5 6 — 95 94 93 92

CONTENTS

FOREWORD

Believe it or not, we all have an area of influence in our lives. Whether we are well-known, or not, there are few of us who pass through life without affecting—for good or bad—the lives of others and there is a need for us to be aware of this powerful influence.

There are those who believe that what they do is of no concern to others. Life is not lived that way. What they do—what we all do—helps or hurts others, whether we want it to or not.

In reading the first edition of You Can Do It!, I was impressed to find so many leaders from such diverse areas of life had MADE time to share their experiences and to give advice to encourage others.

The issue of role models was discussed recently by some NBA players. I thought Karl Malone, the Utah Jazz all-star, put it well when he said, "We don't choose to be role models, we are chosen. Our only choice is to be a good one or a bad one." He's right, like it or not, parents, athletes, business leaders, clergy, celebrities, et al, do influence others by their conduct. Young people especially look up to them and tend to believe that what they do is always acceptable.

Pat Williams is Chief Operating Officer/General Manager of the Orlando Magic, the National Basketball Association (NBA) franchise in Orlando, Florida. The 53-year-old protégé of the late Bill Veeck is widely recognized throughout the sports world as the consumate promoter and astute talent scout, with 31 years sports experience to his credit.

Before assuming the reigns of the Orlando Magic, Williams was general manager of the Philadelphia 76ers for 12 years, and through personnel moves played a major role in bringing the NBA title to Philadelphia. Prior to that, he was general manager of the Chicago Bulls and Atlanta Hawks. While in Chicago, he raised average game attendance at Chicago Stadium from 3,700 to 10,000 per game.

Pat's public persona is that of the ultimate successful sports promoter, the man who brought the NBA to Orlando and signed Saquille O'Neal. His name recognition in the sports community is perhaps as high as any nonplaying sports figure. He is also recognized as one of the country's premier motivational and humorous speakers. Pat has authored 13 books, including his version of the birth of the Orlando Magic, entitled Making Magic.

With his wife, Jill, he co-authored a #1 best seller entitled Rekindles, a recounting of how they saved their marriage through adoption. They also wrote Twelve Part Harmony, a book on adoption. At this writing, the Williams family includes 18 children—four biological and 14 adopted.

(Continued on page 296)

My particular interest in this book, which Bob Budler has put together, is because of the effect it has on young people. My wife, Jill, and I, are raising 18 children in our home. I often think of what author James Baldwin had to say about youngsters: "They've never been interested in listening to their elders, but, they have never failed to imitate them."

We, as parents, need to set good examples for our children to get them off to a good start in life. If they choose to close their ears to our advice, we need to live so they can imitate us. The few minutes it takes to read one of the guest author entries in this book will be time well spent by young people and adults alike.

Mother Teresa once noted: "We may not be able to feed 100 children, but, we can each feed one. Helping out at a time in their lives when they are easily influenced can mean the difference in how they fare in life." This was brought home to me in an incident resulting from a lesson in this book.

A teacher in Ohio had a student in her class who had spent his entire life in and out of foster homes and institutions. By happenstance, just before the Christmas break, she chose the Dave Thomas material in the book for a class discussion. Thomas, who founded Wendy's, like the youth, was orphaned at birth and never knew his maternal parents.

After class, the student told the teacher he'd been depressed and was contemplating suicide over the holiday. He was so moved by what Thomas has done with his life that he changed his mind. That's what one good example can do. Scores of other reports have been received documenting how the book has impacted the lives of other young people.

If we are truly concerned about our families, our communities, and, our nation, then we must all be willing to accept the responsibility of exemplary living. This book is filled with people who have accepted the challenge. Why? Because it is simply the right thing to do. Never before in our history have we so needed to be pointed in the right direction.

Jonathan C. Cutler, of the International Youth Services Conference, observed: "If you are a mentor—even for one youngster at a time—I promise you will leave this world a better place than you found it!"

He's correct—and each of us can do it, too!

INTRODUCTION

SIB-KIS, See it Big, Keep it Simple. That was the word, the formula that I chose almost forty years ago to shape my life and build a business. This book edited by Bob Budler will be one of the few books you will return to many times to help you see it big and keep it simple. Very carefully, Bob has chosen the people you'll meet in these pages. He's captured the essence of the individual philosophy of 137 successful people and has reduced them to one-pagers, which are an inspiration to young and old alike. The two to three minutes it takes to read each one can be life-changing.

Charles E. Jones is known worldwide as a dynamic lecturer, motivator salesman, executive and humorist. His nickname "Tremendous" comes from the enthusiasm he packs into every area of his life.

Charlie entered the insurance business at age 22. Within a year, he received his agency's highest sales award. As a young man he had an encounter with Jesus Christ that added purpose and direction to his ambition. When, at age 37, his agency exceeded $100 million in force he retired to devote all his efforts to lecturing, writing and consulting activities.

Today, he is president of Life Management Services, Inc.; Executive Books; Advisory Board of Investment Timing Service; and chairman of Pneumedic Corporation.

Charlie is a member of the prestigious Speakers Roundtable. He is the recipient of the CPAE Award for speaking skills and professionalism from the National Speakers Association.

He is author of "Life is Tremendous," which earned him the Platinum Award for more than one million copies in print. Two of his speeches, "The Price of Leadership" and "Where Does Leadership Begin?" have been enjoyed by millions on records, cassettes and at conventions. Videos and films featuring his presentations have been used by more than 1,000 companies throughout the Free World.

Charlie resides in Mechanicsburg, Pennsylvania, with his wife, Gloria. They have six children, six grandchildren and one great grandson.

Most of the achievers you'll meet in this book think big and keep it simple. Many of them started with little or nothing. Some in dire circumstances. They saw the big picture, believed in themselves and worked hard to achieve their goals. All of them had one thing more—enthusiasm.

Enthusiasm is one of life's great elixirs. All we need to really make us happy is something to be enthusiastic about. As Van Dyke noted ... "we must never lose life's zest, because the road's last turn will be the best."

The unique use of role models to inspire and motivate makes this book different from other works. Here you'll share the ideas and ideals of winners from all walks of life. Prominent personalities, giants from commerce, industry, education, sports, clergy and other celebrities and entrepreneurs have taken time to write messages to inspire you to personal achievement.

Page after page of understandable, easy-to-read messages provide a treasure of experience and philosophy that you can adapt to your own life. The biographies contain many Horatio Alger "rags-to-riches" stories. Rare is the book that has something for everyone—this one does. Somewhere herein you'll find a message that seems to have been written just for you. Parents report the book generates family discussions. Teachers and youth group leaders are finding it can be an effective teaching tool.

Never in history has the world been in greater need of heroes and role models than today. There are plenty of heroes and role models. The problem is, we never hear about them because the media leans toward the negative. As you read these pages, I hope you'll think about others in your sphere of influence with whom you can share this life-changing gift of YOU CAN DO IT!

I firmly believe that you are the same person today as you'll be in five years except for two things: the people you meet and the books you read. You've done both in reading this book—keep it up and you'll find that life is TREMENDOUS!

GUEST AUTHORS

16

ACKNOWLEDGMENTS

Hundreds of people have contributed to this book. Special thanks are due the guest authors who, in the midst of the clamor of life, made time to share their experiences and thoughts that our nation's youth might draw upon them to enrich their daily lives.

My daughter, Mary Freund, logged long after-work hours to put the book on computer disk. Her four children, Kristy, Sarah, Lisa and Jason proved a good sounding board and their inquisitiveness, as they sought clarification of some materials, made their grandfather do a better editing job.

Mary Ellen Dunne, of the Bensenville Community Public Library staff, saved the author countless hours in research time with her vast knowledge of information sources.

My life's companion, Rita, who has been the "wind beneath my wings" for 53 years, helped with the project until sidelined by Alzheimer's disease. She continues to be a daily inspiration as she demonstrates the greatest test of courage—to struggle without losing heart.

ABOUT THE AUTHOR

Bob Budler is an author, former reporter, editor and nationally syndicated newspaper columnist. For more than 35 years, he headed corporate communications for some of the nation's leading companies.

His first book, Patient: Heal Thyself!, written while he was recovering from heart surgery, has helped thousands of patients and their families deal with the same traumatic experience.

Now retired, he's a "grandpa-preneur" pursuing a free-lance writing career embodying his You Can Do It! philosophy.

YOU CAN DO IT!

BOB BUDLER

EXECUTIVE BOOKS

MECHANICSBURG, PENNSYLVANIA

RICHARD F. "DICK" ABEL
National Director
Military Ministry
Campus Crusade for Christ

Dick Abel became National Director of the Military Ministry of Campus Crusade for Christ in 1992.

The Military Ministry of Campus Crusade for Christ trains and equips service members for personal growth and peer-group Christian influence by strengthening relationships, building leadership skills, helping learners become teachers and emphasizing dependence on the Holy Spirit, prayer and God's word. Outreach is to all service branches, active, reserve and guard members, officers and enlisted ranks, cadets and midshipmen, and dependent family members—both in the U.S. and around the world.

Abel was born in Akron, Ohio, where he graduated from St. Ignatius High School. He earned his Business Administration degree at the University of Detroit and was commissioned in the Air Force. During his military career he was a pilot, leader of an aerial demonstration team, assistant football coach at the Air Force Academy, served on the 7th Air Force staff in Vietnam, and was a public affairs officer for the U.S. Pacific Command. Later he was special assistant for the Chairman of the Joint Chiefs of Staff. He concluded his military career as Air Force Director of Public Affairs.

Dick retired from the Air Force in 1985 and accepted the position as director of legislative and public affairs for the United States Olympic Committee. In 1988, he was elected president of the Fellowship of Christian Athletes, the oldest and largest Christian outreach to athletes and coaches in America. He also is a National Director of the Armed Forces YMCA. His highest recognition is the award of the Air Force Distinguished Service Medal.

Dick and his wife, Ann, have four children and nine grandchildren. The Abels make their home in Poquoson, Virginia.

The Truth Shall Set You Free

Prison is not a place. Prison is the absence of freedom.

This paradox is so evident when we see "prisoners" who are "free" and when we see "free" people who are "imprisoned."

Nearly 20 years ago I came face-to-face with several prisoners—the prisoners of war in Vietnam—as the first American they had seen after being held captive over eight years, some who had been in solitary confinement for four years!

Yet, as I watched them line up on the flightline at the Hanoi airport, I saw the quick winks and the dancing smiles invade their placid faces and I could see that inside there was a freedom that eight years of captivity could not destroy. Later, I stood in awe as I heard their leader speak for the group in a message to the free world: "Thank you for the privilege of serving: God bless America!" This, from a group of men who were captives, not prisoners, expressing their freedom to serve.

How did they do it? So many cited their faith. Larry Guarino, four years in a 6 x 9-foot cell with a cement slab for a bed and no window admitted: "If it wasn't for Jesus Christ, I couldn't have made it." He told me, " 'Larry, you'll make it.' " He expressed his freedom to live.

Robbie Risner used a wood dowel to painstakingly wear a hole through an 8-inch concrete wall—then shared Jesus Christ with the man in the next cell, sharing the freedom of eternity (the man later died). And the group singing of "Amazing Grace," which the guards could not silence, a freedom to share their faith.

Since then, I learned that we can be imprisoned anywhere, even where there are no guards, no bars—where we are captives of anger, hate, depression, loneliness, economics, peer pressure, and, yes, even captive to the fear of death. Traveling the country, I see this kind of imprisonment even in young people. What keeps them captive is drug abuse, sexual promiscuity, even suicides. How does a country turn such a lost generation around? We, as a country, turn around and face God and fight for the freedom to live, the freedom to share, the freedom to serve and, yes, even the freedom to die.

Then, you press on toward the goal of knowing the Truth—for the Truth shall set you free.

Dick Abel

RONALD W. ALLEN
Chairman & CEO
Delta Air Lines, Inc.

A native of Atlanta, Mr. Allen joined Delta in 1963 as a part time analyst during his senior year in college. For the past 28 years, he has served in several positions at the Atlanta-based airline, including senior vice president for personnel and administration. He served as president and chief operating officer from 1983 to 1987, when he was named chairman of the board and chief executive officer.

Allen is a 1964 graduate of the Georgia Institute of Technology where he received his Bachelor of Industrial Engineering degree. He currently serves on the boards of directors of The Coca-Cola Company, National Service Industries, Inc., The C&S/Sovran Corporation, and the Atlanta Chamber of Commerce. He is a member of the board of trustees of Presbyterian College.

He has served as a member of the Georgia Institute of Technology's national advisory board, the board of trustees of Christian City Home for Children, the Metropolitan Atlanta Red Cross, and the United Way of Atlanta.

Delta's growth from the first aerial crop dusting company to the third largest scheduled airline in the U.S. has been characterized by hard work, persistence, and a dedication to customers. "We Love To Fly and It Shows" is the true spirit of the 68,000 member Delta family operating more than 470 aircraft to 158 communities in the U.S. and 57 foreign cities.

Each Day Brings Opportunities

Each day comes to me with both hands full of opportunities...

Those are the words of a woman born in Alabama in 1880, who lost her sight when she was 19 months old, yet inspired thousands of people throughout the world. Her name was Helen Keller. On March 3, 1887, three months before she was seven years old, this exceptional student met an exceptional teacher, Anne Mansfield Sullivan. Their accomplishments are an important lesson in what can happen if we learn to work as a team.

Ludwig Van Beethoven, born in Bonn, Germany, in 1770, grew up in a musical family. It was not until after 1819, when he was completely deaf, that Beethoven composed some of his greatest works, among them the Ninth Symphony.

It was an inventor who said, "Genius is one percent inspiration and ninety-nine percent perspiration." That same inventor, Thomas Alva Edison, is credited with more than 1,000 patents, among them the electric light bulb and the phonograph. Edison's contribution of a small transmitter made the telephone, Alexander Graham Bell's invention, of practical use. Despite a hearing impairment, Edison's genius touches the lives of millions each day.

Franklin Delano Roosevelt contracted polio in the early 1920s, and served as the 32nd President during two of the most challenging decades in U.S. history. FDR is the only U.S. President to have been elected to a fourth term in office.

Two masters of modern music excel at composition and as pianists and entertainers, as well. Yet, neither Georgia-born Ray Charles, nor Stevie Wonder, can see the notes they so easily maneuver, nor the many gold records they have been awarded.

These talented, dedicated individuals share two common characteristics. They have all faced major obstacles, yet have made significant contributions to the quality of life in the world around them. Each of them has accomplished more than most of us could ever dream of accomplishing in one lifetime. Helen Keller summed it up well. *"Each day comes to each of us with both hands full of opportunities."*

Ronald W. Allen

STEVE ALLEN
Author/Actor/Composer
Comedian/Musician/Scholar

Andy Williams once said, "Steve Allen does so many things, he's the only man I know who's listed on every one of the Yellow Pages." It is, in fact, difficult to believe there is only one Steve Allen. Not only is he the only TV comedian from the Golden Age of Comedy of the 1950s still appearing frequently on TV, but he has:

Created and hosted the Tonight Show.

Authored 36 published books.

Starred on Broadway in The Pink Elephant.

Starred in motion pictures, most notably Universal's The Benny Goodman Story.

Written over 4,000 songs, including This Could Be the Start of Something Big, Picnic, Impossible, Gravy Waltz, and South Rampart Street Parade.

Written the score for several musicals, including the Broadway production of Sophie and the CBS-TV version of Alice in Wonderland.

Made some 40 record albums.

Written the stirring Irish drama, The Wake, which won an L.A. drama critics nomination as best play of 1977.

Starred in the critically-acclaimed NBC series The Steve Allen Comedy Hour.

Created, written and hosted the Emmy award-winning PBS-TV series Meeting of Minds.

Been inducted into the TV Academy's Hall of Fame.

Allen is married to actress-comedienne Jayne Meadows.

Most Important Skills

I am pleased to have the opportunity to contribute to this collection of suggestions directed to young Americans. Earlier in the present century I might have spoken of traditional virtues, of the importance of concentration on work assignments or something of the sort. But now, I find it more important to make a few suggestions about the importance of reading and writing.

You can do nothing more important than to learn to read and write well. Without these basic skills you have an almost insurmountable handicap in your journey through life and in the workplace.

Literate manpower has become one of management's top priorities. Management has learned that the creative talents of many valued employees are shackled by their inability to communicate effectively. In this high-tech age, simply learning to cope with industrial jargon is vital to most business operations. If you are deficient in reading and writing skills, promotions will not come your way. Instead, you'll join the ever-growing number of others who are stagnated in menial jobs at the bottom of the employment ladder.

I suggest you make use of all the writing resources available to you. You might start by dusting off your grammar and English textbooks from your school days. Become familiar with your local library, which will offer you a bevy of books, as well as videotapes and on-site programs to improve your ability to read and write. Once you've honed these skills a whole new world will open up to you.

Literacy makes no promises of wealth or fame; in fact, it makes no promises save one—learn to read and write well and you'll at least have a chance to realize your dreams and ambitions.

JAMES H. AMOS, JR.
Chief Operating Officer
The Brice Group

James H. Amos, Jr. is Chief Operating Officer of the Brice Group, Dallas, Texas. An accomplished public speaker and critically acclaimed author, his book "The Memorial" was chosen by the American Library Association as one of the best books published in 1990.

Amos is a former Marine Corps officer and veteran of two combat tours in Vietnam, where he received 16 decorations, including the Purple Heart.

He is recognized in Marquis Who's Who in America, Who's Who in American Executives, Who's Who in Finance and Industry, Who's Who in American Authors and the International Authors and Writers Who's Who.

Jim was recently elected to the Board of Directors of the International Franchise Association and named Chairman of its Public Relations Committee.

As Chief Operating Officer of the Brice Group, Amos has responsibility for the I Can't Believe It's Yogurt, Java Coast Gourmet Coffee, BOXIES Cafe, American Rotisserie and Grill, and Summer Fun Day Camp franchise systems serving customers in more than 1,300 locations in the U.S. and abroad.

The Eagle in Your Mind

Perhaps no symbol has been more prevalent in history and culture worldwide than the eagle. An important part of the literature and history of nations for both the warrior and the poet, a bird of unsurpassed power and majesty, the eagle has often been referred to as the lion of the air.

The Persians bore the eagle's likeness into battle on their spears. The eagle was the symbol of choice for both the Kings of Babylon and Ancient Egypt. In Rome, to see an eagle in the sky on the eve of conflict, meant certain victory. Charlemagne combined Latin and German rule under the double headed eagle. For Prussia, Czarist Russia, Hapsburg Austria and Napoleonic France, the eagle was the bird of war.

In the Golden Age of Greece and mythology, the eagle became the symbol for Zeus, father of Gods. It was the only bird that dwelt in heaven.

Prior to becoming a symbol for the United States of America, the eagle was thought, by the Iroquois Indians, to be a messenger between heaven and earth. Two thousand years ago Solomon said: "The way of the eagle in the sky is wonderful." Isaiah reflected that because of the strength, swiftness, vision and freedom from earthly ties, the eagle was a metaphor for God's care for his children. He would write: "Nut they that wait upon the Lord shall renew their strength; they shall mount up with wings as eagles; they shall run and not be weary and they shall walk and not faint." (Isaiah 40:31)

Eagles are strong of heart, responsible, stable and they soar. But soaring never just happens. Soaring is a result of strong mental and physical effort. It requires clear thinking and a bold, confident, positive attitude. To soar we must embrace the eagle in our mind.

Charles Swindoll said it best when he reflected that we live in a negative, hostile world that says the glass is half empty. Society focuses only on what's wrong instead of what is right; ugliness instead of beauty; destruction instead of construction; the impossible instead of the possible; the hurt instead of the help; what we lack instead of what we have. Our society seems to be engulfed in cynicism and mediocrity, where excellence is lost in the shuffle. Instead of eagles, society if filled with parrots. Parrots don't soar, but simply sit and watch, repeating whatever they hear.

To break this cycle of cynicism, we should adopt the philosophy of "Eagle Excellence" to develop the steadfast character that gives a business, a family and a nation its purpose and pride. To do this we should embrace the eagle in our mind.

(Continued on page 301)

WALLY AMOS
Entrepreneur/Author

Wally Amos has been described as Horatio Alger in a Panama hat and as a walking advertisement for "everything great about America." He's a parable for free enterprise, a hymn to guts, and a promise that opportunity still lives in this nation.

He grew up in Tallahassee, Florida and New York City. After a stint in the Air Force and a career with the William Morris Agency working with such acts as Simon and Garfunkel, the Temptations and Dionne Warwick, he accepted the entrepreneurial challenge "to find a niche and fill it." He borrowed $25,000 and formed the Famous Amos Chocolate Chip Cookie Corporation, which turned out to be an exemplary entrepreneurial effort. His story has been well documented but his fame is not grounded in his unique cookie mix—but rather in quality, substance and a strong positive mental attitude he describes as "the power in you."

In 1979, Wally became national spokesman for the Literacy Volunteers of America, which combats the problem of adult illiteracy. He has travelled throughout the United States speaking to millions of people on behalf of the literacy group; sponsoring workshops; preparing public service announcements; and organizing state programs. He is also TV teacher/host of 50 episodes of state-of-the-art programs for adult basic learners that air on PBS stations. In Hawaii, where he lives, he is on the board of Hawaii Literacy, the Governor's Council, and the Aloha United Way board. In 1990, the Caring Institute presented him its Caring Award which recognizes contributions of those whose deeds help sustain society.

Amos has been the recipient of many other awards. Dr. Amos received an honorary doctorate in education from Johnson & Wales University. He has been inducted into the Babson College Academy of Distinguished Entrepreneurs, and is the recipient of the Horatio Alger Award

The Power In You

I believe there is something only you can accomplish—an idea with your name on it. It's up to you to grab it and do it or it will never get done.

Nothing in life is worth working on more than you. Begin with a positive attitude. Attitude is not the result of success. Success is the result of attitude.

The biggest obstacle that will come between you and your goals is the lack of total commitment. Commitment is never "I'll try." It is always "I will."

Bring enthusiasm to everything you do. Enthusiasm is to your life what electricity is to a light bulb. Nothing happens until you flip the switch.

Everything starts inside of you. You create everything in your world whether you do it consciously or unconsciously. Life is an inside job. You have the power in you to accomplish all your goals and make your dreams come true. You can do it!

Wally Amos

---

and President's Award for Entrepreneurial Excellence. His battered Panama hat and colorful trademark shirt are in the Smithsonian Institution's Business Americana Collection.

Wally is also an author. He wrote his biography, The Face That Launched a Thousand Chips, in 1983. In 1988, he collaborated with his son, Gregory, a free-lance writer, on The Power in You, an inspirational book sharing his philosophy and life experience.

A series of financial reverses deprived him of the company he founded. Today he cannot even use the word "famous" in his name in connection with cookies, food, beverages and restaurant franchises. But, believing in himself, he's back in business with The Uncle Noname Cookie Co. and one percent of net sales goes to Cities in Schools, a dropout-prevention program on whose board he serves.

WALTER H. ANNENBERG
Publisher/Diplomat/Philanthropist

Walter Annenberg has enjoyed a challenging career as an editor and publisher, broadcaster, diplomat and philanthropist.

Born in Milwaukee, he was graduated from The Peddie School, Hightstown, New Jersey (his classmates voted him most likely to succeed), and attended the University of Pennsylvania's Wharton School. He entered the family publishing business in Philadelphia at age 32.

While serving as editor and publisher of the Philadelphia Inquirer, Annenberg saw the need for a publication for teenage girls and established Seventeen Magazine. In 1953, he established TV Guide and turned it into the largest circulation magazine in the United States.

Expanding into radio and television, he pioneered a number of broadcasting concepts, including educational programming via television. He earned the prestigious Alfred I. DuPont Award and the Ralph Lowell Medal for "outstanding contributions to public television." In 1981, Annenberg announced he would give $150 million, over the next 15 years to the Corporation for Public Broadcasting.

Annenberg's performance as U.S. Ambassador to the Court of St. James lifted him to the ranks of respected statesman. He earned the rare distinction among U.S. ambassadors to Britain of being knighted.

His philanthropic donations total over $1 billion; e.g., $21 million to the University of Pennsylvania in 1989; $50 million to the United Negro College Fund.

In 1986, he received the Medal of Freedom from President Reagan. The same year, he was elected to the Wharton School Hall of Fame by votes of the school's students, and received the Linus Pauling Medal for Humanitarianism.

Prepare Yourself

You must be prepared to discipline yourself and to strive to develop affirmative characteristics. Our character is what distinguishes us from others. It is what we really are, not what others think we are. Reputation is what you are supposed to be; character is what you are. Countless successful people, who began with little, disciplined themselves and won life's battle—you can do it, too!

You must prepare yourself for occasional shocks in life because harassment is just around the corner. Success breeds envy. The higher you climb, the bigger target you become.

You must prepare yourself to strive for inspiration from the ashes of adversity. Trouble and difficulty are a real and necessary part of our existence. Without them there are many lessons in life we'd never learn. Poet Robert Hamilton put it well:

> *I walked a mile with Sorrow*
> *And ne'er a word said she*
> *But, oh, the things I learned from her*
> *When Sorrow walked with me.*

MARY KAY ASH
Chairman Emeritus
Mary Kay Cosmetics

Mary Kay Ash started her dream company in 1963 with $5,000 and plenty of determination and perseverance. Under her direction, the company has grown from a small direct-sales company into the largest direct-selling skin care company in the world.

A unique combination of enthusiastic people, quality products, innovative marketing concepts and an ambitious set of goals has turned Mary Kay Cosmetics, Inc., into an American business success story.

Today, more than 325,000 independent beauty consultants sell the company's products in the United States, Canada, Argentina, Australia, Mexico, Germany and 16 other countries.

The Mary Kay success story began after she retired from a long and prosperous career in direct sales. She began thinking about her own dream company, one based on the golden rule and one which would give women unlimited opportunities for success.

Mary Kay is a much sought-after speaker and has received numerous awards and honors. Her latest laurels include the Outstanding Business Leader Award from Northwood Institute, the Circle of Honor Award from The Direct Selling Education Foundation and the First Annual National Sales Hall of Fame Award presented by the Sales and Marketing Executives of New York. She is also the recipient of the prestigious Horatio Alger Award.

Mary Kay is also active in helping find a cure for breast cancer through funding educational and research programs. St. Paul Medical Center in Dallas has named its new cancer research facility, "The May Kay Ash Center for Cancer Immunotherapy Research."

Confidence Keys Success

If you were to ask me, "What is a common denominator among women?" I would have to say it is a lack of faith in their own God-given abilities. Did you ever hear a man say, "If I can," "I hope," or "Maybe"? That seems to be a female disease. Most men have enough sense to bluff their way through and pretend confidence, even if they don't feel it.

At Mary Kay Cosmetics, we try to instill confidence in women by "praising them to success" one small achievement at a time, urging them on to greater success.

From early childhood my mother instilled confidence in me by constantly repeating, "You can do anything in this world you want to do, if you want to do it badly enough—and you are willing to pay the price!" You can do it!!!

Mary Kay Ash

RAYMOND R. BECKER
Executive Director
Illinois Road Builders Assn.

Ray Becker has spent a lifetime and his professional career understanding and dealing with people. His career was somewhat shaped by Karin Walsh, legendary city editor of the Chicago Sun-Times. He hired Becker as a general assignment reporter, when he was one-year out of a monastery, where he studied for the priesthood.

Walsh told him: "I get scores of applications from journalism students each year but I believe you bring a different perspective and may have an innate ability to understand people and why they do the things we report on." A previous one-year stint at the City News Bureau may also have helped Becker get the job. In 1954, he was awarded his Bachelor Degree in Philosophy from DePaul University in Chicago.

Following his newspaper career, Becker became Director of Communications for the Chicago Association of Commerce and Industry. From there, he was "drafted" to serve as Director of Communications for the Chicago Board of Education, during the tumultuous late 60's.

A telephone call from Otto Kerner, then Governor of Illinois, brought him into state government. He served as speech writer for the governor and as Chief of Information for the Illinois Board of Economic Development (now the Illinois Department of Commerce and Community Affairs).

Following his government service, Becker became Director of Public Affairs for Interlake, Inc., a billion dollar steel corporation. After 11 years with Interlake, he accepted appointment as Executive Director of the Illinois Road Builders Association, where he is now in his 14th year.

Becker is part president of the Chicago Area Public Affairs Group, past chairman of the Citizens of Greater Chicago, past chairman of the Alumni Council of the Liberal Arts and Science College of DePaul University, former trustee of the Chicago Laborers' Pension Fund, and currently trustee for the Chicago Laborers' Health & Welfare Board.

Seek The Goodness In Others

My life has certainly been a simple one. No fanfare. No television awards. No notoriety. But it has been enormously successful—in every way—spiritually, emotionally and materially. Why? Simply said: *people.*

People are the reason most of us do the things we do—family members, acquaintances, fellow workers, everyone we come in contact with in our daily lives may influence our actions—and we theirs. Happiness is often the result of what we give to our fellowman—not what we take. As Longfellow once said: "Give what you have. To some one, it may be better than you dare to think."

We are all different as the stars in heaven, but, everyone carries a seed of goodness within them waiting to be called out and cultivated. So, look for the goodness in people with a smile, a hug, a pleasant word or a compliment. When you see goodness in others, you surround yourself with pleasantness, which then becomes a bulwark, a kind of protective coat to shut out some the unpleasantries of life.

Among those surrounding you there is always one who stands out from the rest. One particular man or woman who knows you best, who has the ability to bring out the best in you. One who sees the goodness in you. A person whom you can follow and emulate.

I was fortunate to have a stand-out guy in my life—my older brother, Stan. He was my advisor. My idol. My role model. One whom I followed—and he followed God as a Dominican priest.

I'll always remember a lesson he gave me to stress the importance of education. He said: "Put your nose on a painting—a special work of art or a landscape. Now, every time you learn something, every time your brain is nourished with knowledge, and every time you do a good deed, take a step backward from the painting. Each day brings a step backward until one day—lo and behold—you see the entire painting. Your eyes light up and your imagination expands. You exclaim: "I see it. I see it. I understand!"

Find someone good to follow and, if you are lucky, and that person follows in God's footsteps, how can you not be happy and successful—it's practically guaranteed.

Happiness and success come in recognizing and appreciating the goodness and abilities in others.

Ray Becker

CATHLEEN BLACK
President & CEO
American Newspaper
Publishers Association

Prior to becoming head of ANPA, the major newspaper organization in the U.S. and Canada that represents 1,400 newspapers, Cathleen Black was publisher of USA TODAY, Executive Vice President/Marketing of Gannett, USA TODAY's parent company, and a member of the Gannett Board of Directors.

Prior to joining USA TODAY, Black was publisher of New York magazine. At the time of her appointment in '79, she was the first woman ever to be publisher of a weekly consumer magazine.

A graduate of Trinity College, she completed her term as a member of its board of trustees and has been named to chair the school's newly formed board of regents.

Recently, she was appointed by President Bush to the board of directors of the Points of Light Foundation. In addition, she is active on the boards of the Advertising Council, United Way of America and the board of visitors for the School of Foreign Service at Georgetown University.

She has received numerous honors. In 1990, Ladies Home Journal named her as one of "The Fifty Most Powerful Women in America." The Sara Lee Corporation awarded her their 1989 Frontrunner Award for business excellence. Manhattan College's De LaSalle Medal, the Matrix Award, the Catalyst Award and NOW Legal Defense and Education Fund Award also acknowledged her achievements. She holds honorary degrees from Simmons College, Trinity College, Ithaca College and Capitol College.

Black resides in Washington, D.C. with her husband, Tom Harvey, and their young son, Duffy.

Stretch To Your Limit

You can do it! You certainly can. In fact, the advertising slogan for the Nike shoe campaign may be more appropriate. What is says is, "DO IT NOW!"

When I think about what's important to succeed, I think that the message is singular. We can almost do anything we want to do, if we have courage, self-confidence and a can-do it spirit.

Surely one of life's greatest mistakes is not stretching to one's own limit. It has helped me in my career to not let self-imposed boundaries deter me from surging forward.

You can do it, too—good luck.

Cathleen Black

BONNIE BLAIR
U.S. Olympic Champion

Success under pressure is the measure of a true champion. There are numerous winners in the world of sports but the celebrated athletes are the few who meet the challenge of pressure time after time. Bonnie Blair is undoubtedly celebrated as the speedskater who produces her best performances when it counts.

Bonnie began her race in the 500 meter event of the 1988 Calgary Olympics immediately after her rival Christa Rothenburger of East Germany set a world record. Not to be outdone, Bonnie proceeded to skate the 500 meters faster than any woman had before or has since, capturing the gold medal in a world record time of 39.1. This record stood for five years until March 1994, when at the age of 30, Blair met her ultimate goal of shattering the 39 second mark with a time of 38.99.

Four years later at the 1992 Albertville Olympics, with the world watching and a nation counting on her, Blair came through again. She blew away the field in the 500 meters, defeating her nearest competitor, Ye Qiaobo, of China, by 18 hundredths of a second. The victory made Blair the first woman in Olympic history to win consecutive gold medals in the event, and the first American woman to win consecutive Winter Olympic gold medals. She made history again the 1,000 meters, edging out Ye by just two hundredths of a second to win her second gold of the games, and her fourth Olympic medal overall.

In 1994, Blair skated in her final Winter Olympics in Lillehammer, Norway. Supported by 60 plus members of "The Blair Bunch", Bonnie once again swept the sprint races winning gold medals in both the 500 and 1,000 meter events. By capturing her sixth career Olympic medal, Bonnie emerged as U.S. history's most decorated Winter athlete, as well as the record holder for the most gold medals (5) won by an American woman in any sport.

Hard Work Brings Success

Most people measure my success by the number of gold medals I have. I measure it by how hard I work for my personal best in everything I try. As an athlete, I compete to win and the only way I know how to do that is to go out and skate for my personal best every time, in every race. I try to approach every competition, whether it's the Olympics, the World Cup or a training race early in the season, exactly the same. I pretend every race is the Olympics so when I finally get there every few years, it is not any different than the thousands of races I have competed in before.

The consistency that comes with treating every challenge the same is a major key to success. We have to recognize and honor even our smallest triumphs, the personal best goals we set for ourselves, even it they seem less noteworthy than others. Getting within three-one hundredths of a second of the bronze in the 1500 meters in Lillehammer was just about as thrilling as winning the two golds. Although I just missed getting a medal in that event, it was my personal best time in six years.

Some people drive themselves with rewards from the outside. I cannot do that. Racing year after year, I found that the best and truest motivation comes from inside. Preparing for the moment of success has to become just as important, just as much fun, as the success itself.

For all of us, no matter what the challenge, our performance depends on so many factors, only some of which we can control. But what we can control is attitude, what we bring to the starting line and, since I have been racing for over 26 years, I can confirm that is the most important part of the race, that is where consistency comes from.

No matter what successes I have had, I never expect things to just come my way. I know that once I start expecting to win, that is when I will start losing. Never take anything for granted but do not give up just because certain gifts have not been bestowed upon you either. By developing your natural talents and making a commitment to success, you can easily make up for any advantages that may not have been handed to you. Once you have your first taste of success, you will enjoy it and find it easier to work harder for more.

KEN BLANCHARD
Chairman
Blanchard Training and
Development, Inc.

Few individuals have impacted the day-to-day management of people and companies as has Ken Blanchard.

As a writer in the field of management, his One Minute Manager library of books has collectively sold more than seven million copies. Translated into 20 languages, it is one of the most successful collections of business books of all time.

His textbook, Management of Organizational Behavior, co-authored with Dr. Paul Hersey, is considered standard reading on the subject, and his most recent work, The Power of Ethical Management, co-authored with Dr. Norman Vincent Peale addresses one of the most important issues of the day.

Blanchard is chairman of Blanchard Training and Development, Inc., a management consulting and training firm that he founded with his wife, Marjorie. He earned his B.A. in government and philosophy from Cornell University, his M.A. in sociology and counseling from Colgate University, and his Ph.D. in educational administration and leadership from Cornell University.

He maintains a faculty position in leadership at the University of Massachusetts/Amherst, and a visiting lectureship at Cornell University, where he is also an elected member of the Board of Trustees.

Develop "Get To" Attitude

One of my favorite stories is about Beverly Sills, the great opera singer. It was reported that she gave an afternoon concert one day in San Francisco. During the reception following the concert, a reporter said to her, "I'll bet you hate the fact that you have to give another concert tonight."

Beverly Sills replied, "I don't 'have to' give another concert tonight. I 'get' to give another concert tonight. At one time in my life I was into 'I have to' do things. The minute I would say 'I have to' I could feel all the energy in my body drain away. One day I realized that all over the city people were getting baby sitters and getting all dressed up just to come and hear me sing. I suddenly realized how fortunate I was that 'I get' to give another concert."

That story says so much. Beverly Sills is right. If you have a "have to" mentality in life you will be de-energized. You will spend most of your time quacking like a duck, complaining, and blaming other people for what you "have to" do. Life will become a drain.

To me life is a very special occasion. I get to do exciting things. I get to write short articles like this. I get to speak to groups all over the country. I get to write books. I get to do a lot of wonderful things.

I once heard that it was easy to become successful. All you had to do was work twelve hours a day. You could work the first twelve hours or the second twelve hours. Successful people are people who do things that other people are not willing to do. I, too, feel successful people have an attitude that they "get" to work hard, they "get" to do things. With that positive attitude they have the energy that races them past others that are quacking and complaining about what they "have to" do.

Ken Blanchard

EDDY BOAS
Chairman
Pan-Pacific Seminars

Eddy Boas was born in Holland in 1940 at the outbreak of World War II and spent nearly three years in a German concentration camp with his father, mother and brother. As far as is known, they were the only family that went into a concentration camp and survived as a family.

On returning to Holland they decided to migrate to Australia. In 1948, when Eddy was eight years old, his father passed away. His mother supported the family by taking a job as a cleaning lady. Eddy left school at age 15 to work in a Sydney radio station while attending night school. After six years in radio, he became an office equipment salesman with Olivetti and continued to study at night.

After 19 years with IMS International, he retired in February 1994, to set up his own conference business, Pan-Pacific Seminars, based in Sydney, Australia.

His interests have always been in sports. He has participated competitively in modern Pentathlon (running, swimming, fencing, pistol shooting and horse racing), as well as soccer. He is a qualified soccer referee and for four years was president of the local Junior Soccer Club.

He has two sons in their early 20s. The youngest, Marc, is in the Australian regular army, while his elder son, Philip, is general manager of Pan-Pacific Seminars.

How to Survive

From a young child, survival in a tough world has been part of my life.

It started by surviving World War II and continued until today where survival in a tough business world is paramount to one's success.

To be successful, whether in sports or business, one has to be a team player and have a positive attitude.

To be a winner in life, a positive mental attitude is essential. "Everything is possible—you just have make the effort."

To survive in today's business world you have to be one step ahead of your competitors. Do not be afraid to ask. My mother, who is 80 and is a real survivor, early on in life gave me a saying which I still use today—"Don't be afraid to ask because No you have got and Yes is a maybe." This is so true because many of us think in a negative way while in actual fact the results can be quite positive.

Young people today should not be afraid to ask questions of their peers. Unfortunately, in a negative world where we are continuously told that business is bad and jobs are difficult to get, our young people feel that there is nothing to strive for in life. This is totally wrong, since a positive attitude and a will to win will give you more opportunities in life.

Our leaders, in whichever country, need to set examples for our young people, as well as our handicapped people. Far too often they made excuses for what has gone wrong with this world, instead of being true leaders and showing a positive attitude.

Look upon business as you look upon sports. It's a team effort. No manager is capable of running a business by him/herself. They need a team effort to be successful. The same as the best quarterback can't win a game by himself. It doesn't matter how far he can throw, he needs to have protection and receivers who can catch the ball.

To survive today, think of how well off you are. Look around and you'll always find someone worse off than yourself. Think about the handicapped people, who have made a success of themselves, and compare their accomplishments with yours.

Be proud of yourself for what you have achieved in life and you will survive to go on to better things.

Eddy Boas

PAT BOONE
Author/Entertainer

Pat Boone has enjoyed eminent success as an entertainer and author for more than 35 years but he's most proud of his accomplishments as a father and Christian.

He married his high school sweetheart, Shirley Foley (daughter of country music legend Red Foley). They were married his first year in college. In 1958, he graduated Magna Cum Laude from Columbia University majoring in speech and English. By this time, the Boones had four daughters.

While at Columbia, in 1956, he signed a million dollar contract with 20th Century Fox and subsequently starred in 15 films. The same year, ABC signed him for the Pat Boone Chevy Showroom, making him the youngest performer with his own network show.

As a recording artist, Pat set an all-time record by staying on the charts for more than 200 consecutive weeks. He's sold more than 45 million records.

On cable, he's a co-host on the Shop Television Network and, with Shirley, on the Nashville Network as "RV" travelers. They took part in Gospel America Tour '88 and completed a sold-out concert tour in Hong Kong and Japan. His Pat Boone Radio Show continues successfully on 300 stations worldwide.

His first book, Twixt Twelve and Twenty, *a guide for teenagers, sold more than 800,000 copies, with all royalties going to the Northeastern Institute of Christian Education. In addition to the 15 books he's written, including his most recent* Miracle of Prayer, *he's co-authored two books with Shirley,* The Honeymoon is Over *and* Together: 25 Years With The Boone Family.

Pat has been national chairman and host of the Easter Seal Society telethon for 10 years and he authored The Human Touch, *the Easter*

The Miracle of Prayer

Prayer has been the greatest source of help in my life. Everything I've ever achieved has come as a result of including prayer in whatever I do. It led me to write a book, *The Miracle of Prayer,* to share with others my strong belief in the power of prayer.

Space limitations here prevent my going into great detail, but I assure you the most important prayer you'll ever pray is that which provides the basis for everything else: turning to Jesus Christ and receiving Him as your Saviour. That's where prayer must begin.

I believe it is quite possible to achieve success in any field by employing the right approach to prayer. This has been documented over and over again. Throughout this book some of America's most successful people acknowledge it as well.

Prayer is simply conversation with God. Talk to Him like you would to your own father, your best friend, even your boss. He's all of these to you.

God does want us to be contented and successful. Take your problems to Him, who listens and answers. "Therefore I say to you, whatever things you ask when you pray, believe that you receive them, and you will be given them." (Mark 11:24) Be patient. Keep asking and you'll find that's a written guarantee you can count on.

I also suggest you read Proverbs, a 31-chapter gold mine of human and practical wisdom. It's a fantastic "how-to" book for practical living in this world.

One final word—the greatest doers in human history are all gone. They stand as evidence that human victories, no matter how exciting or encompassing, are relatively short-lived, temporary. There must be more to life. And there is!

Jesus is the only person who got out of this world alive. Make Him your partner, talk to Him through prayer, and you'll be a success—it's guaranteed!

Pastor

Seal story. He's an astute businessman and a partner in many diverse projects but perhaps the most exciting aspect of his life centers around his grandchildren, now a combination of 14 boys and girls.

FRANK BORMAN
Commander/Apollo 8 Mission
Business Leader

A hero of the American Space Odyssey, Frank Borman led the first team of American astronauts to circle the moon, extending man's horizons into space. He is internationally known as Commander of the 1968 Apollo 8 Mission. A romance with airplanes that began when he was 15 years old took him to the Air Force, then to NASA, and to leadership in the aviation industry.

A career Air Force officer, his assignments included service as a fighter pilot, an operational pilot and instructor, an experimental test pilot, and an assistant professor of thermodynamics and fluid mechanics at West Point. When selected by NASA, he was instructor at the Aerospace Research Pilot School at Edwards AFB, California.

A native of Gary, Indiana, he was raised in Tucson, Arizona. He earned a Bachelor of Science degree from the U.S. Military Academy, West Point, in 1950, and a Master of Science degree in aeronautical engineering from the California Institute of Technology in 1957. He completed the Harvard Business School's Advanced Management Program in 1970.

During his tenure as chief executive officer of Eastern Airlines, the industry went through the enormous change caused by deregulation. The company enjoyed the four most profitable years in its history under his leadership.

Recipient of many honors, he received the first Congressional Space Medal of Honor from the President of the United States. He is a member of the International Aerospace Hall of Fame and the holder of the Harmon International Aviation Trophy, in addition to many honorary degrees, special honors and service decorations.

Today he is Chairman, CEO and President of Patlex Corporation and resides in Las Cruces, New Mexico, with his wife, Susan. They have two sons and four grandchildren.

You Have to Pay the Price

After a reasonably successful high school football career, I entered the U.S. Military Academy at West Point. One of the first voluntary actions I took was to go out for football. Of course, I had not been recruited and at the time weighed all of 145 pounds, but the thrill of playing football for Army was one of the reasons I applied for West Point. The other being, I wanted an opportunity to become a military pilot.

I didn't last long in the screening exercises, but rather than quit, I opted for the next best thing and became a student football manager. I have always thought that act was one of the more fortuitous events in my life.

Though the student manager's job was hardly glamorous and the position was held in low esteem, it placed me in direct contact with Colonel Earl "Red" Blaik. This austere man epitomized leadership. In my four years at West Point he produced post-war teams that were among the best ever in college football. And he did this without the enormous pool of talent that was available at the academy during the war years.

His theme for life and success was the title of a book he authored, *You Have to Pay the Price.* By that, he meant that you have to be prepared if you are to succeed in life and that preparation often involves sacrifice, dedication and enormous effort. This rule applies the same if you are preparing for football, science, medicine or any other career. Throughout my military and civilian career, subsequent to my graduation in 1950, Colonel Blaik kept in touch, even though I was only a manager on the Army teams. He offered personal encouragement at all times, advice when it was needed and congratulations when I was successful. This encouragement had an enormous impact on my thinking long after my association with the football team was gone.

Even more important was the indelible stamp that he placed on me and so many of the cadets he coached. The essence of his message was, "You can do it," you can succeed, you can achieve, but you must be prepared "You Have to Pay the Price."

ADAM J. BOZZUTO
Chairman & President
Bozzuto's Incorporated

Adam Bozzuto was born in Waterbury, Connecticut. Today, he resides in Middlebury and is head of one of the largest and most successful food distributorships in the Northeast. He's known for his philanthropy, which is part of his lifelong philosophy to give something back in appreciation for success.

A self-made man, he learned much about life in the "school of hard knocks." During the depression, to help his family make ends meet, he worked in grocery stores doing all sorts of menial tasks. Intrigued by the many facets that go into a retail food operation, he often worked extra hours without pay to learn about the business.

The toughness of the times helped him discipline himself to spend less than he earned. By 1945, at age 29, he had built his own nest egg which he used to found Bozzuto's, in Waterbury, Connecticut. It was the first step toward his goal to become a leader in the food industry.

Well on the way to achieving his goals, he suffered a devastating setback in 1955, when a violent flood swept through Waterbury and wiped out his business in its wake.

From the adversity came a valuable lesson—the importance of the strength of relationships developed in running a business. He was amazed by the support he received, beyond his family, from friends, employees, loyal customers and business acquaintances, who helped him resurrect his business from its watery grave.

Success has not deterred his interest in other people. Today he provides strong support to schools, churches, charitable organizations and the Special Olympics in Connecticut. He still believes happiness is a result of what we give our fellowman—not what we take.

Guidelines for a Happy Life

There are many formulas for success. I think the most important aspect of life is to be happy by enjoying your family, friends and work. Happiness is not always easy to find because we look for it outside ourselves, when, in reality, it comes from within.

I'd like to share with you some suggestions to help you enjoy a sound, secure and happy life:

1. Live a simple life. Be temperate in your habits and avoid selfishness.

2. Spend less than you earn. Avoid extravagance and keep out of debt. It may be difficult, but it pays big dividends.

3. Think constructively. Train yourself to think clear, useful thoughts. Avoid unwholesome ideas.

4. Try to see the other person's point of view. Resist the tendency to want things your own way.

5. Develop good friends and business associates. This support network will be there for you in times of need.

6. Rule your moods, don't let them rule you. Remember, a lifetime of unhappiness can be caused by a moment of emotional instability.

7. Next, give generously. There is no greater joy in life than to bring happiness to others.

8. Be interested in other people.

9. Work with righteous, honest motives. No one who does wrong is ever really happy.

10. Live one day at a time. Concentrate on the task at hand and avoid attempting too much at one time.

11. Develop some means of diversion and relaxation.

12. Finally, and most important, keep close to God. It will do more to bring you happiness than any other single endeavor. And God, in turn, will help keep you close to all other attributes of happiness.

Adam J. Bozzuto

ROBERT J. BROWN
Chairman
B&C Associates, Inc.

Robert Brown was born in High Point, North Carolina, the great grandson of a slave who dug ground to make way for railroad tracks to weave their way through the state.

In 1960, against the advice of many who knew him, he left his job with the Federal Bureau of Narcotics in New York and returned home to High Point to start his own public relations firm.

Clients did not rush to his door. Despite lack of business, each day he would don a suit and tie, pick up his briefcase and head for the office—a room not much bigger than a closet on the second floor of an abandoned theatre. He made calls, wrote letters, searched the newspapers and telephone books for prospective clients.

Finally, as he describes on the next page, a lucky break came his way—and he leveraged it into a successful career.

In 1968, Robert Brown was appointed Special Assistant to President Nixon. His duties included oversight responsibility for community relations, civil rights, emergency preparedness, small towns and day care. He started and developed the U.S. Minority Enterprise Program and initiated the U.S. Government Black College program.

Today his public relations / crisis management firm, B&C Associates, is one of the largest and most respected black-owned firms in the nation. B&C's clients include Dow Jones and Fortune 500 companies such as F.W. Woolworth, SC Johnson Wax, Nabisco Brands and Sara Lee Corporation, as well as a number of small businesses.

Brown has been honored by numerous colleges, universities, and organizations. He holds eight honorary doctorate degrees and six national achievement awards. He was honored in 1990 as a recipient of the Horatio Alger Association of Distinguished Americans Award.

Never Give Up

One day in 1960, I was sitting in the office of my newly founded company wondering if I'd made the biggest mistake of my life. I had left a good job in New York to start this public relations company and clients were few and far between.

My office consisted of a desk, a chair, a telephone and a file cabinet. I had hidden my car behind the pool room because I was three months behind on payments. As I struggled to figure out what my next move was going to be, the telephone rang.

Sitting there, looking at the phone as it chimed away, I wondered if I should pick up the receiver. On the other end could be any number of people I owed money to: the used car dealer saying he was coming for the car, or, the phone company calling to inform me they were on the way to take out the phone.

Then my grandmother's words sounded in my ear: "Have faith in God, work hard, and make sacrifices, and you can achieve anything. Nothing can stop you, son."

I did answer that call, and it resulted in my company's first major corporate client: F.W. Woolworth. After that, one thing led to another and I started to have some measure of success.

To the young people today who are trying to achieve something, I can give no better advice than my grandmother's words.

No matter what kind of adversity you face, be it no shoes, no food, or intangible injuries such as discrimination, remember that faith, hard work and sacrifice will be the key to success.

Never give up.

Know that God will work wonders through your faith.

Robert J. Brown

A major part of his life has always revolved around giving. He and his wife, Sallie, have put many needy children through school, and he is president of the International Concern Foundation, which channels support from the private sector to disadvantaged groups around the globe.

JOHN H. BRYAN
Chairman & CEO
Sara Lee Corporation

John Bryan is a native of Mississippi. He is a graduate of Rhodes College, Memphis, where he received a Bachelor of Arts degree in economics and business administration. He began his business career in 1960 with the family owned and operated Bryan Foods in West Point, Mississippi. In 1968, Bryan Foods was sold to Sara Lee Corporation of Chicago.

In 1974, Mr. Bryan became executive vice president and a director of Sara Lee Corporation. That same year he was elected president, and the next year was named chief executive officer. He was elected chairman of the board of Sara Lee Corporation in 1976.

Mr. Bryan is a member of the board of directors of Amoco Corporation and First Chicago Corporation and its subsidiary, the First National Bank of Chicago. He is the past chairman and a member of the board of directors of Grocery Manufacturers of America, Inc., a member of the Business Council and the Business Roundtable, a trustee of the Committee for Economic Development, and national chairman of the Business Committee for the Arts. Mr. Bryan is also a member of the board of the National Women's Economic Alliance and serves on the National Corporations Committee of the United Negro College Fund.

Active in a variety of organizations in the Chicago area, Mr. Bryan is vice president of the board of trustees and treasurer of the Art Institute of Chicago, is a member of Chicago United, a director of the United Way/Crusade of Mercy, a trustee and vice chairman of Rush Presbyterian St. Luke's Medical Center, a trustee of the University of Chicago, and chairman of the Business Advisory Council of the Chicago Urban League.

Mr. Bryan's awards include the French Legion of Honor, Holland's Order of Orange Nassau conferred by Queen Beatrix, the National Hu-

Focus on Your Objectives

The 1990s mark a great milestone in our history, for they mark the last decade in this millennium. There is something awesome about the closing of a 1,000 year cycle—a time that has seen the Dark Ages, the Renaissance, revolution, and now the age of technology. The year 2000 will be an exciting call to action, as well as a catalyst for change on all fronts. With these changes come enormous opportunities, more specifically, opportunities for leadership.

If you aspire to capture these opportunities—to take up leadership roles—I should like to offer, from my experience, three prerequisites that I believe are the most important for leadership tomorrow or at any time.

The first is integrity. You must guard your honor with all you have. Leadership is based on respect and trust. A reputation for ethical behavior is the cornerstone of successful leadership in business, as in life.

Second is that effective leaders are truly concerned about other people—for leadership demands a genuine respect for those you lead. We cannot accomplish very much alone. I watch a lot of people getting selected for leadership positions. Those selected are most often chosen because their peers want them to be their leaders. Showing respect for your peers, and for those you lead, is just as important as showing respect for those who lead you.

The third point is that leaders must perform. He or she must become identified with accomplishment—whether it's the general in battle, or the coach on Saturday afternoon or the company president striving to meet financial objectives, or the college president aspiring to make his or her institution the very best.

A lot of factors do affect accomplishment. But of those you can control, the most important is this: It is being intensely focused on the proper performance measures of whatever is your assigned task. Tragically, most people scatter their efforts—and even worse many never understand their objectives. Today, this focus on your objectives is usually called vision. It is surely among the critical factors for success.

John H. Bryan—

manitarian Award of the National Conference of Christians and Jews, and the Willian H. Albers Award given by the Food Marketing Institute.

BARBARA BUSH
38th First Lady

Barbara Bush, wife of President George Bush, has lived a life that reflects her husband's varied career in business and public service, her involvement as the mother of five children, and her own energy and commitment to a wide variety of community projects.

Barbara Pierce Bush was born on June 8, 1925, grew up in Rye, New York, and married George Bush on January 6, 1945. They have five children, four daughters-in-law, and 12 grandchildren. By virtue of George Bush's service as a member of Congress, U.S. Representative to the United Nations, Chairman of the Republican National Committee, chief of the United States Liaison Office in the People's Republic of China, Director of the Central Intelligence Agency, and the vice president of the United States, the Bushes have lived in 17 cities and 29 homes since their marriage.

Mrs. Bush has chosen the promotion of literacy and the importance of reading as her special areas of focus. She is a sponsor of Laubach Literacy Volunteers, a world-wide program committed to eradicating illiteracy. She is honorary chairman of the National Advisory Council of Literacy Volunteers of America, Inc., a national volunteer tutorial organization; she is Honorary Chairperson for the National Committee on Literacy and Education of the United Way; and serves as honorary chairman of the Reading is Fundamental Advisory Council.

Mrs. Bush is honorary chairperson of the Barbara Bush Foundation for Family Literacy, an organization whose mission is to establish literacy as a value in every family in America, to support the development of family literacy programs, and to break the intergenerational cycle of illiteracy.

Reflecting her own years as an active volunteer, she encourages volunteerism and the giving by people of their time and energies for the

Three Special Choices

(From Commencement Address, Wellesley College, June 1, 1990)

I hope that many of you will consider making three very special choices in your life. The first is to believe in something larger than yourself, to get involved in some of the big ideas of your time. I chose literacy because I honestly believe that if more people could read, write and comprehend, we would be that much closer to solving so many of the problems plaguing our society.

Early on I made another decision which I hope you will make as well. Whether you are talking about education, career or service, you are talking about life—and life must have joy. It's supposed to be fun! One of the reasons I made the most important decision of my life—to marry George Bush—is because he made me laugh. It's true, sometimes we've laughed through tears, but that shared laughter has been one of our strongest bonds.

The third choice that must not be missed is to cherish your human connections: your relationships with friends and family. For several years, you've had impressed upon you the importance to your career of dedication and hard work. This is true, but as important as your obligations as a doctor, lawyer or business leader will be, you are a human being first and those human connections—with spouses, with children, with friends—are the most important investments you will ever make.

At the end of your life, you will never regret not having passed one more test, not winning one more verdict or not closing one more deal. You will regret time not spent with a husband, a friend, a child or a parent.

Barbara Bush

---

betterment of others and their communities. She also has taken a particular interest in the problem of learning disabilities and has encouraged many national organizations that seek to bring about greater public awareness and effective treatment for the problem.

Mrs. Bush has received honorary degrees from Bennett College, Smith College, Morehouse School of Medicine, St. Louis University, and the University of Pennsylvania.

Mrs. Bush is an exercise enthusiast and also enjoys reading, gardening, the family dog, Millie, and being with her family.

GREGORY J. BUTLER
President & CEO
Market Day Corporation

Greg Butler grew up in Dover, Delaware, where he began his lifelong observation of, and learning from, successful people.

As a young boy, he worked a paper route, mowed lawns and shoveled snow. In his teen years, he worked in a small family distribution business, sold Christmas trees, and started his first business—a snow cone concession at the community pool. From his work experience, he learned the benefits of determination and persistence. Along the way, he was active in the Boy Scouts and lettered in football in high school and college.

Butler chose public service after graduation from Southern Illinois University. He held administrative positions in local government where his leadership team won national recognition for excellence in their field. Among his responsibilities, he developed cooperative relationships between school districts and other units of government, especially focusing on "lighted schoolhouse" programs that made schools available to the community for use after the school day. To provide better nutrition and savings on food for the elderly by establishing food co-ops for neighborhood senior citizen centers.

In the course of this endeavor, he met Trudi Temple, a homemaker, mother and volunteer who had been successful working with parent-teacher organizations to establish neighborhood food cooperatives as a way to help their schools raise needed funds. In the late 70's, they formed a partnership. From that modest beginning, Market Day has evolved as a leader in its industry, serving thousands of schools throughout the nation and helping them earn millions of dollars annually.

Today, Butler and his management team have established a "Partnership in Education" program to encourage business and industry to support local schools.

There Is No Magic Formula

Of all the advice and counsel I've received over the years, none has been as important as watching, working with, and learning from successful people. The lesson in all of this experience is that there is no magic formula for success.

I've felt for many years that success is not measured in dollars. Success is doing what you like to do, doing it well, and in the process, helping others as well as yourself. What you need to keep you focused along the way is a set of guiding values or beliefs that will help you grow through the rough and tumble of everyday life. Here are some of mine:

Read and Learn—The world is changing so fast that we need to anticipate the demands of these changes. Reading is a wonderful way to learn from others, to generate new ideas, and to keep pace with innovation and change. Read the daily newspaper, read books outside your main interests, and read magazines of every kind on a continuous basis. By reading, you're demonstrating your commitment to learning and you'll be better prepared to make life's choices. To this day, I keep the books that have made the greatest impression on my development and refer to them often.

Get Involved—Experience is great teacher. By working and volunteering, young people learn to help others as well as themselves. As a teenager, working after school in my family's small business, I learned valuable lessons from my father and mother who started a business with very little, and made it a success. I learned from every job even the most menial of tasks.

During the holidays, I worked at a local Christmas tree stand. I not only earned much needed spending money, but, I learned valuable lessons about salesmanship and customer service, from another successful entrepreneur.

As a Boy Scout and as a volunteer helping distribute food baskets to the needy, I learned the importance of helping others. These, and many other lessons, all come from the experience of working and volunteering.

(Continued on page 301)

At the heart of Market Days success, is the generation of the co-op spirit and fellowship as friends and neighbors join together to volunteer their time and effort to help their schools.

JOHN CALLAWAY
Broadcast Journalist/Executive

John Douglas Callaway has been a news person since he started selling his dad's weekly newspaper on the streets of New Martinsville, West Virginia, at the age of six. He later went on to become the editor of his high school newspaper and wrote for the college paper at Ohio Wesleyan University until he left school with 71 cents in his pocket and hitchhiked to Chicago in February, 1956.

He intended to make some money, pay off some bills, and return to college. Instead, he ended up living at the Chicago YMCA in a nine-dollar-a-week room and working as a police reporter for the famed City News Bureau of Chicago (his first take-home pay was $34 a week).

After nine months at City News, John became one of the first street reporters for WBBM Radio-TV, the CBS outlet in Chicago. For the next 17 years, he worked as a documentary-maker, street reporter, talk-show host and news director for CBS in Chicago and New York. He helped develop the all-news radio stations nationally for CBS Radio.

For the past 17 years, John Callaway has worked as an executive and broadcast journalist-program host for WTTW, Chicago's Public Television Station. His John Callaway Interviews series was broadcast nationally on PBS. He has hosted the Emmy-Award winning Chicago Tonight with John Callaway nightly news analysis program on WTTW since 1984.

In addition to his public broadcasting duties, John was the founding director of the William Benton Fellowships in Broadcast Journalism program at the University of Chicago in 1983.

John is married to the Chicago actress, Patrice Fletcher. He is the father of Ann Hampton Callaway, one of New York's leading cabaret singers and Liz Callaway, one of Broadway's leading musical theatre performers.

My Prayer for You

Here are my hopes and prayers for each of you:

That you will try to do what you really feel in your heart you need to do. That you will go with your instincts and take healthy chances. That you will try to take the right bite out of life. That you will not try to go it alone. That if you are hurt, lonely and overwhelmed you will seek out those who can help you, or at least talk with you about your troubles. That you will read with a passion and write if you can.

I pray that if you are lucky enough to be blessed with faith that you will try to keep it and honor it and if, by chance, you lose it, that it will someday return.

I hope that you will try to sing your own music, but that you don't listen to yourself sing (that is, don't take yourself too seriously). I hope that you will just do what you do best and let it burst forth gloriously.

I pray that you will do your homework and then do some more homework and then some more. I hope that when you find yourself debating another person that you will take care to acknowledge your opponent's argument and be prepared to make his or her case better than they can. Then your own interests and arguments will come easily.

I pray that you will not be afraid of defeat and that you will know the wisdom of confession. I pray that you will be blessed with delicious intimacy and rich family life and that you will find a life partner whose passions and vision mesh with your own.

I hope you will have the grace and good humor to hold competing truths in your mind, to embrace paradox. I pray that when you experience or encounter tragedy that you can learn and grow from it and that when you experience or encounter the thrilling beauty of life that you will carry it in your heart and mind for all your days.

John D. Calhoun

CURTIS L. CARLSON
Chairman
Carlson Companies, Inc.

Curt Carlson started in business all by himself in downtown Minneapolis in 1938. With $50 in borrowed capital, he began his entrepreneurial effort by founding the Gold Bond Stamp Co. (trading stamps).

Today, Carlson heads an empire of hotels, resorts, the largest travel agency in North America, restaurants and incentive companies spanning the globe employing more than 70,000 employees.

His Carlson Companies is ranked by Forbes magazine as one of the ten to 15 largest privately-held corporations in the U.S., with annual systemwide revenues of $8.1 billion, and plans to reach $9.2 billion in 1992.

One Step at a Time

I have been in business now for over 50 years and have found that if a person is to be successful in life, no matter what one does, he or she must have good self-esteem.

Your opinion of others may vary, but one thing that should never falter is your own self-esteem and confidence that you can do the job. A person should have complete faith in doing the task coupled with the courage to back it up. Forget what others may think or say and leap over the fears and timidity of those who lurk on the sidelines with negative thoughts. They will only impede your progress.

A successful person will make his or her own decisions, set definite goals which are realistically attainable, then shore up that confidence with the ability to reach those objectives and then "go for it!"

I have always tried to work toward goals, whether they be newspaper subscription prizes I sought to achieve while carrying a newspaper route, or when I was a soap salesman for Proctor & Gamble and was seeking one of their bonuses. I was brought up to decide on what it was I wanted and then to work until I had it.

I always wanted to be in business for myself and that makes me an entrepreneur—a category of the human race I have always been most proud being a member. Entrepreneurs are risk-takers and can only exist in the American free enterprise system. They are idealists and provide the spark and create the jobs which make the United States a fantastic place to live, play and to be in business for yourself.

To be in business for myself also meant I had to succeed by myself. I will let others decide whether or not I am successful, but, in the beginning, I remember I set a goal to earn $100 a week. I did not, at the time, set a deadline to reach my goal. Instead, I simply wrote "$100 a week" on a slip of paper and put it in my wallet and began to work toward my goal.

When I finally did attain the $100 a week goal, I threw away the paper and replaced it with one which read "$200 a week." I kept that up for much of my business life, using the paper as a measure of my progress.

What is the lesson here? It is that success is something you must work at slowly—one step at a time.

Curt Carlson

S. TRUETT CATHY
Founder and Chairman
Chick-fil-A, Inc.

Cathy is the originator of the boneless breast of chicken sandwich and founder of the country's third largest quick-service-chicken company— the 550-plus restaurant chain, Chick-fil-A.

He is one of the nation's best-known foodservice entrepreneurs, who launched a national restaurant chain from a single suburban Atlanta diner, The Dwarf House, in 1946. In 1967, he opened the first Chick-fil-A in-mall restaurant in Atlanta's Greenbriar Mall, making him one of the first to pioneer the in-mall, fast-food restaurant concept.

A man committed to running his business based on Biblical principles, he has used his company to create innovative programs to help young people. In 1993, Chick-fil-A awarded $1,102,000 in scholarships to 1,102 of its restaurant employees to help them get started on a college education. The chain will have awarded $10 million in scholarships by 1994.

In addition, the company sponsors youth-oriented programs through its WinShape Centre Foundation, which operates foster home care, summer camps and the Berry College scholarship program. These programs involve approximately 1,500 youths each year and to date have impacted 10,000 individuals.

Cathy's caring lifestyle has earned him scores of awards including the 1992 National Caring Award for being one the "ten most caring people in America." He was also inducted into the Hall of Fame for Caring Americans. In 1991, he received the Shining Light Award in recognition of his youth-oriented philanthropic programs. Readers of Atlanta Business *chose him as the magazine's 1990 Most Respected CEO in Atlanta. Previously, other Georgia CEO's selected him as the 1987 Entrepreneur of the Year. He also is the recipient of the prestigious Horatio Alger Award (1989). His professional dedication and contributions to the*

Put God in Your Life

Some people have called me a self-made man. That's not true. I'm a God-made man. I've learned that if people are going to enjoy the good things in life—peace of mind, security, happiness, abundant well-being—the very SOURCE of their supply is God.

But in our day of modern science, sophistication and vanity, it has not been fashionable to believe in a Maker. Knowledge of God has found little or no place in modern education.

You will find, as you go through life, that in last-resort desperation most people will cry out to Him for help. Wouldn't it seem more reasonable, if there is a compassionate Creator standing ready and willing to give us emergency help as a last resort, for us to seek His guidance and help all along? I suggest that you begin your quest for success by making Him a part of your life.

Through nearly fifty years of business experience there are three keys to success that I've found work for all people under every circumstance:

First, you have to *want* to succeed. You must set a goal for yourself that will arouse ambition. Ambition is more than desire. It is desire plus incentive—determination—*will* to achieve the desire. The right goal will excite vigorous and determined effort.

Second, you have to develop *know-how*. One of the things you need to learn is—*that you need to learn!* Once you've learned enough to choose a goal—you need to acquire additional education, training, experience—to give you the know-how to achieve your goal.

Finally, you have *to do it!* Accomplishment is doing. A half-hearted effort might carry you a little way toward your goal, but, it will never take you far enough to reach it. The Bible counsels us to consider the tiny ant and to be industrious. Without energy, drive, constant propulsion, a person need never expect to become truly successful.

The all-important key to success is having contact with, and the guidance and continuous help of God.

S. Truett Cathy

---

foodservice industry earned him the 1991 Pioneer of the Year Award from the Nation's Restaurant News, *and the International Foodservice Manufacturers Association's distinguished Silver Plate Award in 1988.*

NANCY LIEBERMAN-CLINE
Women's Basketball Great

Nancy Lieberman-Cline may be the best female basketball player ever. A standout in women's amateur and professional hoops, Nancy made history in 1986 by becoming the first woman to play in a men's professional league, signing with the Springfield Fame in the United States Basketball League. That triumph was followed by another first when she joined the 1987-88 Globetrotters-Washington Generals World Tour.

From her introduction to the sport on the playgrounds of her native Brooklyn, at age 7, she led the American team to the gold medal in the 1975 Pan American Games. A year later, she was the only high school member of the silver medal Olympic team.

Nancy attended Old Dominion University leading the women's varsity basketball team to a national championship in 1978-80. After graduation, she turned pro, joining the Women's Basketball League, which eventually folded. Then, in 1984, she won ABC's Women's Supersports competition and then joined the short-lived Dallas Diamonds. She became a role model for female athletes everywhere, leading her team to the WABA title in 1984, after winning the MVP award in the league's All-Star game.

Beyond the basketball court, she was the first female named to President Reagan's Sports Drug Awareness Program and has been a driving force in such charities as the Special Olympics, Just Say No Foundation and the Juvenile Diabetes Foundation. She also conducts free clinics for youngsters combining the teaching of basketball basics and motivational messages to encourage youth to be the best they can be. In 1986, Nancy was named one of the nation's Top 10 Women by Glamour Magazine.

As a respected authority, she has been an analyst/commentator for

(Continued on page 296)

Product of Environment

I really believe that people are a product of their environment. I'm a product of the schoolyards in Harlem, where I played basketball, and my home in Far Rockaway, New York.

When I was 12, my parents got divorced. My brother clung to his studies, for me basketball helped me through the difficult time. I always wanted to play because it made me happy. I grew up like any "little boy" in New York.

My biggest dream was to play in Madison Square Garden. I had my heroes like kids today have Michael Jordan and Magic Johnson. Mine were Walt Frazier and Willis Reed. These guys were the New York Knicks! I wanted to play as good as they did and where they did. I knew that I wanted to be the greatest woman basketball player ever!

I started playing basketball when I was 10. If I wanted to play in games with the boys, I had to be at least as good as them. But that wasn't enough. I started playing with them, and by imitating the way my heroes played, I found I could beat some of them. It came down to respect. I learned not to be afraid to take the A train to Harlem for even more basketball games. It might have scared my mother, but not me. Don't ever let fear beat you.

My attitude of never being afraid and always trying my hardest to beat the best led me through my youth in New York. As I went on to play in college, the Olympics, professional women's and men's basketball leagues, my attitude was always to beat and be the best. I suggest you never stop working, wanting or dreaming—which has remained my motto.

Young people today have a lot of distractions. Don't let bad grades in school, alcohol, drugs, gangs or bad influence keep you from being the best at whatever you choose to do. For me it was basketball. If it's sports for you, terrific! if you want to be the best pianist or musician, great! if you want to be a doctor, go after it! As I did, you CAN make the best of your own situation.

You may be a product of your environment, but that doesn't mean that you can't do something now or later to change or make it better.

Nancy Lieberman-Cline

MARVA COLLINS
Founder
Westside Preparatory School

Marva Collins, an inner-city elementary teacher, founded the Westside Preparatory School in 1975. Her methodology stressing adherence to the phonics system of reading, emphasis on memorization and interdisciplinary learning, enabled her to transform supposedly "unteachable" ghetto children into accomplished readers and overall students.

Mrs. Collins' achievements have earned her recognition from such institutions as the National Education Association, the American Academy of Achievement and the National Urban League.

Her devotion to students and family was the focus of "The Marva Collins Story", a Hallmark Hall of Fame CBS television special starring Cecily Tyson as Mrs. Collins and Morgan Freeman as her husband.

Mrs. Collins continues to teach while presiding over a staff of instructors she has retrained to use her teaching methods. In 1985, with a grant from Prince, the rock star, she founded Westside Prep's National Teacher Training Institute, which seeks to train 1,200 teachers throughout the United States.

Her plans for the future include running a high school and day-care center. Another objective is an adult-education facility because of her belief that many parents need the same education as her students receive.

Her honors include educator-of-the-year awards from Phi Delta Kappa and the Chicago Urban League, a United Negro College Fund Award, the Jefferson Award of the American Institute for Public Service, and designation as Legendary Woman of the World by the City of Birmingham, Alabama.

Howard University, Amherst College and Dartmouth College have awarded her honorary doctorate degrees.

You Must Have Goals

You can do it, all you need to do is remove the "t" from can't and you have can, said four-year old Talmadge to a five-year old, who was a bit ambivalent about attacking the reading of Tolstoy's selection, The Plum Bit.

I have always believed it impossible to put a band-aid on a hemorrhage, and so the very first thing I attempt to do with our students is to teach them self-reliance, self-determination, and the innate belief that "I can't simply means that one refuses to try." Every student at Westside Preparatory School, therefore, is first given an indoctrination as to what the ingredients of a West Side Prepian are.

Each student is taught to believe that life is filled with road markings, and it is our choice as to what marking we choose on this road. For example, we tell them that one road may have the markings, "fun," "play," "drugs," "hard work," "sticktoitiveness," "determination," etc., and it is left up to the individual player in life as to which marking they choose. In other words, the very first lesson our students learn is that there are no free rides in this world and that he or she who rides the back of the tiger usually ends up inside the tiger's mouth.

Therefore, it is not unusual to hear a four-year old say to a hesitant classmate, "You had better finish that work because in this school if you do not work, you do not eat." Ah! There's the rub. Now learning is easy because they have learned the most important rule of all: no pains, no gains, or, the grasp of man or woman, is equal to reach.

Thousands of visitors from all over the world, come to our Spartan, non-government, non-corporate-funded school to see what they call a miracle. I call it common-sense. Ralph Waldo Emerson said, "Man is astounded by common-sense," and that is actually what we do here. I expect the very, very best from our students and they always meet that requirement. I expect the very same from our students that I would from the sons and daughters of Harvard and Yale graduates, and I get it.

Visitors are amazed when three and four-year olds are mastering division, multiplication, and can use vocabulary words that most elite graduate students have never heard of. Not only can the young children use these words, they can also spell and write them. They can supply synonyms, antonyms, and homonyms for the words, too. They can read such great classics as: Boadicea, Suetonious, Father Hidalgo, Mary Queen of Scots, Rachel Carson, Dr. Martin Luther King, Jr., Leontyne Price, and other great works.

While many contemporary, heavily funded government aided schools declare our children illiterates and impossible to teach, I develop the attitude that the good teacher makes the "poor" student "good" and the

(Continued on page 302)

LODWRICK M. COOK
Chairman & CEO
ARCO

Lodwrick (Lod) Monroe Cook was born in Castor, La., and was raised in Grand Cane, La. He received BS degrees in mathematics and petroleum engineering at Louisiana State University in 1950 and 1955, the latter coming after a tour of duty in the U.S. Army. Later, while working, he finished an evening MBA program at Southern Methodist University.

His ARCO career began in 1956 as an engineer trainee. He went on to hold various management and executive positions before becoming President in 1985. He became Chairman of the Board and Chief Executive Officer in 1986. Mr. Cook is also Chairman of the Board of Directors of ARCO Chemical Company.

His interests outside the company focus on education, youth and minority programs. He has had a long association with Junior Achievement and serves on the National JA Board of Directors, of which he is a past chairman. His other national volunteer work includes serving as director of the Points of Light Foundation, trustee of the Aspen Institute for Humanistic Studies, and director of the LSU Foundation.

Mr. Cook's California community involvements include serving as chairman of United Way's Alexis de Tocqueville Society, member of the Board of Governors and Executive Committee of the Music Center of Los Angeles County, director of the America-China Society, trustee of the San Diego National Sports Training Foundation, and chairman of the Ronald Reagan Presidential Foundation.

His business interests include serving as director of the Business Roundtable, Business Council, World Affairs Council, Citizens Democracy Corporation and American Petroleum Institute. He is a member of the Board of Directors of H.F. Ahmanson & Company and Lockheed Corporation.

Mr. Cook is married to Carole Diane Cook and has five grown children and three granddaughters.

Setting Your Sights High

I grew up in a very small town—Grand Cane, Louisiana. It's a wonderful experience for a youth, except for one thing: It's hard to imagine being part of the larger world in any important way. Important things always seem to happen someplace else—in big cities or exotic places around the world.

But, looking back, after many years away from Grand Cane, I can tell you that achievement has nothing to do with where you've come from and everything to do with who and what you become, how you develop your character and talent. Your success ultimately depends on yourself, not your circumstances.

My high school graduating class had only five students, yet it was clear to me that being a good student and a school leader really depended on good work habits and a desire to make a contribution, not class size or elegant buildings. Colleges and employers everywhere seek people with a history of personal commitment, not privilege.

They're also looking for young men and women who have a sense of curiosity about the world. Who could benefit from your help? What activities capture your heart and mind? Science, business, communications, social service? And what institutions or companies are involved in what you like to do?

Careful self-evaluation will lead you to appropriate avenues for your talents and ambitions. The journey will involve no more than the qualities we have discussed—initiative, discipline, curiosity, creativity, diligence and vision.

By doing your best, striving to grow and serve to the extent of your ability, you can travel light years from the humblest beginning. So set your sights high: the world is full of opportunities for service and anxious to make use of your talents.

DENTON A. COOLEY, M.D.
Famous Cardiac Surgeon

One of the world's most successful and celebrated cardiac surgeons, Dr. Cooley is surgeon-in-chief of the Texas Heart Institute. He graduated with highest honors from the University of Texas in 1941 and Johns Hopkins University School of Medicine in 1944. Between 1946 and 1948, he was a captain in the Medical Corps and chief-of-surgery at the 124th Station Hospital in Linz, Austria. After completing surgical training at Johns Hopkins in 1940, he spent a year with Lord Russell Brock in London, where he participated in the first intracardiac operations in England.

Dr. Cooley has been described as the world's most productive cardiac surgeon, as well as one of the most skilled technicians in his field. Even more important, he is an innovator in the field of cardiovascular surgery, constantly revising and improving existing procedures as well as developing new surgical techniques to correct previously inoperable conditions.

In 1969, he became the first surgeon to implant an artificial heart in man. By 1989, Dr. Cooley and his team had performed over 75,000 open heart operations. He has contributed to the development of techniques for repair and replacement of diseased heart valves and is widely known for operations to correct congenital heart anomalies in infants and children.

One of Dr. Cooley's most significant contributions to the field of cardiac surgery and cardiology was founding the Texas Heart Institute in Houston. Within 27 years, since the founding in 1965, the Institute has become a world-renowned leader in research, education and patient care in the field of cardiovascular diseases.

Dr. Cooley is a member or honorary member of over 50 professional

(Continued on page 296)

Take ACTion

Getting what you want from life is not always easy, but it can be done. You can do it through ACTion, that is,

A chievement

C ourage, and

T enacity.

Achievement begins by setting goals. Setting goals sounds simple, yet most of us never take the time to write down our goals. Most of us, in fact, never even identify goals, or if we do, they are of the New Year's resolution type that we never really plan to achieve.

To establish goals and to set a reasonable time frame for achieving them, you must first assess your resources. Ask yourself what is realistic. Then, take action and evaluate your results. Study success. Ask yourself questions. Who is achieving the goals I want to achieve? What are they doing? Guide yourself down the same path as others who are achieving what you would like to achieve.

Once your goals are set, you need the courage to achieve them, even the courage to fail. As infants, we have this type of courage. Take, for example, a ten-month-old infant who is learning to walk. Falls, injuries and failures occur at a shattering rate, a rate that later in life would discourage almost anyone from learning a new activity. The same can be said for many other activities—learning to ride a bicycle, to roller-skate, and to play competitive sports.

You should always maintain this youthful courage. Do not, in your maturity, become flexible. The on-set of inflexibility is insidious, almost never recognized by the victim. It occurs when one stops questioning and evaluating—when one takes the ideas and convictions thus far accumulated and settles them in concrete, protecting them from change or modification. A person afflicted by this deadening phase of inflexibility finds new ideas uncomfortable, even a little frightening. He has arranged his mind, his attitudes, his life so that there is no room for expansion—expansion may be risky. He feels safe. But he has stopped growing.

To continue to grow, to overcome the falls, the failures, the obstacles to success, you need tenacity. You need to be able to pursue your goals, even beyond what you perceive are your capabilities. In my opinion, success is earned in the vast majority of instances. Hard work, determination, and self-discipline are the keys to success. A few achieve success through "luck," but I believe that the harder one works, the "luckier" he becomes. Perseverance toward goals usually provides the rewards of success.

You can choose not to *stumble* through life. Just remember to ACT.

Denton A. Cooley

HELEN K. COPLEY
Chairman & CEO
The Copley Press, Inc.

Helen Copley is one of the foremost women executives in America. Besides heading Copley Newspapers, which publishes 11 dailies, 46 weeklies, and one bi-weekly newspaper, she is also publisher of the San Diego Union-Tribune.

Mrs. Copley succeeded to these positions in 1973, upon the death, at age 57, of her husband, James S. Copley. Her courage in overcoming personal hardships, outstanding effort in reorganizing the corporation, her impeccable integrity and humanitarianism earned her the prestigious Horatio Alger Award in 1990.

Born Helen Kinney in Cedar Rapids, Iowa, she graduated from Benjamin Franklin High School there and later attended Hunter College in New York City. She has received honorary degrees from Coe College, Pepperdine University and the University of San Diego.

Mrs. Copley was the first woman elected to the board of directors of the California Chamber of Commerce (1974-1977). She is active in numerous civic, charitable and cultural organizations, as well as patriotic and professional groups. In 1990, she received the Boys and Girls Club of San Diego Golden Achievement Award for meritorious and unselfish service to San Diego and its youth. She is the first woman recipient of this award in the 28 years of its existence.

Mrs. Copley is a trustee of the Howard Hughes Medical Institute and trustee emeritus of Scripps Clinic and Research Foundation in LaJolla, California.

She was appointed to the National Commission on the Observance of International Woman's Year by President Ford in 1975, and was appointed by California Governor Jerry Brown to the Commission on Government Reform in 1976.

Among the scores of awards she's received is the Golden Plate Award

A Worthy Vocation

I spent a memorable New Year's Eve in West Berlin at the time when the wall had just been torn open between East and West Germany. Everywhere there were toasts to freedom. I was struck by their depth of meaning and feeling.

As a newspaper publisher I feel a deep responsibility toward the development and preservation of freedom for all. Newspapers are a key part of the communication explosion which is now spreading the seeds of freedom in the soil of Eastern Europe.

There is still a question about how the new-found freedom will thrive. It may depend upon how many young Horatio Algers spring forth in the nations where free enterprise has been extinct. In my mind, there is no question that a free press is essential for democratic success at home and abroad.

I urge you to keep informed through our free press. Beyond the electronic media, become an in-depth reader of newspapers, periodicals and books. Take advantage of one of America's most precious resources—your local library. There you can travel the world, share the accomplishments of successful people you can emulate as role models, and you can explore every subject on earth.

I also encourage you to consider journalism as a vocation, and the newspaper field in particular, for your life's work. Not only will it be a self-satisfying experience, it will also enable you to participate in preserving freedom for everyone.

Helen K. Copley

---

from the American Academy of Achievement as one of forty eminent "exemplars of excellence" from the nation's many fields of endeavor.
Mrs. Copley and her son, David, reside in LaJolla, California.

MICHAEL W. COPPS
Chairman & CEO
The Copps Corporation

Michael W. Copps took over as chairman and CEO of The Copps Corporation in 1980. He joined the company in 1970 and climbed the executive ladder while gaining experience in various company functions. He served as real estate and site researcher, personnel director, warehouse superintendent, vice president/warehousing and transportation, and executive vice president/wholesale operations before assuming his present position.

The Copps Corporation is a wholesale and retail food distribution business headquartered in Stevens Point, Wisconsin. The firm distributes grocery products to independent and corporately-owned IGA stores in a 150-mile radius around Stevens Point.

In the early 1980s Copps pulled out of the general merchandise business to concentrate solely on the food business. In six short years, the company built ten new super centers, added significantly to its independent business and doubled sales. They also doubled the size of their distribution facility and are prepared to double business again in the early '90s.

Copps has a bachelors degree and law degree from the University of Wisconsin. He is married with two children, Clint, 16, and Carolyn, 12. His affiliations include serving as a board member of the Independent Grocer's Alliance, Goodwill Industries, and Pacelli Foundation. A Special Olympics ambassador, he is also fund drive chairman for the United Way of Portage County. In 1988, he was named Citizen of the Year by the Stevens Point Chamber of Commerce.

Use Your Ability to Reason

What I want to urge you to consider is exactly the same thing I stress to my own children. The most important gift you have is the ability to reason. You should never act nor should you ever subordinate your thoughts to another person unless it is consistent with your reasoned judgement.

Failure to reason allows bigots and those people preaching prejudices to flourish in various societies. Individuals like Adolph Hitler, James Jones, Saddam Hussein, and countless others, rely on the fact that their following is totally involved emotionally and thus capable of being led without any appeal to reason.

This same sense of reason should apply to your actions in your daily life and chosen profession. First and foremost, you have to listen to yourself over all others, including those whom you consider your superiors. This is the only way you can be accountable and responsible for your actions. You eventually have to say that it is because of the choices I have made that I am where I am and not the choices or forces of someone else. Remember: there is a correlation between your control of your life and your mental well-being.

Other helpful thoughts:

1) The world will definitely let you have what you want. It's an amazing fact, but only five percent of all people in the United States read more than one book a year. That means there is an incredible avenue ahead of you to travel on. A modest amount of discipline will have you surging ahead of the masses. Think of this, there is a proven direct correlation between a large vocabulary and success in any given field. Can you imagine the gift you'll give yourself if you just add a word a day to your vocabulary? It also enhances greatly your power to reason that we talked about above.

2) The strongest language known to mankind is actually unspoken. It's a smile. You'll find that most people who succeed are not power mongers. In fact, they're quite gentle. They intuitively, or by the use of their reason, realize the power and sanctity of a smile. It's appeal is that it shows you as a kind and considerate person. It shows that you respect the dignity of all people, including those below you as well as those above you. If you smile, you're approachable, and its effect is to lay out a red carpet for you to walk on the rest of your life.

3) Do the job that you're doing now to the best of your ability. At various stages in life we all get caught up in some type of job or activity that we don't appreciate. The best advice I can think of is to do the job uncommonly well so that it becomes the stepping stone to the job you do want. A complainer might have a legitimate reason to complain, but

(Continued on page 303)

BOB COSTAS
NBC Broadcaster

Bob Costas began his professional career at WSYR-TV/Radio while studying at Syracuse University in 1973, where he majored in journalism. At age 22, he landed a job at KMOX Radio in St. Louis, Missouri, one of America's most prominent radio stations. He broadcast a wide variety of live, play-by-play, and studio programs for KMOX from 1974 through 1981. One of his primary assignments was play-by-play for the ABA's Spirits of St. Louis team. He did regional NFL and NBA telecasts for CBS (1976-79) and was the radio voice of the University of Missouri basketball games (1976-81) and the NBA Chicago Bulls (1980).

In 1980 he began his career at NBC Sports, initially as football and basketball play-by-play man. From 1983 through 1989, Costas teamed with analyst Tony Kubek on NBC's baseball "Game of the Week" telecasts, forming one of baseball's most popular broadcasting teams. He hosted the network's popular "NFL Live" from 1984 to 1992 and hosted Super Bowls XX, XXIII and XXVI. Bob was one of the hosts for the 1988 Summer Olympiad XXIV in Seoul, Korea and he hosted the 1992 Summer Olympics in Barcelona.

Bob has won the Emmy award as "outstanding Sports Broadcaster" five times and has been named by his peers as the National Sportscaster of the Year in 1985, 1987, 1988, 1991 and 1992. When he first won this award in 1985 at age 33—he was the youngest broadcaster to be so honored. The American Sportscaster Association presented him its Sportscaster of the Year Award in 1989, 1991, 1992, and 1993.

Beginning in 1988, Bob diversified beyond sports broadcasting. He served as a substitute for Bryant Gumbel on NBC's "Today Show," and hosted his own late-night program, "Later—With Bob Costas" from 1988 until February 1994. Bob currently holds a unique position with NBC Sports, News, and Entertainment.

What Is Success?

One definition of success is to do something you care about as well as you are able to do it.

Too often we view success in terms of the most obvious achievements. The larger salary, the promotion to a more prominent position. Finances and professional standing are valid considerations, of course —up to a point—but, ideally they should be an outgrowth of a job well done, in a field which provides personal satisfaction.

The work I do is very visible work, more likely to draw reactions of approval (or occasionally disapproval) on a larger scale. My wife, on the other hand, taught elementary school for many years. She wasn't just a competent teacher, she was extraordinary. She gave her heart to it. It was an extension of her personality. Hardly a week goes by now without her hearing from a student she taught in kindergarten or third grade. A young person now in high school or college remembers her fondly and appreciates the contribution she made to their life. On her terms, my wife is every bit as successful as I have been on my terms.

My sister is a woman in her 30s. What does she do? She's a clown. That's right, a professional clown. She entertains at children's hospitals, birthday parties, whatever. She dresses up like Emmet Kelly and carries a bag of tricks. Her files bulge with letters of appreciation from the parents of children whose lives she has brightened. Could she make more money and enjoy more prestige of a certain kind doing something else? Sure. Could she be as successful, though? What do you think? What she does is a legitimate way of blending her profession with her heart. There is a warmth and childlike quality about her, in or out of makeup. She has found a way to make who she is a part of her work. She is one of the most successful people I know.

Everyone's circumstances, talents, ambitions, relationships, and obstacles faced are different. My only advice would be to think of success in personal terms and not be constrained by narrow prevailing notions of success which may limit you. Identify a legitimate set of goals that have meaning for you, then pursue them with determination and integrity.

Bob Costas

Costas is a native of Queens, New York, who grew up on Long Island. He fell in love with sports as a child while following the New York Yankees' Mickey Mantle. Bob resides in St. Louis, Missouri, with his wife, Randy, and their children, son Keith and daughter Taylor.

WILLIAM E. C. DEARDEN
Chairman of the Board (Retired)
Hershey Foods Corporation

Bill Dearden is a rarity. He's a man who was helped in adversity by his hero, Milton S. Hershey, and then went on to emulate his role model so well that he became head of the empire his late benefactor had built. The odds of that happening are staggering.

When his mother died, Bill's father, an out-of-work Philadelphia factory worker, got him into the Milton Hershey School. It was a wholesome setting for boys and girls who had lost one or both parents and needed financial support.

After graduating from Hershey, where students still live in 85 houses with house parents and must do chores as well as study, Dearden attended Albright College earning his BS degree in economics. He took graduate work at Harvard and Temple Universities. He served in the U.S. Navy in World War II and the Korean War.

Feeling the need to repay the debt he felt he owed the school for what it had done for him, he left a lucrative corporate career to return to serve the school as assistant business manager. It soon became evident that he was a leader and he joined the Hershey Foods Corporation staff. He proved an outstanding planner and sales executive as he scaled the corporate ladder to the top. Under his leadership, the company moved from being a chocolate and confectionery business to become a major, diversified, international food and food related company.

Dearden's many directorships, awards, honorary degrees and other recognitions (too numerous to mention) reflect perhaps the most important lesson he learned from Milton Hershey—to share with others. He is especially happy when he reads the annual reports of the company's continuing success, knowing the school where he got his start still owns 42 percent of the company stock, while maintaining voting control.

Have a Role Model

Write down on paper what you want to be, what will be required to accomplish your plan/dream, the significant milestones you must successfully pass along the way to be on schedule. Why put it on paper? Because that's the only way you will seriously consider the matter and evaluate the alternatives. You should carry it in your wallet and read it every day to remind you where you want to go.

Once established, you must then pursue your plan/dream with a dedication and single-mindedness that will carry you over the rough spots. You must have the courage to stay with it. This means you must be willing to make the sacrifices and put forth the work to make your plan a reality. It won't be easy, but the rewards of success are second to none.

In all of this it pays to have a role model—a hero—someone whose life and deeds are such an inspiration to you that you want to emulate his / her life. Mine was Milton S. Hershey, the man who developed the Hershey bar and made the name Hershey synonymous with chocolate throughout the United States.

A poor farm boy from a broken home, he only had a fourth grade education, received in eight different schools because his family moved so often. At age 13, he was apprenticed to a candy maker in Lancaster, Pennsylvania, and that is where he found his life's work / dream.

At age 19, he completed his apprenticeship and started his own business in Philadelphia in 1876—our centennial year. During the next ten years he failed miserably in the candy business. He returned to Lancaster in 1886 with only the clothes on his back and was ridiculed as a failure.

Despite the criticism, he was determined to be a successful candy maker and borrowed money to start a fourth time in a loft in Lancaster. To make a long story short, this time he was a huge success—so much that in 1900 he sold his caramel business for $1 million. While in the caramel business, he had been experimenting with chocolate and, at age 46, he broke ground in 1903 in a cornfield that is now Hershey, Pa., for his chocolate factory, investing his $1 million in the new venture.

After a slow start, the business grew and with the profits he built a beautiful community for his employees and visitors. He and his wife founded a school for orphan boys because they could have no children of their own. At the school's dedication in 1909, he said if the school graduated 100 children it would be a good thing. However, his business grew so fast that in 1918 he turned over stock of Hershey Chocolate Company valued at $60 million to a trust for the perpetuation of the school. Today Milton Hershey School has an enrollment of 1,200 boys

(Continued on page 303)

ARTHUR J. DECIO
Chairman & CEO
Skyline Corporation

Art Decio, of Elkhart, Indiana, heads a leading U.S. producer of manufactured housing and recreational vehicles with 31 operating companies in 14 states from coast to coast.

He has received presidential appointments to three national commissions and has served on the boards of more than 30 civic, religious, business, educational and financial institutions, including the Federal Reserve Bank of Chicago. Decio currently is a trustee and fellow of the University of Notre Dame, a vice chairman of the National Salvation Army Advisory Board, and a director of Special Olympics International, Washington, D.C.; Banc One Indiana Corporation, Indianapolis, NIPSCO Industries, Inc., Hammond, Indiana; and Schwarz Paper Co., Chicago.

His community involvement is extensive. He is president of the Elkhart General Hospital Foundation and the Elkhart Park Foundation, Inc., serves on the advisory boards of Indiana University and Goshen College, and is a member of the Finance Council of the Diocese of Fort Wayne-South Bend.

Born in Elkhart, he attended Marmion Military Academy and DePaul University, Chicago, and holds honorary degrees from the University of Notre Dame and Indiana State University.

Among his many awards are the 1987 Alexis de Tocqueville Award from the United Way of America, Alexandria, Virginia, for outstanding voluntary service to community and country; the Salvation Army's William Booth Award and its Others Award; and the 1984 Career Achievement Award of the National Italian-American Foundation, Washington, D.C.

In 1989, he was the recipient of the Rev. Howard J. Kenna C.S.C. Award from Notre Dame and its founding religious community, and the Rev. John J. Cavanaugh C.S.C Award for distinguished public service from the Notre Dame Alumni Association. In 1991, he was the first re-

Take Advantage of Today

All of us have a choice. We can waste our time reliving yesterday or daydreaming about tomorrow. Or we can delight in God's great gift—today.

As long as we live, today never will be repeated. It is as unique and fragile as a snowflake. It is 24 hours, 1,440 minutes, 86,400 seconds packed with opportunities.

Our obligation is to take advantage of every second, to make full use of our talents, to never do less than our best.

By being true to ourselves. Each of us is different. Each has been blessed with a special set of interests and attributes. So we must try to understand ourselves and how we fit into the world around us. We must look into our own hearts to learn who we are and what we can be.

By setting goals. Letting life just happen is a formula for failure. We need to decide what we want for ourselves and for all who will be affected by our lives. Then we must outline a plan of action that will bring our goals to reality.

By accepting responsibility. It's easy to blame our problems on our parents or school or society. But blaming others does not solve problems. It only keeps us from seeing the truth. We cannot change others. We can change ourselves.

By increasing our knowledge. The changing world of the 1990s has little room for the uneducated and unskilled. For every person in every walk of life, learning is a lifelong necessity.

By being sensitive to others. All of us were called to help those who are incapable of helping themselves. By listening to others, by sharing our time, energy and resources, we enrich not only them but ourselves.

By strengthening our faith. By giving us today, God opened the door to love and friendship, challenge and adventure, beauty and laughter, to all the treasures of human existence. We cannot return the favor. But we can offer thanks as we work to build a world that lives up to the expectations of all of God's people.

Art Decio

---

cipient of the Indiana Special CAUSE Award, presented by the Indiana Association of Rehabilitation Facilities. The award was created to recognize an Indiana resident who has made a positive difference for persons with disabilities.

Art and his wife, Patricia, have five children.

DR. ARTHUR DeKRUYTER
Founding Pastor
Christ Church of Oak Brook

Arthur DeKruyter as born in Grand Rapids, Michigan, where he was raised by Christian parents, who belonged to the Christian Reformed Church.

His religious education began at Calvin College and Calvin Theological Seminary in his home town, where he received his Th.B. Later, Princeton Theological Seminar granted him a Th.M. and Westminster College in New Wilmington, Pennsylvania, conferred a D.D. degree.

Right out of Princeton, he accepted a call to Western Springs Christian Reformed Church in suburban Chicago, where he pastored for over 13 years. In 1965, he was called to found a new church in Oak Brook, Illinois. The parish started with five families. Today, Christ Church of Oak Brook has more than 5,500 members with about 2,300 families. His "Pulpit of Christ Church" has reached television viewers since 1980.

Since 1972 Dr. DeKruyter has been a member of the board of trustees of Fuller Theological Seminary, Pasadena, California. During that period the seminary has become the largest inter-denominational seminary in the world with over 3,000 students. Because of his reputation and interest in preaching, a Preaching Chair has been endowed and named in his honor at Fuller. In 1989 he was appointed Eastern Europe representative of Fuller Seminary with the assignment of the establishment of an ecumenical seminary in the U.S.S.R. He has made several fact-finding trips to the Soviet Union in this capacity. The seminary officially opened in Leningrad in 1990.

Under his leadership, Christ Church of Oak Brook has become known for its creative leadership in the development of mega-church ministries. Each fall ministers come from the entire Midwest to learn about church growth. Dr. DeKruyter has a special interest in young ministers and makes himself available to a growing number of clergy who seek his advice and counsel.

Principles for Productive Living

The experiences of life are never the same. Every day something new happens. Some people welcome change, and other people become very afraid. Some people see trouble and anticipate problems. I encourage you to see life as a constant flow of opportunities. For me there have been five very simple rules for seizing opportunities and making the most of them.

The first one of these rules is: Be Willing to Learn. Early in life I discovered that the people I wanted to associate with were the people who were better than I. In a sport, I discovered that, when I played with my superiors I played better. In my profession I have always gone to listen to others who were doing it better than I.

When I discovered that I had some potential abilities, I decided to find someone who could help me by example as well as by precept. I traveled distances to relate to these people. I listened to them, I watched them, I imitated them, and then I found my own identity. The most exciting thing is to learn how to do things in a new and better way.

A second thing to learn is: Never Feel Sorry for Yourself. Feelings of bitterness because one feels very sorry for oneself is one of the worst things that can ever happen. Promise yourself that you will never feel sorry for yourself no matter what the circumstances are. Always look to find something for which to be grateful and thankful. That has kept me out of many troubles, and it has kept a very positive attitude in my mind.

A third thing that I had to learn was: I Am Never Alone. Remember that you are never alone. God is always present with you through his son, Jesus Christ. Talk to him. Listen for his guidance. Take time to study the Bible. Learn to be productive in life, to practice inner peace, and to have great hope for the future. Never start the day without talking to God, asking for his presence, his wisdom, and his guidance. Never go to sleep at night without thanking him for being your friend, for being near to you and giving you wisdom, for forgiving your sins and picking you up when you fail, and for keeping you humble in times of success. One day at a time lived in the presence of God will make all things possible.

A fourth thing that is very important is: Keep Your Sense of Humor. We must be able to laugh not only at others but at ourselves. People who insist on doing everything exactly right and are super-sensitive to the criticisms of others lose the joy of living. They often punish themselves for mistakes. They remember for a long, long time the things that others did that hurt them and the things that failed. Learn to be forgiving and put failures behind you. I continue to learn all the time

(Continued on page 303)

DICK DeVOS
President
Amway Corporation

When his father, Rich DeVos, retired in 1993 as president of Amway Corporation, Dick DeVos succeeded him and accepted the responsibility and challenge of helping lead Amway into the next century. At the age of 37, he became president of a multibillion dollar global corporation experiencing rapid growth and expansion around the world.

Amway Corporation was founded in 1959 by Rich DeVos and Jay Van Andel from their homes in Ada, Michigan. Today Amway is one of the largest direct selling companies in the world, with reported annual sales in excess of $3.5 billion and more than two million independent distributors and 10,000 employees in 60 countries and territories. In addition to 400 Amway products, independent distributors sell thousands of other brand-name products and services.

Dick DeVos is well prepared to be president of a large corporation. He began working for the company in 1974, holding positions in various departments during the next ten years. In 1984, he became Vice President/International, responsible for the operation of Amway's affiliate companies in 18 countries. Under his leadership, sales more than tripled, and international sales exceeded domestic sales for the first time in the company's history.

In 1989, the entrepreneurial spirit of his heritage took him out on his own. He started his own company, The Windquest Group, a multi-company management group. When the DeVos family became the owners of the Orlando Magic in 1991, DeVos also became President and CEO of that NBA franchise.

He also contributes his expertise to a long list of civic activities that benefit his community, state of Michigan, and country. These include his service on the Michigan State Board of Education, appointment by Governor John Engler to the Michigan Job Commission, and appointment

Find a Firm Foundation

All young people face the task of building lives they hope will stand tall and weather the storms. The life you build is your decision and your responsibility, but you do not have to be alone in the project. All of us are fortunate to have a foundation of values that have been given to us by our Creator and instilled in us by our parents (and others) that are the principles of a successful life. I've found a key to success is to build from a firm foundation.

When I accepted my responsibilities as president of Amway Corporation, I realized my success and the continued success of the company, its employees, and distributors would depend on the wisdom and values I learned from my father and his partner. We are all uniquely created individuals in this world, but most truly successful people never forget their roots—their family traditions and values. Growing trees and growing people need roots that are deep and strong.

Listening to stories of independent Amway distributors who have fulfilled their dreams of success, I hear the shared values and traditions that have become our company's foundation for success. People who achieve their highest goals in Amway (and in life, as well) have many values in common. Here are a few that I believe are part of their solid foundation:

Integrity—a full-time commitment to doing what is right, not what is convenient.

Excellence—striving to achieve the full potential of your God-given talents.

Responsibility to others—reaching out to help those less fortunate than ourselves.

Faith—believing God has a plan for this world, and that we are all part of that plan.

Worth of the individual—realizing each individual's role—large or small—is important to an organization or community, and that each person is special.

Freedom—everyone should be free to believe as they wish and to pursue their highest goals.

Family—honoring the traditions of our parents and making your family a priority.

(Continued on page 304)

---

by President George Bush to the White House Commission on Presidential Scholars. His awards include the Distinguished Service Awards from the Association of Independent Colleges and Universities of Michigan, Northwood University, and the Grand Rapids, Michigan Jaycees.

MIKE DITKA
Football Great
NBC Analyst

Mike Ditka holds the unique distinction of being a Super Bowl champion as a player, assistant coach and head coach.

His career in the National Football League began in 1961 when the Chicago Bears selected him in the first round out of the University of Pittsburgh, where he was an All-American end. He made an instant impact by earning NFL Rookie of the Year honors.

Mike played five more seasons with the Bears, earning a Pro Bowl trip each year. Known for his intensity, after dislocating his left shoulder, he played the 1964 season in a harness, and virtually one-handed caught 75 passes, then an NFL record for tight ends and still an all-time Bears mark.

After two years with the Philadelphia Eagles, he joined the Dallas Cowboys. He played four seasons with Dallas, where he caught a touchdown pass in their 24-3 win over the Dolphins in Super Bowl VI.

As a coach, in nine seasons as a Dallas assistant, Ditka helped the Cowboys win three NFC titles and a Super Bowl. His eight years in Chicago have included three trips to the NFC title game, five division crowns, and a Super Bowl victory.

The final accolade to his outstanding playing career was bestowed upon him in 1988 when he became the first tight end inducted into the Pro Football Hall of Fame.

Ditka is a highly sought after motivational speaker and is actively involved in numerous charitable endeavors including Misericordia, Fellowship of Christian Athletes, Sports Teams Organized for Prevention of Drug Abuse and Say No to Drugs. He has established the Mike Ditka Endowed Scholarship at the University of Pittsburgh.

Conceive, Believe, Achieve

I remember telling the Bears football team back in the fall of 1984, "What your mind can conceive, and your heart will believe, you can achieve."

This is not just an idealistic statement, but rather the motivational factor by which all of us should live. Does it work? The Bears team, which won the Super Bowl in 1985, is evidence that it does.

The human will is a great and powerful force. It enables us to do far more than we feel we are capable of doing.

I truly believe we must set in our mind the goals we want to achieve, then we must find the methods and apply the work ethics that will help us reach these goals.

In order to achieve anything in life, we must make a commitment and have a deep conviction that we will relentlessly pursue our goals. We must exercise great discipline and sacrifice in order to find success. We must be sure that the goals and rewards we seek in life are worth the price we will have to pay. Success does not come easy.

Every single person is a creation of God and has a God-given talent. We must find that talent and then maximize it to the best of our ability. In other words we must be the best we can be.

You can do it, just as I can do it. We can do it and the team can do it.

An avid golfer, he plays in various charity events. He was part of CBS-TV's playoff coverage and played himself in an episode of the popular television series, "L.A. Law." He is now an analyst for NBC-TV.

GRACE E. EASLEY
Poet

Grace E. Easley was born on January 24, 1928, in McComb, Missis-sippi. Her father worked on the Illinois Central Railroad, and her mother took care of Grace until she died with pneumonia at a very early age.

After that Grace was sent to St. Mary of the Pines, a Catholic boarding school for girls, which was run by the School Sisters of Notre Dame, at Chatawa, Mississippi, near McComb. Her father faithfully visited her every Sunday, always telling her colorful stories of the railroad, to which he devoted his life.

On one occasion, one of Grace's teachers scolded her for spending too much time on her poems, and not enough on her books, to which Grace replied, "I could sooner stop breathing, than I could stop writing." That has remained true until this day.

Grace is a lover of nature, animals and of all things beautiful. Her po-ems reflect her feelings and have been widely published.

Lesson

They said "you'll never make it,"
And they thought that they were right,
But I kept on plodding onward,
Because I hoped I might.
They shook their heads in wonder,
That I lacked the sense to quit,
But I held my chin up higher,
And I didn't mind a bit.

They said "you'll never make it,"
As the problems multiplied,
But I had to make an effort,
And to know at least I tried.
So I dug my heels in deeper,
Though sometimes my spirits lagged,
And I shouldered what was lightest,
And the rest I sort of dragged.

And I found to my amazement,
At the ending of the day,
That what they said I couldn't,
I had managed anyway.
It only took three little words,
"Lord help me," and I rid
Myself of doubt, and all they said
I'd never do—I did.

Grace E. Easley

JOHN J. EDL
President
Noble Production & Recording, Inc.

John Edl is a successful small businessman who epitomizes what being an entrepreneur is all about. He founded his company with only $400 capital. During the firm's early years, he performed all of the company's research, administrative, development, sales, advertising, promotion and service functions himself. A hands-on technician, he enhanced his knowledge of electronics and business by studying technical manuals, attending seminars, and taking courses offered by companies in his field of interest.

Starting is a one-room home-based studio he developed Noble into a corporate entity which today includes a full-service photo studio and a state-of-the-art video communications center with network special effects capability.

Upon returning from service in the U.S. Air Force following the Korean War, ohn worked for various companies honing his management, production and service skills. This experience convinced him that he could make it on his own. The rest is history.

Long active in community affairs, Edl served 22 years on the Board of Fire and Police Commissioners in Bensenville, Illinois, where he has lived for 41 years. For 16 of those years he chaired the board which was recognized for its innovation in the development of testing and training programs used throughout Illinois. He created the Fire and Police Commission Manual and other courses still being used at the University of Illinois.

From the outset, John was encouraged by his parents and his wife, Elaine, who functioned as a "Jill of all trades" as the twosome handled all duties of the business until they could hire additional staff. The Edls are good role models for would-be entrepreneurs, who are willing to work hard, take risks, and make sacrifices to achieve their goals.

Entrepreneurial Challenge

Being a successful entrepreneur is one of the most rewarding experiences one can have in life. Aside from the financial rewards, nothing can match the satisfaction and pride that comes from knowing you succeeded on your own.

I think the primary reason that people limit themselves is fear. It's a real demotivator. My success came because I could not afford to fail—so I did not tolerate it. This doesn't mean that I didn't have setbacks and make mistakes, everyone does. I learned from them and kept moving toward my goal.

What keeps a person moving forward? Desire. To be a success on your own you must have a burning, all-consuming desire to realize your dream. You've got to want to reach your goal with such intensity that you are willing to make the sacrifices, and put in the long hours and hard work necessary to achieve your objective.

The long-standing entrepreneurial challenge to "find a niche and fill it" still applies today. In our gadget oriented world the most overworked phrase is state-of-the-art. It pertains only to equipment and has nothing to do with skill and experience. It's a fact that 80% of the people who own VCR's, which represent state-of-the-art, can't program the equipment. I found my niche in adapting ever-changing equipment and technology to the needs of the marketplace.

Finally, you must be in touch with your God. When all is said and done life boils down to just the two of you. Worldly success passes away. I think of that every time I see a beautiful sunset. Do you realize that stunning sight takes place despite the many layers of pollution between the earth and sun. Only God could accomplish that breathtaking experience. Think then what He can do with any pollution which might exist in your mind. All you need do is ask for His help. He should be your best partner in whatever you do—if He is, your success will be assured.

CHRIS EVERT
Professional Tennis Champion

Chris Evert, master of the baseline, was the world's No. 1 ranked seven times during her 16-year professional tennis career that included 18 Grand Slam titles (three Wimbledons, seven French Opens, two Australian Opens and six U.S. Open Championships), before she retired in 1989 at age 34.

Chris won 1,309 matches, holds 157 singles titles, and won at least one Grand Slam singles title for 13 consecutive years, each a record for either men or women in professional tennis history.

In 1985, the Women's Sports Foundation named her "Greatest Women Athlete in the Last 25 Years."

Chris is in her unprecedented ninth term as president of the Women's Tennis Association. She oversees the overall operation of the player's organization and helps coordinate the activities of more than 1,500 players.

In 1990, she was among nine Women of the Year selected by Glamour Magazine in honor of her outstanding commitment to social causes. Chris serves as spokesperson for Clean Start, the public/private funded program to help drug addicted pregnant women and their babies. She organized and hosted the Chris Evert/Phar-Mor Celebrity Tennis Classic which raised nearly $1 million to benefit the program. It is administered through Chris Evert Charities, Inc. and the Governor of Florida. Chris also raised $350,000 to build a drug treatment center in Delray Beach, Florida.

A board member of the President's Council on Physical Fitness and Sports, she was presented the Flo Hyman Award by President George Bush in 1990 in recognition of her contributions to sports.

Chris is married to Andy Mill, the former Olympian and No. 1 American skier for seven years. The Mills have two children, Alexander and Nicholas Joseph.

Have a Passion in Life

My dad, Jimmy Evert, a teaching tennis pro, thought tennis provided a wholesome atmosphere to raise his five children. In between teaching us how to hit ground strokes and two-handed backhands, he sprinkled in some fatherly advice that has helped me on and off the court.

"Never lose your temper" was a cardinal rule. I've seen some big matches lost and meaningful relationships broken because a person became upset. Learn to control your temper by realizing that it's not the situation that angers you—it's your reaction to the situation. I remembered that even on center court at Wimbledon.

Sports provide a natural high. Drugs cannot match the feeling one gets in winning a hard-fought match. Tennis, in particular, is most exhilarating because you're on your own—no one can make the shots for you.

Sports and other special interests offer you ways to avoid drugs and crime. I believe everyone should have a passion in life, especially kids. Mine was tennis. You should have a reason to wake up each morning—some activity that makes you stretch to your own limit.

Doing something worthwhile, working hard and doing it well breeds confidence. When you're confident any reasonable goal is within your reach—go for it!

Chris Evert

BOB FELLER
Baseball Hall of Famer

Robert William Feller was born on November 3, 1918, in Van Meter, Iowa. He played baseball throughout his grade school and high school years. In his spare time, Bob played catch with his father, which helped to develop a pitching arm capable of throwing a baseball at over 100 miles per hour.

Bob played four years of American Legion baseball, as well as amateur and semi-professional ball, before signing with the Cleveland Indians at age 16. In his first start, he struck out 15 St. Louis Browns. Later the same year, he fanned 17 Philadelphia Athletics, setting a new American League record. In 1938, he established a new major league record by striking out 18 Detroit Tigers.

Two days after the Japanese attack on Pearl Harbor, he enlisted in the United States Navy. He served three years aboard the U.S.S. Alabama, earning eight Battle Stars. After his discharge, Bob returned to the Indians and soon established an American League record of 348 strikeouts in a single season, pitched three no-hit games and 12 one-hitters.

The first pitcher in major league history to win 20 or more games before age 21, he played in nine All-Star games, two World Series, and was elected into baseball's Hall of Fame in 1962. In 1969, he was selected "Greatest Living Right-Hand Pitcher" as part of Professional Baseball's Centennial Celebration.

He has authored three books, Strikeout Story, How to Pitch *and* Now Pitching. *Feller and his wife, Anne, live in Gates Mills, Ohio. Bob heads the Cleveland Indians Speakers Bureau, takes part in various baseball promotion events, and is involved in numerous corporate activities.*

Disposition Is Important

There are a lot of things that go into the makeup of a baseball player. One seldom-noted attribute is disposition.

Physical assets, such as the ability to hit a ball hard, to throw with speed and accuracy, and to run fast, are all necessary. But, without proper disposition, the athlete blessed with natural ability will not make the grade in the major leagues.

The disposition of a pitcher can often be most accurately measured by watching how he pitches when he is behind and is apparently pitching for a losing cause. Baseball scouts will not make up their minds on a young pitcher in the minor leagues until they see how he pitches when he's getting beat.

Disposition means a person is industrious. In baseball they call industriousness "hustle." It's a word players hear every minute, every hour of the day in spring training—and through the season. Some otherwise worthy players never make it to the big leagues because they have the wrong disposition.

The late Lou Fonseca, one-time American League batting champion and an excellent batting instructor, often used Ty Cobb as an example to young players he spoke to in clinics. Most people don't realize that Cobb was not a great natural hitter. He studied opposing pitchers and players. He studied himself and made adjustments in his batting stance, even developed his famous "hands-apart" grip on the bat. His concentration on a winning performance was so steady, so relentless, that it made a great difference in this great player.

I suggest all young people develop a good disposition toward everything they do. With the proper attitude and "hustle" you can be a success. It is only with the proper disposition that you will gather the strength to meet the stresses and crucial moments that come to all human beings.

Bob Feller

ERIC J. FELLMAN
President & CEO
Peale Center for Christian Living

Eric J. Fellman is President and CEO of the Peale Center for Christian Living. Founded by Dr. Norman Vincent Peale and Ruth Stafford Peale, the Center's mission is to help people discover their personal spiritual potential through positive thinking principles. Its main work includes publishing PLUS: The Magazine of Positive Thinking to 750,000 subscribers, audio and video cassettes and seminars for both clergy and business leaders.

Mr. Fellman is also director of Positive Communications, Inc., a subsidiary of Peale Center that produces and distributes programs presenting positive values to schools, businesses, and the general consumer market. The flagship product is PCI "Positive Kids Video Program." "Positive Kids contains eight half-hour videocassettes that teach positive-thinking principles to children in kindergarten through fourth grades."

As secretary of the independent Positive Thinking Foundation, Eric assists in soliciting funds for non-religious applications of positive-thinking principles. The foundation is the sponsor of America's Awards for unsung heroes, whose selection committee includes Senator Bill Bradley, Disney's Michael Eisner, broadcaster Walter Cronkite, philanthropist Ross Perot and Father Theodore Hesburgh.

Eric is a graduate of Moody Bible Institute, the University of Wisconsin (B.A.), and Wheaton College (M.A.), with a strong background in journalism.

Since joining the Peale Center, Eric has taken a strong interest in the Biblical basis of positive thinking. He is currently collating his work on this subject into a seminar entitled, "The Power Behind Positive Thinking," which he hopes to be the basis for his first book.

On October 13, 1991, Eric was ordained to the Gospel ministry at

The *POSITIVE THINKING Balance*

When I came to work for Dr. Norman Vincent Peale in 1985, the task of helping carry on his message of Positive Thinking seemed overwhelming. He must have sensed my apprehension for he said to me one day, "This message of Positive Thinking is really simple, it just isn't easy to live day in and day out. It takes practice and it takes balance."

Over the next nine years, until his death on Christmas Eve, 1993, Dr. Peale took a little time every now and then to teach me those principles.

His famous book, "The Power of Positive Thinking" begins with the simple command, "Believe in yourself, have faith in your abilities." Living out that principle takes balance.

You have to believe in yourself first, because the world out there will often seek to tear you down. Once I was hurrying through Los Angeles International Airport, trying to catch a flight back home to the east coast. Just as I approached the check-in counter, a woman grabbed my arm and exclaimed, "Eric, it is so good to see you, I can't believe we are running into each other here at Los Angeles airport."

Turning to look at her I was surprised to find I had no idea who she was. When she said, "Boy, Harry will sure be sorry he wasn't with me to see you." I was even more befuddled, but said, "Well, it's great to see you, too!"

Then she pulled forward two children who were standing behind her and said: "Look at Sammy and Mary, haven't they grown since you last saw them?" Still I didn't have a clue who she was, but said gamely, "They sure are getting big."

Fortunately, she was in a big hurry, too, and we said a quick goodbye, promising to get our families together soon. Shaking my head I started back to the counter when another woman stopped me and demanded my autograph! "Lady, I said, "you've made a mistake, I'm no one whose autograph means anything."

"Oh yes you are," she insisted, "I saw that woman latch on to you. Now I know this is Los Angeles, home of famous people and it won't hurt you to give me your autograph."

Seeing she wouldn't be convinced, I reached for her pen just when the airline person handed me my ticket back and said, "There you go Mr. Fellman, you are all set."

(Continued on page 304)

---

the Trinity Baptist Church in New York City. He and his wife, Joy, and their three sons, Jason, Nathan and Jonathan live in Pawling, New York.

KARL FLEMKE
President/Chief Executive Officer
Junior Achievement, Inc.

Karl Flemke is President and Chief Executive Officer of Junior Achievement, the oldest, largest and fastest growing economic education program in the world. It is the leading organization in creating business/education partnerships to inform youth about economics and the private enterprise system.

More than 1.7 million young people are enrolled in Junior Achievement this year in programs in the United States and over 70 countries worldwide.

He joined Junior Achievement in 1958 as head of operations in New Bedford, Massachusetts. Receiving many honors, both from Junior Achievement and from the communities in which he lived and worked, he went on to head Junior Achievement operations in Pittsburgh and Los Angeles. In 1980, he was promoted to the position of National Vice President and in 1982 he was named to his present position.

Karl was born June 12, 1931 in Wethersfield, Connecticut. He is a graduate of Wethersfield High School and the University of Pittsburgh.

Flemke is president of National Associations in Colorado Springs (NACS), a member of the Board of Trustees of the United States Air Force Academy Falcon Foundation, serves on the Board of Directors of Bank One, Colorado Springs, N.A., the Colorado Springs Chamber Foundation, Pikes Peak United Way, and the Broadmoor Golf Club. He is the past Chairman of the Colorado Springs Nonprofit Center Advisory Board, a member of the Advisory Council of Alfred University College of Business, and also the Executive Education Advisory Board of the University of Colorado School of Business.

Karl and his wife, Mary, who has a doctorate in Education from the University of Southern California, have three children.

98

Observation on Leadership

During my 36-year career with Junior Achievement, I have had the opportunity to work closely with many of America's top business leaders. They were all smart, hardworking, results-oriented and successful.

Those whom I admired the most possessed the following common traits:

Humility—They realized that the perks they enjoyed were really conveyed to the position and not to the individual. They understood and acknowledged that their success was attributed to the efforts of many and not just to their leadership.

Balanced Life—Despite the tremendous demands of the job, they made time for quality relationships with their families and still found time to contribute to their community and nation.

Unselfishness—They put the institutions' best interest before their own.

Sense of Humor—They were able to laugh at themselves and had the ego strength not to take themselves too seriously. One of the most successful business leaders I have ever known has a number of rules by which he lives. One of my favorites is … have a belly laugh every day and you'll live to be one-hundred!

GERALD R. FORD
38th U.S. President

President Ford was born in Omaha, Nebraska, and raised in Grand Rapids, Michigan. He worked his way through the University of Michigan by serving nurses and interns in the university hospital and washing dishes at his fraternity, DKE. He earned his varsity M on three Michigan football teams, including the 1932 and 1933 national champions.

After earning his Bachelor of Arts degree from Michigan, he went on to Yale to earn a degree in law. While there, he served as assistant football coach and freshman boxing coach.

In 1942, after a brief stint in the law profession, he entered the U.S. Navy, serving almost four years during World War II, and participated in 3rd and 5th Fleet operations aboard the aircraft carrier USS Monterey for two years in the Pacific theater. He was discharged in 1946 as a Lt. Commander.

In 1948, he married Elizabeth Bloomer. They are the parents of four children and are the grandparents of five granddaughters.

President Ford was elected to the U.S. House of Representatives in 1948 and re-elected every two years through 1972, serving 25 years in the House. He was elected Chairman of the Republican Conference in 1963 and chosen Minority Leader in 1965.

In November 1963, President Lyndon Johnson appointed him a member of the Presidential Commission investigating the assassination of President John F. Kennedy. He subsequently authored (with John R. Stiles) Portrait of the Assassin *(1965).*

President Ford was nominated vice president to succeed Spiro T. Agnew, who resigned. He succeeded to the presidency following the resignation of Richard M. Nixon, serving from August 9, 1974, to January 20, 1977.

Be True to Yourself

I can't stress enough how important this period of time is in your life. By forming good morals and learning the meaning of right and wrong now, you are forming a pattern that will follow you throughout life.

I encourage you to set goals and strive for excellence in all you do. The experience, knowledge, and discipline you acquire during your youth will be of immeasurable benefit in your adult life and how you affect this nation and its people.

I have had the privilege of working closely with Mrs. Ford raising funds for the Betty Ford Center for Alcohol and Drug Abuse. I have seen first-hand how alcohol and drugs can affect one's life. It is so easy to slip into dependency; therefore, I ask you not to give into peer pressure. It's okay to say NO! Celebrate your life by being true to yourself.

Warmest, best wishes for success and happiness now and in the future.

Gerald R. Ford

Since leaving the White House, President Ford has lectured at 178 colleges and universities. His autobiography, A Time To Heal, *was published in 1979. The Gerald R. Ford Library, in Ann Arbor, Michigan, and the Gerald R. Ford Museum, in Grand Rapids, Michigan, were dedicated in 1981. President Ford has always been very active in various charitable events and is the recipient of numerous awards and honors from many civic organizations. Numerous public and private colleges and universities have bestowed honorary doctor of law degrees on the former president.*

PAUL FULLMER
President
Selz, Seabolt & Associates

His first "real" present was a typewriter. Paul Fullmer's parents were right on target with the gift because he never wavered from a writing career.

Like most youngsters, he loved sports. But, Fullmer soon realized that he wasn't going to be a great athlete (bad eyes and no speed were just two of the reasons!). So, sports reporting in high school was a natural outlet for Paul and the new typewriter.

He started covering the sports teams of his high school (Immaculate Conception in Elmhurst, IL) for the school paper, and soon began writing, too, for the local weekly paper. By his senior year he also was covering the conference for the dailies and the Catholic weekly in Chicago.

Notre Dame was next and he had his eye on a sportswriting career until he interviewed with Thomas Stritch (nephew of the former Cardinal in the Chicago Archdiocese and head of the Notre Dame Journalism Department), who quickly informed Fullmer, "We don't turn out sportswriters here. If you plan to be successful here, you'll learn to be a good all-around journalist." He did that, but he also served as sports and associate editor of the Scholastic, Notre Dame's weekly news magazine.

After graduation in 1955, he worked for two years as a reporter and columnist at the Aurora, IL Beacon-News, before joining the Chicago-based public relations firm, Selz, Seabolt & Associates, Inc.

Fullmer has worked for the same firm for more than 30 years, and was elected president in 1979. Selz, Seabolt was a founding member of Pinnacle Worldwide, an international consortium of independent public relations firms, and Fullmer was elected to a two-year term as Pinnacle president in 1990. He also is the former president of the Chicago Chapter of the Public Relations Society of America.

(Continued on page 296)

"Fast Track"

Young people spend a lot of time talking about the "fast track." How long should I stay in this position? Should I jump to another company? What about the big move cross-country to a new and exciting challenge?

In short, they focus on the positive side of mobility and quick advancement. Seldom do they examine the downside of the equation.

This is even more critical today in a more sluggish economy. In this era of corporate restructuring, leveraged buyouts, downsizing and mergers, senior management may well be looking for a real sense of old-fashioned LOYALTY.

Many fast track young professionals have been caught in the "last in, first out" crunch. What had been the fast track quickly became the last track. They don't have friends or even more importantly, mentors, to help position them in the new structure.

As one of the rare breed who has spent nearly his entire professional life with one organization, I strongly believe that the majority of young people can build their own version of the fast track without job hopping.

My advice to young people has always been to identify with an organization that provides an opportunity to learn—to grow professionally. Do not accept a position or a promotion unless you can learn a great deal from your boss. It's important, therefore, for you to find out during the interview how much time your future boss will have to work with you. If the response is, "As soon as you get up to speed, you can run your own ballgame," that job isn't for you. All you'll do is run in place and repeat the same mistakes.

If the boss indicates you'll work as a team and outlines challenges that are interesting, you're onto something good. That's when you begin to build your own "fast track" within the organization. Work to free your boss of details so he/she can concentrate on the bigger picture.

There are a very few superstars in this world. And, there are even fewer shortcuts. There's no substitute for common sense, a smile, hard work, persistence and loyalty. To me that is the "fast track"—to business success and personal satisfaction.

Paul Fullmer

GEORGE GALLUP, JR.
Chairman
The George H. Gallup
International Institute

Besides serving as co-chairman of The Gallup Organization, Inc., George Gallup, Jr. is presently chairman of The George H. Gallup International Institute and Executive Director of the Princeton Religion Research Center.

He was born in Evanston, Illinois on April 9, 1930. In addition to his BA degree (Department of Religion / Princeton University), he also holds six honorary degrees.

This percentage specialist inherited a passion for facts and figures from his late father, who pioneered opinion polling. His professional activities cover the fields of health / drug and alcohol abuse, survey research, education, children and youth, religion and public affairs.

Gallup is chairman of the board of the Quill and Scroll Honorary Journalism Society, an honor society for high school journalists. He also serves on a score of other boards in the professional areas in which he works.

He loves the theatre and has performed in more than 40 theatrical productions over the last 30 years, mostly Gilbert and Sullivan. His favorite sport is soccer, which he played and coached until age 45. Presently, he is an eager but unskilled tennis player.

Gallup has written numerous articles on survey research, religion, health, urban problems and many other topics. His 10 books include Varieties of Prayer *(1991) and* The People's Religion *(1989).*

Anyone Can Be a Success

The best way for me to respond is to share our discoveries from a national Gallup Poll on the topic of "success." The survey was based on a sample of 1,000 persons listed in Marquis' *Who's Who in America,* and reported in a book called *The Great American Success Story,* published by Dow Jones Irwin in 1986.

One of the lessons of this book (which I wrote with my brother, Alec, and William Proctor) is that anyone can be a success. Although many people automatically assign themselves to the status of an also-ran, the results of our study show that most of us have the potential to be high achievers. For example, common sense, which high achievers consider the most important personal characteristic for success, is something upon which we all draw.

Also, successful people place a lot of importance on old-fashioned virtues and list hard work, the desire to excel, goal setting, and caring about others, as essential to achieve success.

One of the happiest surprises for me was that the achievers we interviewed are not overly aggressive or insensitive people who are only out for "number one." In our society, we tend to admire the wheeler-dealer who scores by aggressive but not necessarily admirable behavior. In contrast, our survey respondents prove that personal success often involves a great social consciousness as well. They care about others, they volunteer their time to aid the needy, and the large majority give money to charity.

George Gallup, Jr.

THOMAS G. GARTH
President
Boys & Girls Clubs of America

As president of the Boys & Girls Clubs of America, Tom Garth heads the nation's fastest growing youth development organization with a primary focus on young people from disadvantaged backgrounds.

Garth was instrumental in changing the name of the national organization (formerly Boys Clubs of America) to better reflect the growing number of girls served. B&GCA serves more than 1.9 million girls and boys through more than 1,500 affiliates across the country.

As a youth, Tom was an active member of the Boys Club of St. Louis, where he took special interest in sports and community service projects. He credits much of his later success as a club professional to his early experiences as a member.

Returning to St. Louis in 1956, after serving in the Army, he sought a career that would enable him to work with children and help them gain a foothold in the world. "My club experience had provided me with a purpose and a direction," he says. "I wanted to provide guidance for other young people who so desperately needed it."

Education Is A Must

Growing up in any generation means facing an uncertain future, but being a youth today means you must adjust to a host of stark realities that far exceed what most of us experienced when we were young.

Youth is, or should be, a time of learning and preparation for the challenges and responsibilities of the future. My advice is that you get an education. Stay in school and give it your best effort and attention. Fight for it, if you must. Suffer for it, if need be. But get it!

As our rapidly advanced technology wipes out more and more unskilled and semi-skilled jobs, never before have the penalties for the neglect or abandonment of one's education been more severe. Stay in school and seize every opportunity to improve your knowledge and skills.

Your most important decision is to determine what you want to do. Don't hesitate to ask your teachers or vocational guidance counselors to assist you in your efforts to make the right career decision. You stand a better chance when you get into an endeavor suited to your educational background, interests, personality and other characteristics.

Whatever you want to be, you must believe in your ability to do it, regardless of your present circumstances. There are countless men and women, many in this book, who may have had two strikes against them in the beginning, but, they won life's ball game by so preparing and disciplining themselves that they knocked the ball out of the park—and won! It is important for you to understand and believe that you can do almost anything in life—if you prepare yourself to reach your goal.

Career progress appears to come faster for some than others. As long as you are doing your best every day and remain dedicated to your objectives, don't worry about it. Your chance will come soon enough. Work hard and believe You Can Do It!—then you WILL succeed.

Thomas H. Harth

LEONARD A. GENTINE
Chairman
Sargento, Incorporated

Leonard A. Gentine is a man who has achieved success in the true spirit of American entrepreneurship. At one time, he was running a funeral parlor, a mink ranch, and a mail-order cheese business, all at the same time—and all were doing well!

He was born and raised in Milwaukee, the only child of a French immigrant father and Wisconsin farm girl mother. His father insisted that he learn a trade so his formal education ended with high school and he went to work in a Milwaukee factory. He became interested in the mortuary business while moonlighting as a $4-a-day hearse driver for a local funeral home. Leonard applied for a mortuary apprenticeship and completed a two-year course at the Wisconsin Institute of Mortuary Science, while continuing to work nights at the Falk Corporation.

With limited resources, he and his wife, Dolores, went into the funeral business in Plymouth. Gentine commuted 60 miles to work each day to work the night shift on his factory job, until the funeral home was solvent.

His entrepreneurial spirit led him into taking a short course in genetics and becoming interested in mink ranching. Before long he was operating a 10-acre mink farm with 250 head of mink.

Capitalizing on the popularity of Wisconsin cheeses, he launched a deli and mail order cheese business from a carriage house behind his funeral home in Plymouth. Four years later, he founded the Sargento Cheese Company in 1953.

The packaged cheese product caught on. Sales soared. More product innovations followed and today Sargento ranks as the second largest-selling brand of natural cheese in America's supermarkets.

Opportunities Await You

People often say that there just aren't as many opportunities today as there were 50 years ago. I don't agree.

I think young men and women are better prepared, better fed, and better educated than my generation. And while career opportunities have changed, the important thing is that the opportunities are there. It's up to you to explore them and to find your place—your niche—in the business place.

You may have to take a few risks along the way, but the risks are worth taking. The road to success is lined with a few failures, but look on those as experiences, not failures.

It has been said that there's no substitute for experience and I can vouch for that. My career path took a very winding route which is another way of saying that I had more than my share of different jobs. And that's the lesson learned. Look on every job experience as a positive forward step in your career path.

I don't care if you're bagging groceries or delivering pizza during your summer break, take the approach that this is going to be your permanent job—your career job. Keep in mind that the mere fact that you'll be dealing with different kinds of people, in different environments, in different situations, is going to help you. It's going to give you better insight on how people react in different situations and it will prepare you better for the decisions you'll be called upon to make later in life.

Don't be afraid to change directions in your career. Just because you're a graduate engineer, for example, doesn't mean you shouldn't take a sales job. I'm not advocating job-hopping, but I am suggesting that you not close the door to any opportunity.

Don't expect to find the perfect job because it probably doesn't exist. And don't be afraid to take risks as long as you have confidence in your abilities. You can do it!

Leonard H. Sentino

SUE LING GIN
Founder/Chairman/CEO
Flying Food Fare, Inc.

The owner, chairman and chief executive officer of Flying Food Fare, Inc., Ms. Gin has been in business in Chicago for nearly 30 years. She is among the few successful self-made female entrepreneurs in the country.

Born in Aurora, Illinois, of immigrant parents from Canton, China, Ms. Gin completed her first business deal at age 17 in her hometown. Hearing that a Shell gasoline dealer intended to demolish a large house to clear the way for a new gas station, she negotiated a deal whereby she purchased the house for $1,000, had it moved a few blocks to a lot she had purchased for that purpose, installed a foundation, and rehabbed the house into a six-unit apartment building.

Shortly thereafter, she moved to Chicago where she enjoyed successful careers in insurance and real estate before undertaking the creation of Flying Food Fare, Inc., an airline catering and institutional food service concern.

Ever the opportunist, she turned a happenstance into one of her biggest entrepreneurial achievements. She was a passenger on a Midway Airlines breakfast flight when she was served a frozen sweet roll. Ms. Gin wrote the chairman of the airline and told him that she could provide them with better food service. Midway's chairman let her bid competitively on the airline's entire food contract. She won; and thus was born Flying Food Fare, which today provides over 10,000 meals daily to two dozen airlines, both domestic and foreign.

Sue Gin currently serves on the boards of the Chicagoland Chamber of Commerce, DePaul University, Georgetown University, Commonwealth Edison, and the Chicago Network, a women's organization, among others.

With her various businesses prospering, Ms. Gin is now pursuing other interests, including education, economic development, and trade issues.

Success Demands Hard Work

I firmly believe that the secret to success is work—hard work. Very little is gained by working "just enough to get by." The person who has the best chance of getting ahead is the one who arrives early, leaves late, gives that little extra, and enjoys what he or she is doing. Never work at anything that you do *not* enjoy doing; you will always be handicapped in your search for success.

At times, I have been called a tough taskmaster. That's because I believe that everyone should be obligated to do his or her best at all times. Unfortunately, most people find that difficult to do. The late Earl Nightengale, who was a pioneer in the motivational field, found, after extensive research, that all worthwhile achievements were accomplished by only five percent of the population!

Think about that: 95 percent of the work force is content not to do any more than is required by the basic demands of the job. What a terrific opportunity that gives those individuals who want to maximize the full potential of their talents!

I strongly advise young people to be cautious of the "something for nothing" philosophy that is so prevalent in today's society. The easy way and the fast buck are illusions and stumbling blocks along the road to prosperity and success. The longer you live, the more you will realize there is no such phenomenon. Everything worthwhile must be earned.

Young people should establish goals for themselves. These goals should be difficult, but not impossible to reach. Put your heart into it, and believe in yourself. Sure, you'll make mistakes—but learn from them. Your best education will come from doing things, not reading about them in a textbook. If you apply yourself, you can become one of the five percent who will achieve success!

Some of these areas will be assisted by the William G. McGowan Charitable Fund, which was established by the estate of her late husband, William G. McGowan, a founder and long-time chairman of MCI Communications. The Charitable Fund is headed by Ms. Gin and her brother-in-law, Monsignor A. Joseph McGowan.

Perhaps the Monsignor best summed up this extraordinary woman when he described her as "a combination of Mother Teresa and Lee Iacocca. She's one competent, tough businesswoman."

BILL GLASS
President
Bill Glass Ministries

Evangelistic crusades and a successful prison ministry are as much the trademarks of Bill Glass in the '90s as was his outstanding pro football play in the '60s. He has now been in full-time evangelism longer than he played pro football (12 years).

A native of Texarkana, Texas, he went to Baylor University after an outstanding high school grid career in Corpus Christi. He helped the Baylor Bears to four bowl games and was named consensus All-American and All-Southwest Conference in 1956.

After a year in the Canadian Football League, Glass played four years with the Detroit Lions and seven with the Cleveland Browns, the team with whom his name is most closely associated. He was named to four Pro Bowl teams, and played on Brown teams that won the NFL championship in 1964 and division championships in 1965, 1967 and 1968. Glass is a 1985 inductee into the College Football Hall of Fame and is also in the Texas Sports Hall of Fame.

Even while receiving laurels for his athletic prowess, Glass was beginning his Christian ministry. He attended Southwestern Theological Seminary in his off-seasons, receiving a bachelor of divinity degree in 1963. As the years passed, his preaching ministry expanded until he was leading interdenominational crusades drawing thousands of people per night—sometimes in the football stadiums in which he excelled as a player.

His highly successful Prison Ministry began in 1972. This mission outreach has grown to become the largest evangelistic prison ministry in America. His "Bill Glass Prison Special" on television was nominated for an Emmy.

He has written nine books including "Expect to Win," "The Commit-

"Ud'en Ud'en" Attitude

I have a little grandson, Billy Ray, and he is fantastic! I remember the day he was born. I thought he might be president or a pro-football player like his father and grandfather before him. On the second day of his life we were told he had Down's Syndrome. This meant that he could never be president because he will always be a little bit or a great deal retarded. He can never be an athlete. This wasn't the little boy we had looked forward to. We felt cheated.

But almost from the beginning, Billy Ray had an unusual amount of love. He'd sit in my lap sometimes for 30 to 40 minutes and hug, kiss, and talk to me. He calls me "Gams Gam." At first, we thought we were cursed to have a Downs child. We soon realized we were actually most fortunate. Sure there are hard times and difficulties, but overall, what a joy he is!

One time I was over at his house and he was on the floor playing with his little car making motor-like sounds, "ud'en ud'en." He looked up at me and smiled and went "ud'en ud'en." I smiled at him and he went "ud'en ud'en" again, but this time he frowned. I got the picture. He wanted me to get down on the floor and play with him. I knelt down on one knee and took his car and went "ud'en ud'en." He liked that pretty good but not real good because I was still on one knee.

Billy Ray was on the floor down on his belly. He was asking me to get down on my belly. I really didn't want to because I was dressed in a suit on my way to an important engagement. But, before I knew it, he had me spread eagle on the floor and playing with him.

We were having a great time until some friends of my son came in. They had to step over me to get into the room. They said, "Oh, Mr. Glass, we've always wanted to meet you." I didn't even have time to shake hands because when Billy Ray wants to play "ud'en ud'en" I do so.

No man or woman ever stands quite so tall as when you bow your knee to play with a small child. And no man is ever so much a fool as when he is too tough or macho that he can't even play "down on your belly" type children's games.

(Continued on page 305)

---

ment of Champions," and "Plan to Win." His latest, "How to Win When The Roof Caves In," was published in 1988.

Glass and his wife, the former Mavis Irene Knapp, make their home near Dallas. They have three grown children—Billy, Bobby and Mindy.

RONALD D. GLOSSER
President/Chief Executive Officer
Hershey Trust Company

Ron Glosser is the youngest of nine children from Conesville, Ohio. At the age of four his father died and his mother kept all nine children together.

As a graduate of Ohio Wesleyan University, with a Bachelors Degree in Business, he later had the privilege of serving as Chairman of the Board of Trustees for his alma mater. Following service in the United States Air Force, Glosser's entire career has been spent in the banking industry with Cleveland Trust, The Goodyear Bank and National City Bank. Since 1989, Ron has served as President and CEO of Hershey Trust Company, in Hershey, Pennsylvania, and is Chairman and CEO of The M.S. Hershey Foundation.

Glosser's early childhood experiences influenced him greatly and thus his work in Hershey takes on added significance. The Milton Hershey School, which is the sole beneficiary of a trust created by Milton and Catherine Hershey, provides an excellent educational and residential experience for over 1,000 disadvantaged youngsters from throughout America. Since the school's inception in the fall of 1910, when four orphan boys were enrolled, it has served the needs of over 17,000 children. The program is pre-Kindergarten through 12th grade. Upon graduation, the students are provided financial assistance to continue their education. In recent years, over 80 percent of the students have taken advantage of this program. The children are cared for in 89 separate homes by loving houseparents.

Glosser's community involvement is extensive having served as President of the Ohio Bankers Association, the boards of Robert Schuller's Hour of Power and Lloyd Ogilvie Ministries. He currently serves on the National Cabinet of the Peale Center for Christian Living, Guideposts,

Count Your Blessings

When confronted with periods of discouragement, take the time to write down all of your blessings in detail. On a recent morning, after a rather sleepless night, I felt guided by God to write all of the blessings of the past year. When this was completed, it was as though God said to me: "Now if I had told you at the beginning of the year that you were going to have some very serious challenges, but that I was prepared to eliminate all those from your life, with the provision that you also be willing to give up all your blessings, what would you have chosen?" It was clear to me that my blessings outweigh all of life's difficulties, you will find it to be true in your life.

There is a wonderful old hymn, "Count your blessings, name them one by one. Count your many blessings, see what God has done." You will be lifted out of discouragement and your feet planted on a pathway leading to a more promising tomorrow.

Ronald D. Glosson

Worldwide Leadership, Inc. and the Salvation Army. He recently received an honorary degree from Lindsey Wilson College.
Ron and his wife, Lily, have five children.

CONGRESSMAN FRED GRANDY
U.S. Representative
Sixth District, Iowa

Fred Grandy, elected in 1986, is in his third term of serving the Sixth Congressional District of Iowa. His district is the second largest producer of corn and soybeans in the nation.

Grandy, a Republican, became the ninth Iowan ever to become a member of the prominent House Committee on Ways and Means when he was appointed in January, 1991. The committee, responsible for all federal revenues, has jurisdiction over issues ranging from taxes, the budget, and trade to social security, medicare, and health care. In 1989, he became the first Iowan ever appointed to the House Ethics Committee.

After only four years in Congress, Grandy is recognized as a leader of domestic issues. As a former member of the House Agriculture Committee, he was a major contributor to the 1990 Farm Bill (the five-year blueprint for U.S. agricultural policy) and authored major groundwater legislation which was incorporated into the bill.

While Grandy has been active for Iowa's concerns, he has also introduced important legislation to improve health care and education. He has received awards for his continued support of American business and his voting efforts to reduce the federal budget.

Grandy was born in Sioux City in 1948. He received his bachelor's degree in English literature with high honors from Harvard in 1970. His public service began as a legislative aide and speech writer for U.S. Rep. Wiley Mayne (R-Iowa), who represented Grandy's home district.

Following his tenure with Rep. Mayne, Grandy pursued his long-time ambition in the theatre. He appeared in several successful off-Broadway plays and two films. In 1975, Grandy began his role as "Gopher" on the television hit series, The Love Boat.

Grandy is married to novelist Catherine Mann.

Something Greater than Self

When I attended the 25th reunion of my high school class, I was astounded so many people in their early 40s were growing old, getting fat and becoming bald. And the men didn't look much better.

I thought if they look this way to me how must I look to them? This was such a terrifying revelation that my first impulse is to advise all young people: If any of you are thinking of growing up, reconsider.

Then I paused and reflected upon the sight of my classmates at midlife and I was comforted. Because everything I witnessed confirmed the teachings around which I molded my life. I refer to the wisdom of Lennon—John, not Vladimir—who said life is what happens when we are making other plans. My friends and companions in the class of 1966 did not meet my expectations or their own. Thank goodness.

There was the kid from Nevada, Iowa, who had planned to be a doctor and discovered halfway through medical school that he couldn't stand to be around things that were sick. So what became of him? He is now one of the premier elephant trainers in the United States and currently in charge of large animals at the National Zoo in Washington, D.C. More important, he loves what he's doing. So does the guy who most of us believed would be the first among us to make the FBI's Ten Most Wanted list. He was a disappointment, too. In the 25 years he's been loose in the world, he has gone from cab driver to cardiovascular surgeon.

Then there was the round-faced kid from Sioux City. He planned on being a big shot lawyer until he took the law school entrance exam—and got a score that wouldn't have gotten him into a good bowling league. He bounced around in show business for 15 years before deciding to try his hand at politics and public service.

As someone whose life has been a mysterious combination of careful planning and complete accident, I can say that certain things will probably be revealed to you when you least expect it. William Butler Yates called it "heaven blazing into the mind," James Joyce referred to it as an epiphany, Luke Skywalker knew it as The Force. I can only describe it as a moment when that which has been confusing becomes clear, and that decision which was opaque becomes obvious.

Let me illustrate with an example from my own life. In early 1986, when I was exploring my candidacy for Congress, I found myself in a high school gym in Paullina filled with angry farm families who were not enthusiastic about listening to a Hollywood actor discuss the crisis in agriculture. I was despondent, even before confronting this hostile audience, because political pundits in Washington were giving my only a 30 percent chance of winning.

(Continued on page 305)

JAMES P. GRANT
Executive Director
UNICEF

James P. Grant has been UNICEF's executive director and an undersecretary of the United Nations since 1980.

Born in China in 1922, he received a B.A. from Berkeley in 1943 and a Doctorate in Jurisprudence from Harvard in 1951. His long career in the field of development began with service in China in 1946-47 for the United Nations Relief and Rehabilitation Administration.

In the 1950s and 1960s, he held a succession of high-level positions with the U.S. Agency for International Development and the State Department, and served as president of the Overseas Development Council from its establishment in 1969 through the beginning of his tenure at UNICEF.

He has received numerous honorary degrees from American and foreign universities, as well as awards for his work for Third World development and the world's children.

He says his biggest satisfaction (aside from the births of his three sons) was helping to bring the world together for children at the World Summit for Children, which took place on September 30, 1990. It was the largest gathering of world leaders ever to assemble and discuss any issue, and they committed themselves to providing all children, everywhere, with a better life.

Never Stop Asking Why

Most healthy children, at around age two or three, go through a period sometimes referred to as "the whys," when they constantly bombard their parents with questions about why things are the way they are. No answer seems to satisfy children in this stage of innocent inquisitiveness, often to the exasperation of adults.

A few months later the "why" phase is over. I suspect that, all too often, it is because children soon learn through bitter experience that grownups get uncomfortable or even angry when asked too many questions—especially hard-to-answer questions about why the world is as it is.

My colleagues and I at UNICEF have never gotten over "the whys."

We look at the world in which one out of every five people—over a billion human beings—lives in dire poverty and we ask "why?" We ask why it is that every day 40,000 children die of largely preventable causes. We ask why more than 100 million children are denied primary education and more than 30 million live on the streets. We ask about military budgets, about environmental destruction, about bias against women and girls, about foreign aid that doesn't aid people.

I would like to invite young people to join us in asking these and other critical questions as we approach the 21st century, for you will be inheriting the planet—whatever shape it may be in—from the adults of the last decade of the 20th century. The problems we face may be complex and immense, but their solution starts with each one of us asking "why?" Young people make the best activists because of their energy, enthusiasm, and ability to imagine better ways of doing things.

I urge you to continue asking the hard questions and challenging the adult world to provide sensible answers. It's your right—and our responsibility.

James P. Grant

LT. GEN. HOWARD D. GRAVES
Superintendent
U.S. Military Academy

On July 22, 1991, Lieutenant General Howard Dwayne Graves became the 54th superintendent of the U.S. Military Academy, West Point, N.Y.

Born in Roaring Springs, Texas, General Graves grew up in the Texas panhandle, in and around Amarillo. He graduated from the U.S. Military Academy in 1961 with a Bachelor of Science degree and a commission as a second lieutenant in the Corps of Engineers. After graduation, he attended Oxford University in England for three years as a Rhodes Scholar where he earned Bachelor of Arts, Master of Arts and Master of Letters degrees.

General Graves has broad experience as a commander of military units and installations. In Washington, at the national command level, he has held several key joint service assignments. Those include military assistant to the Secretary of Defense; vice director of the Joint Staff; and assistant to the chairman of the Joint Chiefs of Staff. In the latter assignment, he served as the principal military representative in critical international negotiations.

In addition to his academic work at Oxford University, he served as an instructor, assistant professor and associate professor at West Point. As Commandant of the Army War College, he was responsible for the final level of professional military education for senior officers of the Army, including many who held key command and staff positions in Operation Desert Storm.

Among General Graves' military awards are the Defense and Army Distinguished Service Medals, the Defense Superior Service Medal, the Legion of Merit with Oak Leaf Cluster, and three Bronze Star Medals. He is also a master parachutist.

General Graves and his wife, the former Gracie P. Newman, have two children. Gigi (Mrs. Eric Kail) is a graduate of Georgia State Univer-

Try and Don't Quit

On June 14, 1911, Dwight D. Eisenhower climbed the long hill from the little railway station at West Point to the administration building where his initiation process began. This is how he described it:

> My main impression of that first day was one of bewilderment and calculated chaos. By the end of the day we were all harassed and, at times, resentful, shouted at all day by self-important upperclassmen, telling us to run here and run there; pick up our clothes, bring in that bedding, put our shoulders back, keep our eyes up, and to keep running, running, running. I suppose that if any time had been provided to sit down and think for a moment, most of us would have taken the next train out. But no one was given much time to think.

Eisenhower made it through that day and four years at West Point and went on to make historic contributions to world history. Like him, thousands of other young people, myself included, have endured that first day at West Point with all its frustrations and self-doubts. Now, years later, as Superintendent of West Point, I can see myself again and again as new cadets enter, each filled with doubts about whether they can do it. But, before even the first day passes, they have surprised themselves by how much they can do. And as they keep trying, their confidence keeps growing. Of course, some don't make it; but it is because they don't want to. Those youngsters who refuse to quit nearly always make it.

Another opportunity for me to see the power of determination is when the West Point cadets sponsor the Special Olympics. The cadets cheer on the young athletes who give their all to compete well, and after the race is run the hugs they share are a simple, deeply-felt reward for their determination. When Special Olympians surpass their innate potential, they have achieved in their own way more than some world-class athletes. And, the cadets who have encouraged these athletes have also achieved something of great worth. Greatness is measured in many ways.

If you try and don't quit, you will achieve great things, I am sure of it. How will you measure that greatness? I hope by how many people you have helped, not by how many things you acquired; by the high moral standards you followed, not by a lack of them; by a humble trust in God, not by avoiding Him. The prophet Isaiah taught us long ago the secret

(Continued on page 306)

---

sity. Greg, a graduate of the Military Academy's Class of 1988, is an Army first lieutenant currently stationed at Fort Carson, Colorado.

DR. JOHN HAGGAI
Founder & President
Haggai Institute for
Advanced Leadership Training

The son of a Christian immigrant who fled his native Syria during Turkey's harassment in 1912, Dr. John Haggai makes his home in Atlanta, Georgia. But his field of operation is the world. Dr. Haggai, founder and president of Haggai Institute for Advanced Leadership, and his associates (American and Asian) established the institute to provide advanced training for credentialed Third World Christian leaders in culturally relevant methods of evangelization in their own nations. The institute maintains a permanent training facility in neutral Singapore and plans a second major training facility, scheduled to open in 1993, on the Hawaiian island of Maui.

An alumnus of Moody Bible Institute (named Alumnus of the Year in 1975) and Furman University, Dr. Haggai holds four honorary degrees, the latest received in 1991 from Korea's Han Nam University.

His first book, How To Win Over Worry, *has been a best-seller since 1959, eclipsing the two million mark. Additional books include* My Son Johnny, New Hope for Planet Earth, The Leading Edge, The Steward, How To Win Over Loneliness, How To Win Over Pain, How To Win Over Fear, Be Careful What You Call Impossible *and* Lead On!.

Dr. Won Sul Lee, for 13 years the secretary general of the Association of International University Presidents, has dubbed Haggai "the leader of leaders." And as he leads the globe-encircling Haggai Institute, he builds bridges between the East and the West—between cultures, creeds, and countries.

Lovers and Leaders

I define leadership as the discipline of deliberately exerting special influence within a group, to move it toward goals of beneficial permanence that fulfill the group's real needs.

Many people associate the exertion of influence with power. To them, the strong leader so captivates the minds of others that they follow him (or her) without a murmur.

But I doubt if this so-called "strong leader" can be relied upon to select goals of beneficial permanence. Someone who sees strength as the *sine qua non* of leadership will often prefer immediate goals geared to his own self-aggrandizement.

So what motivates good leadership, if not power? My answer is: love.

Love, because the leader deals not with hardware (like a mechanic) or with ideas (like a philosopher) but with *people*. Power-holders (and many leaders today are just that) deal with others on an I-it basis. They aim to gain influence or popularity by being invulnerable. Love-givers (if I may use that term) do the opposite: they serve the needs of the group, and in doing so expose themselves to the danger of rejection.

To talk about love in leadership might sound sloppy. But a moment's thought will show that true leadership is impossible *without* love.

The love I'm talking about goes beyond emotion. It is an act of the will. A world leader once said to me, "John, to do what you do, you must have a great love for the Third World." I replied, "If you're talking about feelings I have to tell you I feel no more love for the Third World right now than I do for this desk. But yes, I have great love for the Third World!"

Love is a military commander risking his life for his men.

Love is a corporate CEO improving safety standards in his factories.

Love is a busy professional using precious time off to look after a neighbor's handicapped child.

Love is practical.

Ultimately, it's only the leader who loves who will gain respect.

Of course love is also a high-risk form of leadership. To love truly (whether your spouse, your children, or your employees) you must accept the possibility of being hurt. I find it highly significant that a person I rate the greatest leader of all suffered exactly this fate, becoming a "man of sorrows, despised and rejected." I mean, of course, our Lord Jesus Christ.

And yet who, more than He, has achieved goals of beneficial permanence and fulfilled humanity's real needs? No one. And two thousand

(Continued on page 306)

T. MARSHALL HAHN, JR.
Chairman & CEO
Georgia-Pacific Corporation

A native of Lexington, Kentucky, Hahn graduated Phi Beta Kappa from the University of Kentucky with a bachelor of science degree in physics at the age of 18. He had earned his Ph.D. from the Massachusetts Institute of Technology by the time he was 22—after a two year tour of duty in the Navy.

After graduating from MIT, Hahn held a variety of positions, including head of the nuclear-accelerator laboratory at the University of Kentucky, chairman of the Physics Department at Virginia Tech and dean of arts and sciences at Kansas State University.

He was president of Virginia Tech when he was 35. During his 13 years there, he helped build the university into a major educational center and nearly tripled enrollment.

Hahn was elected to Georgia-Pacific's board of directors in 1973 while still at Virginia Tech. In 1975, he joined the company as executive vice president and was elected president the following year. He became chief executive officer in 1983, and added the responsibilities of chairman of the board in 1984—the titles he holds today.

Hahn has been recognized by industry securities analysts as the top CEO for both the forest product and lumber industry, as well as the paper industry in recent years. He is active in business and civic activities at both the national and local levels. He is a director and former chairman of the American Paper Institute, serves on the Business Council of Georgia, and is a member of the Conference Board.

Never Stop Learning

Today's highly structured society has led to perceived decline in the importance of individual responsibility and initiative. Certainly, more than our forefathers, we consider ourselves more members of a group rather than individuals in today's organizations, corporations, and communities. With our problems so complex and our organizations so large, young people may feel that their ideas or individual contributions have little impact. Yet the future of our nation, and perhaps the world, rests with you as individuals.

As most of us have known since we were very young, there is a great deal of social pressure to conform. Yet the major accomplishments in our entire history have been achieved largely by people who were highly individualistic—who did not behave according to the standard of their class, their people, or their time.

That has been the story of many of the world's great scientists, philosophers, and political leaders who started with the courage of their convictions and ended up leading the world into new frontiers of knowledge or accomplishment. Perhaps the most important component of individual success, however, is the ability to inspire others toward accomplishing shared dreams, to enhance individual effort through teamwork.

With our shared goals we have built hospitals, schools, and communities as well as industries, believing that the only way we could succeed was together—as individuals working together to build our great nation.

The ability to fully develop and utilize our skills—both as individuals and as members of a team—begins with education. The most complex challenge facing our nation's educational institutions and its businesses is preparing our workforce and our workplaces for today's and tomorrow's intensely competitive environment. While I am optimistic that the next decade will be a period of great economic opportunity, there is mounting concern that we will not have the traditional abundant supply of effective workers needed to fuel the growth.

Georgia-Pacific's modern plants and mills provide an excellent example. Our facilities are well equipped with state-of-the-art control systems that provide information on quality, production costs, and scheduling. They are systems that require a multi-faceted and well-educated workforce. There is concern because it is estimated that by the end of this decade three of four jobs will require more than a high school education. That means we must have a workforce that is better educated and better trained than any before it, with willingness to change and to continue the educational process.

(Continued on page 306)

MONTY HALL
TV Producer/Humanitarian

Monty Hall was born in Winnipeg, Manitoba, Canada. His show-business career began while he was a student at the University of Manitoba, where he earned his Bachelor of Science degree.

To pay his way through school, Monty worked for Radio Station CKRC singing, acting, writing, emceeing, and engineering. He performed in school productions but found time to become a five-letter man in athletics and was president of the student body in his senior year.

Upon earning his degree, he moved to Toronto, to work for the Canadian Broadcasting Corporation. He created Canada's longest running radio quiz show "Who Am I?"

In 1955, Monty moved to New York City to do a five-year run on NBC's "Monitor" and did numerous other shows including the New York Ranger hockey broadcasts. Hall was New York's first soccer play-by-play man. He then became emcee of "Video Village" and moved to Hollywood with the show.

During a frantic year, he commuted from CBS to NBC studios performing all day on "Video Village" and producing his first show, "Your First Impression," at night. This was followed by his creation of "Let's Make a Deal," which was among the longest-running game shows in television history.

Monty's life away from television has been as important as that on stage. His charitable and philanthropic activities have brought him more than 500 awards.

In 1975, he was elected president of Variety Clubs International, the world's largest children's charity; in 1977, he became chairman of the board, and in 1981 was honored with the lifetime title of international

(Continued on page 297)

It Takes Pluck

On my television show "Let's Make a Deal," the contestants depend on luck to select the right door. In the game of life, it takes "pluck" more than luck to be successful.

I found that to be true when I moved from Toronto to New York, in 1955, after early success in radio and television in my native Canada. I spent days and weeks on end, hoping to get an appointment; and even getting appointments found instant rejection. It appeared the American networks weren't holding their breath waiting for me—the rest is history.

I was ready for the challenge. My youth had been one of much illness and poverty. My loving mother nursed me through harsh illnesses and pulled me through some tough times. When I finished high school, we did not have enough money to send me to college, so I took various jobs to raise the tuition.

While working in a clothing firm, I was subjected to some demeaning criticism by the boss. I came home that evening filled with frustration and tears. My mother sat me down and recited the wonderful Rudyard Kipling poem "If" to me—"If you can keep your head while those around you are losing theirs," etc.

She was a pillar of strength to me and an inspiration. She convinced me that no amount of adversity should ever stop one. In later years, I translated that for some actors who came to me in despair. I told them, paraphrasing my mother's remarks, that "if you believe in yourself, no amount of rejection should deter you from reaching your goals." If someone tells you that you are "not good," don't accept that as gospel. You are "not good" when you yourself think that you are "not good," not when someone else tells you.

Branch Rickey, the famous general manager of the old Brooklyn Dodgers, used to say that "luck is the residue of design." He might have said "the residue of desire," for it is a combination of talent and courage (pluck) that will keep you in the fight, until that "lucky" day when someone recognizes your talent.

Monty Hall

MERLE HARMON, SR.
Chairman & President
Fan Fair Corporation

Merle Harmon broadcast major league baseball for 35 years. He was the voice of the Kansas City A's, now in Oakland, the Milwaukee Braves, Minnesota Twins, Milwaukee Brewers, and Texas Rangers. With the Milwaukee Brewers, he and Bob Uecker became one of the hottest broadcast teams in baseball history. His baseball assignments included playoffs, All-Star games, and the World Series. He broadcast three no hitters, including two perfect games, and was on hand to describe Nolan Ryan's record setting 5,000th strikeout.

Beyond baseball he covered a Super Bowl, countless bowl games, NCAA championship events, ABC's Wide World of Sports and Sports World Shows. He co-anchored the World University Games in Moscow, where he survived an auto crash, a Russian hospital, and a bout with the KGB.

His evolution from broadcaster to sports retailer was a natural one. Merle was one of the first to realize that fans would eagerly drape themselves in clothing worn by their favorite player or team. Teaming his business and sports experience, he founded his chain of Merle Harmon Fan Fair stores in 1977. Today there are more than 150 of the stores featuring official and personalized gifts for fans of amateur and professional teams. To devote full-time to his new enterprise, he stopped broadcasting Texas Rangers games after the 1989 season. However, broadcasting is still in his blood and he occasionally announces college football and basketball games.

Harmon holds degrees from Graceland College in Iowa and the University of Denver. In 1971, he became the third recipient of the National Association of Intercollegiate Athletics Outstanding Alumnus Award. The two previous winners were President Nixon and Congressional Medal of Honor winner and former American Football League Commissioner Joe Foss.

Brighten Someone's Day

I have always admired and, in a way, envied those who work with their hands. Carpenters, artists, mechanics, doctors, and architects, among others. Those who build houses, create paintings, fix automobiles, repair bodies, and design magnificent structures. When the job is completed, they can step back, view their work, and proclaim, "I did that."

For my first few years in broadcasting, I felt that I was not contributing anything worthwhile to society. I could not rationalize that announcing a game on radio or television could be compared to the importance of the work done by those whose hands had saved lives or built a cathedral or skyscraper.

Then one afternoon, after visiting my wife in the hospital where she had delivered our second child, the hospital administrator stopped me in the hallway. He asked, "Do you realize how important your job is to many of our patients?" I was surprised by the question.

He went on to say: "I can walk down this corridor, from one end to the other, and never miss a play when you are on the air. For those few hours you bring listening and viewing pleasure, which may be the best therapy for patients who need to get their minds off their health problems. Some patients have many visitors, others have none, so you may be the one who brightens their day."

I have never thought of my job in that light and his observations had a profound affect on me. Thereafter, every time I sat down in a broadcast booth, I felt a real purpose in what I was doing.

Think back to the last time someone came up to you and, without particular reason, told you how much she or he appreciated what you did, or merely offered a simple and sincere compliment. Remember how it brightened your day?

When's the last time you did that? Why not begin today? It's a habit that will bring you much happiness throughout your life—and you'll make a lot of other people feel good, too.

Merle Harmon

Merle and his wife of 46 years, Jeanette, have four sons and a daughter. Three of his sons and his daughter are involved in the corporation.

PAUL HARVEY
ABC Radio News Commentator

"Hello Americans! This is Paul Harvey. Stand by ... for news!"

Every day, 23.8 million loyal listeners wait to hear his skilled blend of news and views delivered in his patented rapid-fire, stop and start style. Today, Paul Harvey News is the world's largest communications conglomerate—comprised of 1,350 ABC radio affiliates, plus another 400 stations on the Armed Forces Radio Network. In addition, his syndicated column appears in 300 newspapers.

It all began in Tulsa, Oklahoma, where he was born. At age 14, he was already doing spot announcements at Station KVOO. He continued broadcasting while attending Tulsa University.

He credits his wife, Lynne, whom he has always called Angel, with keeping his career on an upward track. They met in St. Louis, at Station KXOX, when he was earning $29 a week and she came to the station for a school news program. He invited her to dinner and proposed to her that very evening!

After their marriage, they decided to pool their talents in a news career and cast their lot in Chicago, the center of all national radio broadcasting at the time. When Paul Harvey News was launched, Angel became producer and general manager.

Paul says the most important news event he ever reported was the birth of his son, Paul, Jr., who is now part of the family enterprise. A concert pianist, he gave up his musical career to become a writer for The Rest of The Story, which began as a segment of the news program but is now a separate series.

Paul Harvey has received countless awards, including his '94 Peabody Award for lifetime achievement, as well as 11 honorary degrees and 11

(Continued on page 297)

Get Up When You Fall Down

If there is one common denominator in the biographies of men and women the world calls successful it is this: They get up when they fall down.

We all fall down. Only a comparative few are willing and able, again and again, to pick themselves up, dust themselves off and keep on keeping on.

This is not to say that all men are otherwise "equal"; they are not.

The "all men created equal" thesis has misled us; it's simply not true.

The Gettysburg Address was delivered before the human I.Q. was mathematically measurable.

Vice Admiral H. G. Rickover, Godfather of the atom sub, said: "The greatest disappointment ever suffered by true believers in democracy was when they awakened one morning to discover that the I.Q. of humans ranges from zero to two hundred; we are that far from being equal."

Lincoln was, of course, a splendid example of the fallacy of his own statement. In lifting the line from our Declaration of Independence, he removed it from its proper context. The Declaration of Independence goes on to specify "equal *rights,* to life, liberty," so forth.

People are not created equal. We do not have the same coordination, the same respiration, the same pulse rate, the same fingerprints, the same tolerance for disease or the same I.Q.

Yet we have sought to run many of our institutions and to re-order our society as if that semi-sacred cliché were true. The truth is that some persons are built for leadership and some are not, and the sooner we get back to encouraging the uncommon men and women, the better it will be for all of us; including those of us who may be "less equal" than others.

When Christ was on earth he recognized the inequality of men by reciting the parable of the talents.

In your own family, members demonstrate different attitudes. Environment and heredity have been similar, yet some individuals, within the same family, are better able to solve problems.

There are other factors which can contribute to individual accomplishment: health, perseverance toward a single goal, an extraordinarily compatible marriage partnership . . .

But I am convinced there is no power on earth which can keep a first class man down—or hold a fourth class man up.

And that one controllable factor in success is that those who deserve it—get up when they fall down.

Paul Harvey

CHICK HEARN
Sports Broadcaster

"You want baseball, you go to Vin Scully. For football, it was the late Ted Husing. But basketball is Chick Hearn." Those accolades came from Jim Murray, the Pulitzer Prize winning columnist of the Los Angeles Times. The occasion was Chick Hearn Night at The Forum, home of the L.A. Lakers basketball team.

Hearn has been the Voice of the Lakers for 32 years. He's broadcast 2,625 consecutive games dating back to November 1965, missing only two—both because of snowstorms. In perspective, he called his first Lakers game when Magic Johnson was one year old!

His first major broadcasting job was doing Bradley University basketball games. This was quite a feat because he had no college education or formal broadcast training. A strong work ethic, determination to succeed and an understanding wife were his motivation.

In 1951, he was lured to Los Angeles to be USC's football announcer. He also worked for NBC and CBS. His work log includes two Ali fights, seven Rose Bowls and several major golf tournaments. He also has appeared in numerous movies and his star in on Hollywood's Walk of Fame.

Hearn is credited with helping build the Lakers' following, especially in the early years, when the team was a nonentity in an area dominated by baseball's Dodgers. His radio broadcasts, enlivened by his enthusiasm and creative verbiage, caught on. To this day, thousands of fans bring their radios to the game to hear his commentary as they sit courtside. With the advent of television, Hearn inspired introduction of simulcast broadcasting.

His Chickisms have changed basketball's vocabulary. He coined terms like slam dunk, airball, dribble drive, stutter step, give and go, and no-harm no-foul, all now part of every sportscaster's phraseology.

Attitude Is Important

I don't know any hard and fast rules to tell you how to get where you want to go. Life is filled with too many complications and uncertainties for that.

I live in a world of words. There is one word which I feel controls everything we do. That word is ATTITUDE! It will bring us whatever we want, or, will keep us from reaching any of our goals. If I approach a broadcast with a bad attitude it will soon become evident to my listeners. A poor attitude has killed a lot of promising athletic and business careers. Be assured, attitude will play an important role in any success you achieve.

I encourage you to do something you enjoy by selecting a career suited to your inclinations and talent.

Don't expect or ask for something for nothing. There isn't anything worth having that can be achieved without effort.

Always give more than you get. Keep putting in extra effort and extra thought to make what you do become your best effort—every time.

Never be satisfied. Set high goals for yourself. If you achieve them, set new ones.

Learn your abilities and limitations. You might ponder the famous prayer which says: "God grant me the strength to change those things which can be changed, the patience to bear those things which cannot, and the wisdom to know the difference."

'Chick' Hearn

ROLAND A. HEMOND
Executive Vice President
and General Manager
Baltimore Orioles

In 1989, in his second season with the Baltimore Orioles, Roland Hemond was named Major League Executive of the Year. It was the third time in his career he'd won the award, the second in the '80s. The honor came in the wake of the Orioles' amazing 32½ game improvement over '88, third greatest turnaround in major league history.

The accomplishment was not new to Hemond. In fact, the energetic executive has engineered three of the major league's ten best turnarounds since divisional play began in '69. As general manager of the Chicago White Sox, Hemond's '71 club improved 23 games over the previous year and his '77 team climbed 26 games above the '76 White Sox.

One of the more active trade makers, he has made 121 trades involving 335 players in his 39 years in baseball. He made 17 trades in his first 17 months with the Orioles as the Baltimore club rebounded as a contender.

Happenstance played a key role in his success. A chance meeting with blind World War I veteran, Sgt. Leo C. McMahon, led to an introduction to Charlie Blossfield, general manager of the Hartford, Connecticut, Chiefs of the Class A Eastern League. Newly-discharged from the Coast Guard, Hemond accepted a job with the Chiefs, an affiliate club of the Boston Braves.

A subsequent two-week tryout in the minor league office of the Braves ended up being a lifetime baseball career, with the Braves in Boston and Milwaukee through 1960, as Scouting and Farm Director for the California Angels, general manager with the White Sox from 1961 through 1985, a year in the Commissioner's Office, to his present assignment with the Orioles.

Develop Champion Qualities

Baseball is my business, but, it's more than that. I love my job and still get the same thrill out of the game I did when I was a kid. That's important. You need to enjoy what you do for a living, whatever it may be.

All players in professional baseball have ability. My job, and that of our manager, coaches, and entire organization, is to develop that ability to capacity. I look for three qualities in each player beyond natural talents.

First, an athlete must believe what he is doing is worthwhile. It is important that a player is aware that he has more responsibility than just putting on a pair of spikes or hitting a home run. Whether he likes it or not, he automatically becomes a role model for our nation's youth. It's true that baseball is just a game, but it has much to offer beyond the baselines. So, a player must believe there is a purpose and dignity in what he does for a living.

The second factor that makes a champion player is his desire to be one. The greatest quality of a championship club is a collective, dominating urge to win. Some great teams have lost the World Series to less talented ones, which simply wanted to win more. It's the same in life—desire drives people to achieve their goals.

Show me a championship team and I'll show you one which has mastered fundamentals—the little things that often spell the difference between winning and losing. Countless players, who have the ma terial requisites for greatness—youth, speed, power, even desire—still fail. Why? Because they can't master the basics; a pitcher can't hold a runner on base, a runner doesn't know how to slide, outfielders can't hit the cutoff man, batters can't bunt—just to name a few. Learning fundamentals is essential in sports and business.

Begin early in life to develop these qualities—believe in what you are doing, desire to be the best you can be, and master even the smallest skills required for your vocation. If you do, you'll reach home plate often and score a lot of runs in your life.

THEODORE M. HESBURGH,C.S.C.
President Emeritus
University of Notre Dame

Father Hesburgh guided Notre Dame's destinies for more than three decades, after he took office at age 35. He raised the school from a glorified Catholic liberal arts undergraduate institution to a status in academe equal to that of its football team in the annals of sports.

The public-spirited priest became a national figure through his work in religious ecumenicism, with philanthropic foundations, and for the federal government. Father Hesburgh held 14 presidential appointments over the years, which involved him in virtually all the major social issues. He distinguished himself as an ardent defender of academic freedom and as a champion of civil rights.

During the Hesburgh era, he expanded the university's campus and broadened its intellectual horizons. In two historic moves, the university government was transferred from exclusively clerical control to the predominantly lay board of trustees, and admission of women ended Notre Dame's all-male tradition.

He has received 120 honorary degrees and is the holder of the United States Medal of Freedom, as well as the prestigious Meiklejohn Award from the American Association of University Professors.

His principal retirement role is to develop two Notre Dame institutes that he was instrumental in founding—the Institute for International Peace Studies and the Kellogg Institute for International Studies.

Father Hesburgh was educated at Notre Dame, the Gregorian University of Rome, and the Catholic University of America, from which he received his doctorate in sacred theology. His autobiography, God, Country, Notre Dame *was published by Doubleday in November, 1990.*

You Can Make a Difference

When one is young, the whole world stretches out ahead, beckoning with dreams and hopes.

Thanks to spending most of my adult life at the University of Notre Dame, I have known many young people who want their lives to make a difference in the years ahead. Many of them have their doubts about whether or not one person can make a difference.

I have always told them: you can make a difference, can help make a better world, more just, more peaceful in the years ahead, if you really believe it is possible, if you try.

I know it is possible because, so often, I have seen it happen. In fact, every step forward the world has made in history may be traced back to one person, or a small group of persons, who had a vision, attracted other dedicated people to share the vision, and then made it come true.

Of course, all this has its costs: one must become educated to the limit of one's capabilities to become competent in one's chosen field, whether it is ministry, medicine, law, science, business, education itself, or whatever.

A man named Albert Schweitzer, a minister and medical doctor drew the world's attention to the medical needs of sub-Sahara Africa, attracting many talented doctors to help him, winning the Nobel Prize for Peace in the process.

Mother Teresa, a poor Catholic nun, was so touched by seeing elderly homeless people and abandoned infants dying in the streets of Calcutta that she decided to change the scene. Eventually thousands of generous and capable young men and women of many nations joined her to work with the poorest of the poor, all over the world. She, too, won the Nobel Prize for Peace.

Jim Grant, as the new director of UNICEF, the U.N. agency for children, was appalled by the fact that 40,000 children die needlessly every day, mostly in the Third World, mostly through the effects of malnutrition. He organized a simple five point program for child survival. Already it is saving more than two and a half million children who otherwise would have died in the early years of their lives.

John Kennedy asked his brother-in-law, Sarge Shriver, to organize a Peace Corps. It was almost impossible, but Sarge did it. Today, about a quarter of a century later, more than 125,000 young Americans have served poor nations all over the world, seeing their own lives much

(Continued on page 307)

BONNIE McELVEEN-HUNTER
President & CEO
Pace Communications

Bonnie McElveen-Hunter was born in Columbia, South Carolina, in 1950, the daughter of a dynamic and determined school teacher and a career pilot in the U.S. Air Force, Madeline and John T. McElveen. She is the eldest of three children. Her brother, Dr. John T. McElveen, is a neurotologist at Duke University, and her sister, Tweed McElveen, is the owner of McElveen Designs & Antiques, an interior design and home furnishings business. She likes to say she had the privilege of growing up rich in every way except money. Those wonderful beginnings equipped her for what she hopes she is doing today in business, and that is making a life—rather than just making a living.

Mrs. Hunter grew up an Air Force "brat" and lived in eight states and Germany. She attended high school in Bellevue, Nebraska, and graduated from Stephens College in Columbia, Missouri, with a degree in business administration.

Today she is president and CEO of Pace Communications, a publishing company she compares to a three-legged stool, the legs representing custom/contract magazine publishing, inflight magazines, and a consumer/newsstand magazine. Pace Communications currently publishes United Airlines' inflight magazine, Elegant Bride Magazine, Furniture Retailer Magazine, ASTA Agency Management Magazine, IGS Grocergram, Amtrak Express Magazine, Carlson Voyageur Magazine, and Nautilus Magazine.

Mrs. Hunter is a member of the Young Presidents' Organization, the University of North Carolina at Greensboro Business Advisory Board, the Board of Visitors of Wake Forest College, the Greensboro Board of First Union National Bank, the United Arts Council of Greensboro's Renaissance Campaign, as well as the Greensboro Development Corporation.

Ten Commandments for Failure

When I was invited to participate in this book, I immediately thought of my mother's "pearls of wisdom:" paint a picture and a child will live up to it, so paint a success story every day; mediocrity is the greatest sin; work is the greatest privilege; and time is precious—use it wisely. In our vocabulary, *can't* was a word that did not exist. In fact, it was written on a piece of paper, put in a shoe box, and buried with full burial rites, never to be used again.

We were taught growing up that two options exist in our lives through the choices we make, success or failure. I decided that since success is an all-too-frequently-used term, I would share with you my Ten Commandments for Failure—for failure is never an ending but an opportunity for a new beginning.

Commandment 1: Thou Shalt Have Little Faith. As a Southern minister put it, fear is like being nibbled to death by the minnows. Fear keeps us from reaching our goals and taking risks. If you are going to lose, fight a battle with a worthy foe—make sure you have been swallowed by a whale!

Commandment 2: Thou Shalt Pick Thy Partners with Wanton Abandon. Why is it we spend more time selecting a car that we will drive for only a short time than we spend selecting the people and the company we intend to keep for a lifetime? I have shared a belief with my business partners and friends of 20 years, Gene Johnson and Bill McGee, that it is more important to "select your partners than to select your business." It has served us well.

Commandment 3: Thou Shalt Make the Quick Buck. As long as we have freedom in our economic system, there will be charlatans looking for the "quick buck." Doing wrong in many cases has been a shortcut to making good, but the "quick buck" is its only reward. It's a lousy way to make a living and, more importantly, a life.

Commandment 4: Thou Shalt Have No Enthusiasm. The definition of enthusiasm is "to be possessed by God," and I can assure you that nothing great has ever been accomplished without it—or Him! Enthusiasm is contagious—try it!

(Continued on page 307)

She feels strongly that her accomplishments have been facilitated by a wonderfully supportive family, divine intervention, and a mother with a low tolerance for failure! She is married to Bynum Merritt Hunter, an attorney in the law firm of Smith Helms Mulliss & Moore in Greensboro, North Carolina, and has a ten-year-old son, Bynum Merritt Hunter, Jr., whom she affectionately calls the "Chairman of the Board" of their family.

CONGRESSMAN HENRY J. HYDE
U.S. Representative
Sixth District, Illinois

Congressman Henry Hyde is currently serving his tenth term in Congress, representing Illinois' Sixth District. He serves on the Judiciary and Foreign Affairs committees.

A graduate of Georgetown University, Hyde received his law degree from Loyola University in Chicago. He is a combat veteran of World War II, a former trial lawyer, and in 1987 served on the Iran-Contra investigating committee.

Recognized as one of the Republicans' most competent and motivated legislators, Congressman Hyde has made a difference on a variety of issues, and increasingly on foreign policy from his seat on the Foreign Affairs committee.

He is considered by many as the best debater in the House. In the high-stakes Iran-Contra situation he was the minority's most effective partisan weapon, according to the National Journal, which also gave him a most appropriate accolade: "Hyde's effectiveness may be grounded most of all in his willingness to do his homework and, because unlike many members of Congress, he appears to do his own thinking."

Hyde's rhetorical skills are credited with helping the GOP win over Democrats on key issues. As one fellow Congressman put it, "If you don't have a Henry Hyde articulating your views very forcefully, very well, and with intelligence behind them, it's hard to attract people to come over."

The community-minded Hyde has received honorary degrees from Lewis University, Allentown College and Midwest College of Engineering. Among the many honors conferred upon the Congressman are: The National Security Leadership Award, American Security Council; Distinguished Service Award, Disabled American Veterans; Exceptional

(Continued on page 297)

Freedom Works

We have just come to the end of what I think must be regarded as one of the sorriest centuries in human history. Thanks be to God, we in the United States have been spared much of the horror of the 20th century. But we—you—should never forget that you shared this century with martyrs: martyrs for the truth, martyrs for freedom, martyrs for faith.

The good news is that, in the providence of God, the 20th century is ending in a far better way than we might have expected. Much of the world, after the travails of two world wars, a forty-year cold war, and innumerable small wars, seems to have learned a great truth: freedom works!

But freedom works only if we know what freedom truly means. Lord Acton, a great Catholic historian of the 19th century, put it best: "Freedom is not the power of doing what we like, but the right of being able to do what we ought."

In this, the 200th anniversary year of the American Bill of Rights, we need to think—you need to think, as citizens and voters who will be responsible for leading America in the 21st century—about this business of rights and obligations. About the most we can bring ourselves to say to someone else is, "I'd prefer that you do such-and-such." And we think of that as a humane, decent way to live in a democracy.

The trouble is, our inability to say to each other, "You ought to do this, or that," could spell the end of this great American experiment in freedom. I challenge all young people: care enough about each other to be able to say, "You know, you really ought to..."

Perhaps the most precious, and least appreciated freedom we posses, is our free will. We are allowed to even choose the wrong way, but we are compelled to make our own decisions in using this God-given gift.

In using your free will, I urge you to remember the soul, the capacity for goodness, mercy, compassion, sacrifice, creativity, and grandeur that is in each of you—and that is in every human being you will meet on your life's journey.

Sometimes that soul is hard to find in others. It's even hard to find within ourselves sometime. But it is there. There is no finer gift you can give to your country, and the world, than if each of you nurtures the soul within you, and to help those around you discover and nurture theirs.

Henry J. Hyde

BO JACKSON
Baseball/Football Player

Bo Jackson was the American League's Comeback Player of the Year in 1993. He's been overcoming great odds since he was a youngster. During his early years, he lived with his mother and nine brothers and sisters in a three room house without indoor plumbing. Sometimes all they had to eat was grits and margarine. Sometimes they had nothing at all.

Blessed with extraordinary natural athletic talent, he saw sports as his way to be somebody, as he noted in his autobiography, Bo Knows Bo. In high school he became one of the greatest athletes in Alabama history as he set records in baseball, football, track and field. In baseball, he pitched two no-hitters and set a national high school record hitting 20 home runs (despite missing seven games because of track meets), while batting .447 in his senior year. That same year, he became an all-state running back gaining 1,173 yards on 108 carries, an amazing average of almost 11 yards. He also played defensive end.

A Heisman Trophy winner at Auburn University, in 1985, he was also selected as College Player of the Year by The Sporting News. He finished his collegiate career as Auburn's all-time leading rusher.

The first player selected in the 1986 college draft, he spurned a multi-million dollar offer to play football for the Tampa Bay Buccaneers. Instead, he signed a professional baseball contract with the Kansas City Royals. Strictly a baseball player for one season, he stunned the sports world in 1987 by signing a contract with the Los Angeles Raiders, announcing that he intended to play pro football in the fall, while continuing to play baseball in the spring and summer.

His dual sports career ended in 1991 when he suffered a hip injury. He subsequently underwent hip replacement surgery. Despite some medical experts saying he'd never play sports again, he undertook an exhaustive

(Continueed on page 297)

Start With Education

It doesn't matter where you start, it's where you finish that counts. One of the best ways to start is to get an education. The first thing you must do is to learn to read and write. Without these two basic skills you can't do anything. Before long even unskilled jobs will not be available to non-readers.

Get as much education as you can. Don't tell me you don't like school. Neither did I. Most youngsters don't. I was a juvenile delinquent. My mom even whipped me with a switch and warned me I'd end up in reform school if I didn't mend my ways. It took me a while before I saw the light. For me sports turned me around.

I became involved in track, Little League and Pony League baseball. Before I knew it, I was so occupied with athletics that I didn't have time to get into trouble. If you don't like sports, find something else, but, get involved in something you like. Then work to be the best you can be.

As for school, I found myself concentrating on my favorite subjects—English and science. Guess what? I soon was getting good grades. You may not get as much kick as scoring a touchdown or hitting a home run to win a game, but, getting good grades will give you confidence in yourself and it's great for your self-esteem.

When I left college without a degree, my mother was upset. I promised her that I'd complete my education and I am. I also promised her that I would return to baseball after my hip replacement surgery. I did that, too. Unfortunately, she did not live to see me do it.

I mention this because promises force us to set goals. We all need to have goals. They give us something to work toward. Young people who can determine early what they want to be have a great advantage over those who have no goals.

So, get an education. Set a goal you have to stretch to reach. Then give it all you've got and you'll find that You Can Do It, too!

KAY COLES JAMES
Secty. of Health & Human Services
Commonwealth of Virginia

Kay Coles James has devoted more than 20 years of leadership and service to both the public and private sectors. An ardent advocate of the traditional family, she was Vice President of the Family Research Council prior to being appointed Secretary of Health and Human Resources for the Commonwealth of Virginia in 1993.

Possessing dynamic insight into family policy, with skills sharpened by varied personal and professional experiences, Mrs. James was appointed by President Reagan and reappointed by President Bush as a Commissioner on the National Commission on Children. During the Bush Administration she also served on the White House Task Force on the Black Family; as Asst. Secretary for Public Affairs at the U.S. Department of Health and Human Services; and as an Associate Director for the Office of National Drug Policy.

Her community work extends beyond government service. In 1993, she was appointed a member at large to the Fairfax County School Board in Northern Virginia, the tenth largest school district in the nation. She is also on the Advisory Board of Women to the World International, which assists women in improving their lives by increasing their knowledge and marketable skills.

In 1990, Mrs. James became Executive Vice President and Chief Operating Officer with the One to One Partnership in Washington, D.C. During this time she formulated specific objectives for this national monitoring program and facilitated relationships between corporations and socially and economically disadvantaged youths.

Mrs. James received a Bachelor of Science Degree in history and secondary education from Hampton Institute; an honorary law degree from King College, Bristol, Tennessee; and an honorary Doctor of Humane Letters from Roberts Wesleyan College, Rochester, New York.

Never Forget Your Heritage

As an African-American woman who has been blessed by my Creator in more ways than I can count, I want to give a word of encouragement to all who wrestle with a sense that their race deters them in their quest for success and self-esteem.

We must never forget where we have been if we are to fully appreciate where we are and have a realistic dream for where we want to go. A detailed awareness of our heritage is important if we are to celebrate it and embody it in the totality of our being.

Celebrating one's heritage begins with recognition of the fact that we are uniquely different as Black, Asian, Hispanic ... minorities. The truth is, that even as individuals, we are each different, one from another—a minority of one.

Whatever our race, we must not allow ourselves to fall prey to the lie that we are victims. We, especially in the Black community, must return to those values which have been central to our tradition; faith in God, loyalty to family, honest toil and an inner toughness that has allowed us to survive over two hundred years of slavery, oppression and blatant racism.

If we are to achieve a level of civility that will allow us to walk the corridors of power rather than the streets of despair, we must strive, on our own if need be, for excellence in education. Education leads to communication, which leads to understanding. It is understanding that will ultimately break down the racial barriers which exist in our society.

The ultimate key to success, regardless of race, lies within the hearts of people. The popular cry that I am the way I am because of outside influences must not be our cry. To change our society and to uplift our people, we must first change ourselves, then our institutions. We must not see ourselves as victims but must be overcomers. We can be and we will be if we look back to our heritage ... a proud heritage ... and build upon it.

Her tireless and unfailing commitment to preservation of the family in America stems from her devotion to her own family, husband Charles James, and three children with whom she resides in Northern Virginia.

DEE JEPSEN
National Campaign Director
Enough is Enough

From 1979 until 1982, Mrs. Jepsen worked as a full-time, unsalaried assistant to her husband, former United States Senator Roger Jepsen from Iowa. In 1982, she became a special assistant to President Ronald Reagan, serving as liaison between women's organizations and the White House. She is currently director of a national women's campaign against child pornography called "Enough is Enough."

The mission of the campaign is to greatly reduce sexual violence and to prevent children, women, men and families from becoming victims by eliminating child pornography and removing hard-core and illegal pornography from the marketplace. Since its national launch of "Enough is Enough," in 1992, the response has been tremendously positive. Since that date, women from all walks of life are attending educational meetings and training seminars and are working in their communities to change the way America thinks about pornography.

Dee's wide range of activities found her serving as an officer in the Republican Congressional Wives' Club and in the Ladies of the Senate where she organized a weekly Bible study for Senate wives.

In 1983, Religious Heritage of America selected her to receive its Business and Professional Award for her dedication to the affirmation and strengthening of Judeo-Christian principles in American life.

Dee is also an accomplished artist and writer. Her first book, Women: Beyond Equal Rights *received the Award of Excellence from Religion Media at the Annual Angel Awards. Her most recent book,* Jesus Called Her Mother *was released in 1992.*

Senator and Mrs. Jepsen currently live in the Washington, D.C. area. They have six grown children and nine grandchildren.

When We Give, We Receive

The older one becomes the more aware one is of the brevity of life. This time on earth is an opportunity to make a difference, a chance to serve both God and our fellow man. If we do not use the gifts our Creator has given us to have a positive impact on our corner of the world, instead waste our limited time simply seeking to serve and entertain ourselves, I believe we will be eternally sorry.

What could be more important than having an influence for good on the lives of others, especially young children who are just setting their life course, or helping the poor and needy, protecting the innocent and vulnerable, standing for justice, or ministering compassion. What better legacy could we leave when we pass from this worldly scene?

I know that many times I have failed to live by such an altruistic standard, but I know that when I have, I am the one who receives the most. It is so very true that when we give, we receive ... and the world is a little better.

Dee Jepsen

PAUL JOHNSON
Mayor
Phoenix, Arizona

Paul Johnson was elected mayor by an acclamation vote of the Phoenix City Council in February, 1990, to fill the term vacated by former mayor Terry Goddard. Johnson had been the District 3 representative on the Council since 1986. Though, unusually young as mayors go, Johnson, at 32, subsequently won election with an astounding 99.8 percent of the vote.

A native of Phoenix, Johnson started a construction firm at age 20. After helping the company grow into a successful construction, building, and investment firm, he turned it over to his family to devote his own time to city government.

Johnson lists his priorities as jobs, the environment, and holding the line on government spending.

He attended the John F. Kennedy School of Local and State Government at Harvard University. At age 32, he is the youngest mayor in Phoenix history—and the youngest mayor of a major American city.

Mayor Johnson and his wife, Christa, have two sons—Paul and Justin.

Make the World Better

As mayor of Phoenix, I am called upon to deliver several commencement addresses each year. The message I give to all young people is always the same—and always brief.

Advice is one thing that all commencement speeches have in common. Most of it you can forget. And most of it you will. Joan Rivers, for example, told a graduating class, "Wherever you go in life, always remember that it's not WHO you know that matters—it's "WHOM." And this is what Bob Hope told a group of graduates: "The whole world is out there waiting for you. Don't go!"

My advice is simple. Joan Rivers is wrong. It's not WHO you know or WHOM. It's WHAT you know and how hard you try to do the best you can. That's what matters. And that's why she's wrong. Bob Hope fares a bit better but he's only half wrong. The whole world IS out there waiting for you. But I say, "Get out there and stare it in the face and make it better. Be visionary. Be adventuresome. Take chances." You simply have to.

WILMA H. JORDAN
President & CEO
The Jordan Group, Inc.

Wilma Jordan formed The Jordan Group in 1987. She oversees the firm's activities which include a full range of investment and advisory services for the publishing industry. Clients include U.S. and international companies.

Ms. Jordan was formerly chief operating officer of the Esquire Magazine Group, which consisted of Esquire and New York Woman magazines, the Esquire Health and Fitness Clinic, Esquire Press and Video divisions.

Fresh out of business school at the University of Tennessee, Ms. Jordan was one of the founders of Collegiate Marketing and Management in Knoxville. The company published publications aimed at college students. Later the company was named 13-30 Corporation, reflecting its specialization in marketing to 13 to 30-year-olds.

In 1979, 13-30 bought then-moribund Esquire magazine. Ms. Jordan and her partners engineered a dramatic turnaround of Esquire, one of the most celebrated success stories in the publishing industry. The achievement earned the 1983 Magazine of the Year Award from the American Society of Journalists and Authors.

Ms. Jordan is a member of the board of directors of the LIN Broadcasting Corporation, Ringier America, and Guidepost Magazine, Inc. She is a member of both the Women's Forum, Inc., and Advertising Women of New York, was inducted into the YWCA Academy of Women Achievers in 1985, and serves on the University of Tennessee College of Business Advisory Council.

In addition, she is an active fundraiser for the Patricia Neal Stroke/Trauma Rehabilitation Center in Knoxville, and chaired the first Patricia Neal Center Ball at the Waldorf-Astoria in 1987.

Courage and Tenacity

I believe courage and tenacity make a winner—every time.

It is easy to be safe, to follow the road taken by others; but what of significance has ever been achieved by a concern to be safe? I like the advice that John D. Rockefeller gave to young people, when he said: "Strike out on new paths rather than travel the worn roads of accepted success." That takes courage.

Too many people think of security instead of opportunity. That's a natural tendency. Whenever you have a choice between going forward and playing it safe, my advice is to go for it. Use common sense in deciding your course of action, then put everything you've got into it.

A half-hearted effort won't get it done. It might carry you a little way toward your goal, but it will never get you far enough to reach it. Be tenacious, no matter how rough it gets; be determined to stay with it—and you'll become a success, too!

Wilmer H. Jordan

MICHAEL S. JOSEPHSON
President
Josephson Institute of Ethics

Michael Josephson has had successful careers in business, law and education before entering the area of ethics. A graduate of UCLA and the UCLA Law School, he was a law professor with an impressive academic career spanning almost 20 years.

During that period, he was founder and chief executive officer of a publishing company and a national chain of bar exam preparation courses. In 1985, he sold his businesses and, shortly thereafter, left academia to found and serve as president of the Joseph and Edna Josephson Institute of Ethics, a non-profit corporation he founded and named after his parents. He personally paid the start up and operational expenses of the Institute through 1989 with contributions of over $1 million. Josephson takes no salary or other reimbursements for any of his services. All fees and honoraria go directly to the Institute.

The purpose of the Institute is to increase the ethical consciousness and commitment of America's leaders through intensive workshops, speeches and publications, including a magazine aptly titled Ethics: Easier Said Than Done. Josephson personally conducts nearly 100 programs per year for leaders in government, journalism, business, law, education and the nonprofit community.

In 1993, Josephson organized the Character Counts Coalition, a partnership of over 30 of the nation's most influential youth-influencing organizations to combat youth violence, irresponsibility and dishonesty by stressing the development of character built on six core ethical values: Trustworthiness, Respect, Responsibility, Fairness, Caring and Citizenship. The Coalition reaches over 25 million young people.

In addition, Josephson has become one of the foremost ethicists in journalism assisting the Associated Press Managing Editors Association in drafting a comprehensive and controversial code of ethics.

Character Counts

I've been lucky to achieve a number of different forms of success, enough to give me a perspective on what does or does not generate the kind of happiness we think success will give us. Though I would have doubted it in my earlier years, I can now say without question that most achievements people call success gave only a short buzz of pleasure. The only real and lasting feelings of success I have experienced occur when I act with a sense of purpose beyond self-interest, when I do something that makes me feel that the world is at least a tiny bit better because I was in it.

Whether or not you are rich, famous or powerful, you are a person of value when you can look back and say "I made a difference." And, in my experience, the power to make a difference has nothing to do with money or position. It has to do with seeing and seizing opportunities to be of genuine service, to make a contribution by acts of kindness or integrity that warm the soul or light the path of another.

I competed effectively in business and in the law profession only to realize that when "winning" becomes the way we measure our lives, we can easily lose sight of the price we pay. If you are not willing to lose, you have to be willing to do whatever it takes to win. Lily Tomlin put it well when she said, "the problem with the rat race is even if you win, you're still a rat." How much wiser is the observation: "if you want to know how to live your life, think about what you want people to say about you after you die and live backwards."

I was at a law professor's convention when a man came up to me and said: "You probably don't remember me, but I want to thank you for changing my life." I was embarrassed to admit I didn't remember and he said, "That's O.K., I didn't expect you to. You visited my law school years ago to give a speech. I was thinking of dropping out and you talked to me after the lecture and gave me confidence. I finished school and I was just appointed the first Mexican-American dean of an American law school." The feeling of pride and satisfaction I get from re-living that story is still strong and powerful.

A lot of people thought I was crazy when I quit law teaching and sold my legal education company to start a non-profit institute to improve the ethical quality of society by teaching ethical decision making and the importance of character. All I can say is I have never worked harder nor felt better. I know the work of the Institute hasn't eliminated violence, disrespect, dishonesty, injustice and irresponsibility, but it has made a difference. Out message that character counts has reached millions of people and I know at least some of them make ethical decisions more often.

The poet Edmund Hale once said, "It is true I am only one person

(Continued on page 308)

DONALD R. KEOUGH
Chairman of the Board
Allen & Company Incorporated

Donald R. Keough is chairman of the board of Allen & Company Incorporated, a New York investment banking firm. He was elected to that position on April 15, 1993.

Mr. Keough retired as president, chief operating officer and director of The Coca-Cola Company in April 1993 and at that time he was appointed advisor to the board. His tenure with the company dates back to 1950. He held various key positions prior to being named president to the company's Foods Division in 1971.

Subsequently, he held the offices of the president of Coca-Cola USA and was later given the responsibility for the company's business in North and South America. Mr. Keough was elected president, chief operating officer and director of The Coca-Cola Company in 1981. From 1986 to 1993, he served as chairman of the board of Coca-Cola Enterprises, Inc., the world's largest bottling system.

Mr. Keough serves on the boards of National Service Industries, Inc., H.J. Heinz Company, The Washington Post Company, The Home Depot and McDonald's Corporation. He is immediate past chairman of the board of trustees of the University of Notre Dame and a trustee of several other educational institutions. He also serves on the boards of a number of national charitable and civic organizations.

Mr. Keough has received various honors in his career including honorary doctorates from the University of Notre Dame, his alma mater Creighton University, Emory University and Trinity University, Dublin. The University of Notre Dame's highest honor, the Laetare Medal, was presented to Mr. Keough in May 1993.

"You Can Do" Philosophy

"You can do it!" For some people, this is little more than a tired cliche. For many of us, however, it is a statement that is both real and empowering.

For me, in fact, it addresses a basic reality of life—that we are put here "to do," and very little of what we "do" can be limited to who we "are." The "you can do" philosophy is a truth I have learned one day at a time over more than six decades.

People arrive at a certain position in life not by chance or luck. To a large degree, it is the result of having the will to succeed and being totally committed.

As president of The Coca-Cola Company, I had the good fortune to help lead a business that sells the best known product in the world, Coca-Cola. It is sold in nearly 170 countries, and every day there are new and wonderful challenges to meet.

But selling Coca-Cola is also a job that has very little in common with selling coffee in Omaha, Nebraska, which was exactly how my career began back in 1950.

Did I know back then that eventually I would assume the responsibilities and face the challenges that I enjoy today? Of course not. I did know, however, that selling coffee was a good opportunity for me and that with a little hard work it was something I could be good at and even master.

In life, it is so important to set short term goals so as to enjoy periodic achievement. It is difficult, if not impossible, to move from an entry level position to chairman of the board in one giant stride. It is possible, though, to set interim goals and move up the ladder in smaller steps. If you work hard you can achieve a goal and be ready for your next goal and next victory. Before you know it your ultimate objective will be in sight.

By joining that little coffee company, it was like I had jumped into a small creek and started swimming. That creek turned into a river, and that river turned into a gulf. Finally, I found myself in an ocean of opportunity called The Coca-Cola Company. All I have ever done is just kept swimming as hard as I could, and today I am swimming harder than ever.

Taking the first plunge into that first creek is often the toughest challenge. But once you feel the water on your skin and learn that you are not going to drown, you will grow stronger and stronger. Before long, you are well on your way toward the ocean, and the realization that you can indeed do it!

HENRY (HANK) KETCHAM
Cartoonist Creator of
Dennis the Menace

Hank Ketcham created Dennis the Menace in October, 1950, and it was syndicated to 18 newspapers the following March. Today Dennis the Menace, who marked his 40th birthday in 1990 while remaining a lovable five, is distributed by North America Syndicate to more than 1,000 newspapers in 48 countries and is translated into 19 languages.

Ketcham was born March 14, 1920, in Seattle, Washington. He became interested in drawing at the age of seven when a local art director doodled cartoon sketches to amuse him. The bug bit him and Ketcham practiced cartooning in every spare moment of his school years.

He entered the University of Washington in 1937, as an art major, but after a year the cartooning urge lured him to Hollywood and the Walter "Woody Woodpecker" Lantz animation studio. Moving to the Walt Disney studios, he worked on "Pinocchio," "Fantasia," and other Disney productions until World War II, when he enlisted in the U.S. Navy.

After the war, he plunged full-time into the highly competitive free-lance cartooning market. He quickly became one of the country's most successful and prolific cartoonists, selling his work regularly to Collier's, The Saturday Evening Post, Ladies Home Journal, Liberty, and The New Yorker, as well as to advertising agencies. By this time, Ketcham was also married and the father of a boy named Dennis.

Since the early days, Ketcham has expanded his lovable imp's popularity through a variety of other media. The hit network television series which ran from 1959 to 1963 still appears on stations around the country.

Dennis' civic mindedness has made him a popular spokesman for many worthy causes, including The Boy Scouts of America, UNICEF and the International Red Cross. His image appears on myriad licensed products, from lunch boxes to greeting cards. The Dennis the Menace

(Continued on page 298)

I discovered this anonymous message many years ago. It has been an inspiration to me ever since. Without persistence, Dennis would not have endured all these years. I share this message with you, hoping it will motivate you to diligently pursue all your goals in life.

Nothing in the world can take the place of persistence.

Talent will not; nothing is more common than men with talent.

Genius will not; unrewarded genius is almost a proverb.

Education will not; the world is full of educated derelicts.

Persistence and determination alone are omnipotent.

Hank Ketcham

TERESA KETTELKAMP
Deputy Director
Illinois State Police

Teresa Kettelkamp is the highest-ranking female State Police officer in the nation. In her position, she carries the rank of colonel and is now first in command in the Division of Internal Investigation.

Teresa is a graduate of Quincy College, B.A. political science, State Police Academy, and the FBI National Academy. While in graduate school at the University of Illinois–Chicago studying sociology she planned to go to law school when she became interested in the Illinois Bureau of Investigation.

From school, she joined the IBI in a clerical function, but found the investigative end more interesting. She soon became a special agent working on the Organized Crime Squad, General Assignment Squad, and Covert Squad, doing undercover work, before joining the Operational Services Command.

Prior to her present position, she worked in the Division of Criminal Investigation, Division of State Troopers, and Division of Internal Investigation.

Teresa keeps fit playing tennis, swimming, and jogging. Music is one of her diversions. Among her favorites is Phil Collins' "Another Day in Paradise," about the homeless, one of her concerns.

Work Hard, Have Faith

When my daughter was born, I made a banner for her bedroom which read: *Girls Can Do Anything.* I wanted to start her out in life with this positive affirmation because, as I looked at this precious newborn, I wanted with all my heart for her to always feel that life's opportunities are limitless. I truly believe that what any person believes in his or her heart can be achieved. I've always liked what Henry Ford said, "Whether you think you can or think you can't, you're right." I believe this to be true.

The older I become, the more reflective I am about who I am and how I was able to achieve the success I have. My not-so-secret secret is that I am where I am because I worked hard and have faith in a faithful God. Some other beliefs I hold which I think will benefit young people are:

- Learn early in life that validation of your worth comes from within yourself—never externally. Get to know yourself and know that you can believe in yourself.

- Life should be lived one day at a time. Living in the past and/or worrying about the future eliminates your today. In keeping with this, learn to forgive those who do you harm. Law enforcement is constantly facing crimes based on grudges and revenge.

- Time and good health are precious—manage them wisely.

- It is important to achieve and maintain a balance between work, family, play, and your spiritual life. Reading the Bible daily will help you accomplish this personal goal.

- You should treat others as you want to be treated. There will always be people in your life who can use your help—particularly children and the elderly.

- A God does exist—make God an integral part of your life. If you don't, you're doing too much yourself.

A career in law enforcement is worth considering because it can positively touch so many lives. There are many levels of law enforcement (city, county, state, and federal) and much diversity within each level that make it a very rewarding career. Law enforcement is also filled with many challenges for you to use your God-given talents to make the world a better and safer place. How can you beat that?

Jm Kettelkamp

PHILIP H. KNIGHT
Chairman & CEO
NIKE, Inc.

Phil Knight was selected Oregon's Business Person of the Decade by business leaders from throughout the state, who made him their unanimous choice for the honor.

Knight holds a BA business degree from the University of Oregon and an MBA from Stanford University. He is a certified public accountant and spent two years as an assistant professor of business administration at Portland State University.

At the University of Oregon, where he was a star middle distance runner, he and his coach, Bill Bowerman, liked to tinker with shoe designs. They chipped in $500 to start Blue Ribbon Sports in 1964, concentrating on distributing Japanese made shoes in the USA.

Seven years later, BRS started making its own shoes and, in 1972, marketed its first NIKE products in time for the Olympic trials. Knight combined economical Far East production with innovative designs and adroit marketing to turn athletic shoes into a major growth industry. He still runs 20 miles per week and personally tests new NIKE shoes.

Knight serves on numerous boards, and is a member of various civic, corporate and education committees. He is married and the father of two children.

Simple Advice

My best piece of advice is very simple: Don't be afraid to fail—the only time you have to succeed is the last time you try!

JACK D. KUEHLER
Former President
IBM Corp.

Jack D. Kuehler, former IBM president retired in 1993.

He came to IBM with a B.S. degree in mechanical engineering from Santa Clara University, a year's experience designing jet engines for General Electric, and three years in the Army assigned to the Atomic Energy Commission.

Kuehler advanced through various technical and managerial positions. By 1981, he was group executive of the Information Systems and Technology Group. The following year he became an IBM senior vice president, and in 1985 assumed executive responsibility for the worldwide development and U.S. manufacturing for IBM's technology and computer systems. He was elected to the board of directors in 1986, became an executive vice president in 1987, vice chairman of the board in 1988 and president in 1989.

While working full time as an IBM manager, and later as an executive, he earned a master's in electrical engineering from Santa Clara University. Kuehler also has two honorary doctorates of science from Santa Clara and Clarkson Universities.

Among many other activities outside IBM, Kuehler is a Fellow of the Institute of Electrical and Electronics Engineers, a Fellow of the American Academy of Arts and Sciences, a trustee of Santa Clara University, a member of the board of directors of Olin Corporation, the National Association of Manufacturers, National Action Council for Minorities in Engineering, and the New York State Business Council. He is also a member of the National Academy of Engineering.

Jack and his wife, Carmen, live in Connecticut. They have five children.

Like What You Do

Not many of us know early in our lives exactly where we're headed in our careers. But that's really not very important. What is important is that we work at something we like, work hard at it, and do it to the best of our ability. Liking what we do and doing it well usually go hand in hand.

What if our very first job doesn't work out? That's no catastrophe. There's always a second chance, and anyone who says there's only one is just plain wrong.

It seems to me that at least three things are important to living a fulfilled life.

First, become involved—in your church or synagogue, your neighborhoods, your schools, in protecting our fragile environment—wherever your interests and your talents lead you.

Second, believe in yourself, and set your sights high. And remember, history has told us over and over that one person really can make a difference.

And third, have some fun along the way. Take time to drink in the sunshine and smell the roses. We can't know the end of this fascinating journey. But rather than curse the inevitable bumps and the twists and turns, relax and smile at the infinite delight and wonder along the way.

Jack D Kuehler

W. DANIEL A. LAMEY, CAE
Secretary General
Junior Chamber International

Dan Lamey was born in Stellarton, Nova Scotia, Canada. He graduated from St. Mary's University, in Halifax, with a Bachelor of Commerce degree. Virtually all of his working life has been spent in the ever growing field of voluntary association management. In 1989 he earned the field's professional designation of certified Association Executive (CAE) from the American Society of Association Executives (ASAE).

In the midst of his university education, he took leave from his full time studies to take his first association job, working for the Association of Student Councils student travel co-op from 1972 to 1973, by running their office which served students in universities and colleges of the Atlantic Provinces of Canada.

After graduation he became a management trainee for the Bank of Montreal. After three years of what he feels was excellent practical management training, he became national Executive Director of the Canadian Junior Chamber, also known as the "Jaycees".

Having originally intended to return to the "normal" business world, he found that the vocation of association management was where he wanted to build his career in a broad field with endless opportunities. In 1980, he became national Executive Director of Canada's largest national service club, The Association of Kinsmen Clubs. He gained international experience by serving the World Council of Young Men's Service Clubs, of which Kinsmen was a member, as General Secretary. He also managed the international development projects which the Kinsmen organization funded, in such countries as Zambia, India, Bangladesh, Panama, Mauritius, The Philippines, Kenya and Ethiopia, all of which he visited.

In 1986, his career path led him to the United States, when he accepted the position of General Secretary of Junior Chamber International, an

Let the World Come to Your Life!

It is, perhaps, a cliche to say that the world is getting smaller. Of course, the distance around the equator or between Memphis and Tokyo is the same as it was 75 years ago. But, in a communication sense or in terms of time, the world is truly getting smaller—a fact that can change your future.

Remember that when you were three years old your "world" was a big place, even though it may have been confined to your house or apartment? That world was nonetheless interesting, sometimes mysterious and often exciting. A closet or a basement was only to be explored by the most adventurous of spirit.

As you grew older, your "world" also grew. Growing beyond your neighborhood, even your hometown or city—you came to feel comfortable in this bigger—yet still interesting and mysterious world of yours. If you are like the average young American, however, you may set limits on your known world that do not go beyond the boundaries of your city or state, but in all likelihood, definitely do not go beyond the boundaries of your own country (visits to Tijuana, Mexico or Niagara Falls, Canada notwithstanding).

News reports, National Geographic studies and countless other commentaries attest to the fact that young Americans are less informed about the world outside their own country than earlier generations. Even more critical is the fact that they are much less informed than similar young people from other countries. While there is more information about the rest of the world available than ever before, too many tend to ignore it and, as a result, their known world stops growing at an early age.

The world outside our country is not maps, capitals and governments; it is people—people who are pursuing their own future, building their own lives and facing many of the same-or-greater-challenges as you. To be truly successful in coming decades you and countless millions of other young Americans are going to have to tune in to this larger world—expanding your comfort zone beyond the borders of your own state and country—becoming a person who really lives life in the world beyond the United States—someone for whom the world is a part of daily life.

(Continued on page 309)

---

organization based in Coral Gables, Florida, that counts over 420,000 member "Jaycees" in 105 countries and territories.

Lamey's voluntary involvement is extensive and includes several organizations in the business, professional and charitable fields.

RICHARD E. LAPCHICK
Director/Center for the
Study of Sports in Society

Richard E. Lapchick brought his experience as a civil rights activist, scholar, and author to Northeastern University in Boston, where he is founder and director of the Center for the Study of Sports in Society.

Since its inception in 1984, the Center has attracted national attention to its pioneering efforts to ensure the education of athletes from junior high school through the professional ranks. The Center helped form the National Consortium for Academics and Sports (NCAS), a group of 100 colleges and universities that have adopted the Center's programs. A requirement for membership is that institutions bring back any athlete on scholarship in a revenue sport in the previous decade, who did not graduate, to allow the athlete to complete his or her education at the expense of the university.

To date, 6,060 athletes have come back to NCAS schools, including 4,482 college athletes whose eligibility had expired, 1,482 current professional athletes, and 138 Olympians; 2,639 have graduated. Nationally, the NCAS has enrolled more than 1,719,000 students in its outreach program. Lapchick serves as president and chief executive officer of the NCAS.

Considered one of the nation's experts on sports issues, he serves as an advisor to the Reverend Jesse Jackson and the Rainbow Commission on Fairness in Sports and to the Players Association of the National Basketball Association, National Football League and Major League Baseball on the issue of racial hiring practices in sport.

A regular columnist for The Sporting News, he is a prolific writer. His seventh book: Five Minutes to Midnight: Race and Sport in America in the 90's, is an autographical account of the role Lapchick and his father played in trying to end racism in sport. His is the son of Joe

(Continued on page 299)

We All Can Make a Contribution

We all start from the same place. We all have the capacity to make a contribution to the world, a world so much more complex for this new generation. We need to be there for our young people to give them hope that they do have a role to play; that they don't have to be afraid of the future because it is theirs to shape.

I happen to believe that playing sport can help shape their future.

In addition to achievement, good health and fun, the more obvious benefits of sport, there is so much more to learn from sport. It teaches self-discipline, about limits and capabilities, about dealing with failure and adversity, about teamwork and cooperation, hard work, group-problem solving, competitive spirit, self-esteem, self-confidence, and pride in accomplishment.

In a time when our races are so divided, sports bring us together to make friends. Good sports programs become an alternative for those with idle time that could otherwise lead them into patterns of alcohol and drug abuse. These are all qualities that can be translated into being a good student, member of the community or corporate citizen. Athletes must understand these qualities are transferable into other areas of their lives. Those of us in sport need to teach that.

Part of the problem may be that young people see superstars and they feel ordinary. A true story about a superstar may help with some perspective.

They say that true genius is very rare. But most acknowledge that Albert Einstein was perhaps the greatest genius, an intellectual superstar, in the second half of the 20th Century. He seemed so extraordinary that when he died, scientists at Columbia Presbyterian Hospital decided to examine his brain to see what was so different. They held a press conference after hours of examination. The surprised scientists and doctors told the expectant world that Einstein's brain was just like yours and mine.

To young people who don't like sport, I encourage you to get involved in something—the arts, music, or anything that captures your imagination. It will make a difference in your life. You are somebody who can make a contribution, whether it be in the world at large, or, within your own family.

Richard E. Lapchick

167

MICHAEL LEVINE
Businessman/Author

Michael Levine is the founder of Levine/Schneider Public Relations, one of the largest entertainment public relations firm in the country. In 1991, the company was named P.R. Firm of the Year by Performance Magazine's annual reader poll.

Called by the Hollywood Reporter trade paper: "one of Hollywood's brightest and most respected executives," the 39-year old Levine boasts a powerful and impressive client roster in all areas of the entertainment industry including film, television, music, books and special events.

His clients have run the gamut from movie stars Charlton Heston, Jon Voight, Michael J. Fox, Demi Moore and Mickey Rooney; sports stars Kareem Abdul-Jabbar and Dorothy Hamill; television personalities Hal Linden, Mary Hart, Linda Evans, Suzanne Somers and John Larroquette; music's Fleetwood Mac, Michael Jackson, Tom Petty and David Bowie; and comics Sandra Bernhard and George Carlin.

Levine is a frequent lecturer at major universities including speaking at the prestigious Harvard Business School on the subject of media opportunities in the 90's. He also moderates a quarterly lecture series called the Thought Forum, which are evenings of intellectual challenge featuring prominent speakers discussing some of today's important ideas.

Levine's the author of a series of address source books. His The Address Book—How To Reach Anyone Who's Anyone, is considered the standard for such reference books. It continues to be well received through six sequel editions. His latest—The Kid's Address Book was published in 1992. Guerrilla P.R., his first hardcover book, was published in 1993 and is considered an important work on the subject.

He serves on numerous boards including D.A.R.E. America, Entertainment Industries Council, the Felice Foundation and Neil Bogart Cancer Laboratories.

Lessons From Life

In the representation of nearly 100 celebrities, ranging from Charlton Heston to Barbra Streisand to Janet Jackson, I have learned a couple of things, including:

- There are a whole lot of people running very fast, but in the wrong direction.
- The person who commits a mistake and doesn't correct it is committing a second mistake.
- Experience is a hard teacher because it gives the test first and the lessons afterward.

And also ...

- Always remember that some ideas are so stupid that only intellectuals can believe them.

EUGENE LOOPER
Banking/Financial Consultant

It's a long way from a tenant farm in rural South Carolina, in the shadow of Appalachia, to the halls of academia and banking's leading institutions. Charles Eugene Looper made that journey and today is one of the nation's leading banking/financial consultants.

His trek took him to Furman University, where he earned a B.A. degree and won a fellowship to Louisiana State University where he received his Master of Arts degree.

After a three year hitch in the U.S. Navy, primarily at sea on a destroyer as a Lieutenant Senior Grade, he resumed his education at Georgetown University, where he earned his Ph.D. in public law.

Prior to entering the banking field, he served as an instructor in Georgetown's School of Foreign Service and as professor of political science at Furman University. Later, while studying monetary theory at London University's School of Economics, he realized that an education without capital was unproductive, which led him into banking.

He began at Wachovia Bank & Trust Company, in Winston-Salem, before becoming vice president at the Southeast Banking Corporation in Miami, Florida. At the same time, he served as a part-time professor in the School of Administration at the University of Miami.

Mr. Looper has received scores of honors and has been active in civic, philanthropic and political activities throughout his career.

He has authored numerous publications, including a prophetic article in The Bankers Magazine in 1981 titled "Early Warning Signs of Banking Trouble."

Capital and Savings

> The shades of night were falling fast
> When through an Alpine village passed
> A youth who bore mid snow and ice
> A banner with a strange device,
> Excelsior.

You may have read Longfellow's poem "Excelsior" and wondered where the ambitious, self-denying, courageous young man carrying the banner with the strange device was going. Many people carry banners with strange devices but with no well-formulated goals, no direction, and gain little achievement. Well-formulated goals are those which enhance the essential elements for achievement: knowledge and capital.

The catalyst is monetary capital. With knowledge you formulate ideas and plans; with monetary capital you purchase resources and energy for conversion of knowledge into products and services.

Knowledge capital is created by education and thinking. Monetary capital is created by savings. At this writing, our country is in a recession. Individuals who have not cultivated the habit of savings find themselves in a precarious position. Installment buying has been made so easy that it is common to spend out of proportion to one's income. Early habits cling to us through life, so, learning to save should be embraced as soon as an individual becomes an income producer. It is essential to personal success.

Thus, a great imperative in a free society is the obligation to save a portion of what is produced or earned. It is no surprise that the countries with the highest savings rate are the most productive and the most democratic. Underdeveloped countries are those deficient in both knowledge and monetary capital which consequently fail to provide the essential of freedom; adequate production of goods and services required for individual mobility.

So it is with the individual—knowledge not energized by capital is academic and frequently misdirected as empty and frustrated idealism. Growth and development for such individuals and countries depends largely upon the quality of education afforded and the acceptance of the necessity to preserve a portion of what is produced. The squirrel who fails to store a part of the fall harvest of nuts seldom survives the winter.

SID LUCKMAN
NFL Football Great
Business Executive

The most-fabled quarterback in Chicago Bears history, Sid Luckman has achieved equal success in the business world.

Brooklyn-born, his high school team won the New York City championship. He was an All American at Columbia University, where despite the athletic schedule, he made time to work several jobs to pay his way enroute to a Bachelor of Arts Degree.

Bears owner-coach George Halas handpicked him as the team's No. 1 draft choice in 1939 to make him quarterback of the intricate new T-formation, which only the Bears used. With the T, Sid led the Bears to world championships in 1940, 1941, 1943 and 1946.

He played 12 years for the Bears making All Pro eight times and was the NFL's most valuable player three times. His records include seven touchdown passes against the Giants and five in the World Championship game against the Washington Redskins, still a record. He's a member of both the College and Pro Football Hall of Fame.

After retiring as a player, he served as a Bears assistant coach and was a vice president of the team, as well. He also assisted Notre Dame, West Point, Columbia University, the University of Pittsburgh, Maryland University and Holy Cross to acclimate them to the T-formation system.

Formerly vice chairman of Cellu-Craft, a manufacturer of flexible packaging, he now serves the firm in sales and consulting. Sid also serves on the boards of various corporations.

He founded the Estelle Luckman Foundation for cancer research in memory of his wife, Estelle, his high school sweetheart, who died in 1981. His three children and various civic and philanthropic endeavors take up his time, when he isn't watching his beloved Chicago Bears.

Spend Your Time Well

Football fans continue to marvel when a quarterback runs a two-minute drill at a crucial time in a game. This studious use of time is often the difference between victory and defeat. People tend to forget it took hours of practice to achieve the coordination it takes to make it work when the game is on the line.

In life, not a minute should be wasted. Time is one of our most precious, mysterious and unappreciated possessions. Precious because none of us knows how much time we've been allotted in this life.

Mysterious because, despite being the only truly constant in our lives, (there will always only be 60 seconds in a minute), time somehow quickly slips away. I'll always remember what the late George Halas, my dear friend, coach and hero, told me shortly before he passed away: "It seems like only yesterday when we were winning all those championships for the Chicago Bears." An avid reader, he quoted Thomas Aldrich who wrote: "All the best sands of life are somehow getting into the wrong end of the hourglass."

Time is unappreciated, because we seem to forget that each minute can be used only once—then it's gone forever. We have no control over the passage of time—the clock keeps ticking—whether we're wasting it or doing something worthwhile with it. So, it's up to you what you'll do with yours.

Unlike the movies, which back-peddle in time, or, fast-forward into the future, we must live life one second at a time. If we could live every 120 minutes as a two-minute drill, as we try to reach one of our goals, we'd never waste one precious moment.

Inevitably, time does slip away. For some, it simply disappears and nothing is left behind. For others, like Mr. Halas, who helped found the National Football League, when time is gone—monuments remain.

What will you have left, when time runs out for you?

Sid Luckman

MANUEL LUJAN, JR.
Former Secretary of the Interior

Sworn in February 3, 1989, as the 46th Secretary of the Interior.

Served in the House of Representatives from New Mexico 1969-1989. Was senior Republican on the House Interior and Insular Affairs Committee and the Energy and Environment Subcommittee; vice chairman of the House Science, Space and Technology Committee; member of the President's National Commission on Space. Received National Science Foundation Distinguished Service Award.

In Congress, was a leader in battle against wasteful government spending, co-sponsor of seven major environmental protection bills including the Clean Air Act of 1970 and the Clean Water Act, promoted education through support of student loan programs, and backed scientific research to help meet the challenges of the 21st century.

Raised in Santa Fe, N.M., and earned a B.A. from the College of Santa Fe. Also attended St. Mary's College in California. Has received five honorary Ph.D.s.

Organized private sector fund that has provided hundreds of $500 scholarships for students attending college in New Mexico.

Personally inspected cleanup efforts of Exxon Valdez tanker spill in Prince William Sound and serves as a Federal Trustee in assessment of damages. Took steps to improve transportation of oil, to insure continued safety in federal offshore program, and increase cooperation with industry to step up oil spill cleanup research.

Married to the former Jean Couchman of Sante Fe. The Lujans have four children.

Take Pride in America

As Secretary of Interior, I am responsible for the protection of much of America's natural heritage—our parks, wilderness areas and public lands.

Our public lands give Americans some of the best recreation opportunities anywhere in the world including camping, hunting, fishing, sightseeing and just plain relaxation. Today these lands are being threatened, sometimes by the very people who use them. We have problems with litter, vandalism, pollution and overcrowding. And with more than 500 million acres to protect, there is no way that only Interior employees can be effective policemen for these treasures.

But there is one thing I know for sure, Americans love their land and are willing to work to protect it. So, we have started a program at the Department of Interior called Take Pride in America. It is a very simple and practical program. Its message is that public lands are your lands. If you want to continue to enjoy them and assure they'll be around for generations to come, you are going to have to help take care of them.

This challenge has gone out to America. The response has been amazing. From a small town garden club to major corporations, the country has responded. We have clean-up drives, recycling programs, volunteers repairing trails and painting buildings. There is an ever-expanding outreach to people everywhere showing them how heartfelt pride in God's gifts to America can assure these gifts will be here to bless future citizens with special joys of a bountiful and beautiful land.

The invitation to Take Pride in America is addressed to everyone. Accepting it is the best gift people of all ages can give to our blessed land. I especially encourage young people to heed this call by making your lands part of your life.

Manuel Lujan Jr.

GERALD L. MAATMAN
President & CEO
Kemper National
Insurance Companies

Gerald Maatman joined Kemper in 1966 as director of Loss Control Engineering after serving on the faculty of the Illinois Institute of Technology, from which he earned his bachelor of science degree. He earlier has served as an executive with the Illinois Inspection and Rating Bureau. He directed the 1968 formation of the Kemper Corporation subsidiary National Loss Control Service Corporation and was its first president.

Before being elected Kemper National president in 1987 and chief executive officer in 1990, Maatman was executive vice president in charge of Kemper Corporation's regional property-casualty insurance companies and Kemper's Information Services Group. He is also a director of Kemper National and chairman of its executive committee.

Maatman is co-chairman of the Advocates for Highway and Auto Safety, a coalition of insurers, consumer groups and others interested in promoting auto safety. The group will attempt to reduce deaths, injuries and economic costs associated with motor vehicle crashes and fraud and theft involving motor vehicles.

He is also a director of the Institute for Civil Justice, National Commission Against Drunk Driving, the National Fire Protection Association, Junior Achievement of Chicago, National Down Syndrome Society, and Underwriters Laboratories, Inc. He is also on the Leadership Council of the Network of Employers for Traffic Safety and is a member of the Society of Fire Protection Engineers.

Born in Chicago in 1930, he now lives in North Barrington, Illinois, with his wife Bernice. They have two grown children.

Outwork Your Peers

The next decade or two will be a time of great challenge for both business concerns and their managements. Communication advances, increased competition in world markets and greater volatility of our financial systems are but some of the factors which will make it increasingly difficult to achieve future business success.

On a personal level, young aspiring professionals will continue to be faced with competition from increasing numbers of well educated peers. What then can a young adult do to maximize his or her chances of achieving a significant level of business success?

Without question, the single most important ingredient for success lies in "out-working" your peer group. This includes not only mastering the elements of your current job and performing in a superior manner, but also remaining alert to ways in which your group's operations can be further improved.

The ability to handle and lead other people is a second most important element in this picture. Aside from developing effective verbal skills to assist you in selling your ideas, it's important to gain a good understanding of human nature (i.e., learning why people act differently under varying circumstances) and to develop the knack of creating "win-win" situations where both yours and the other party's personal goals can be satisfied. Another important characteristic of any good leader is the ability to lead by example and also to be able to put oneself in the other person's shoes and to act accordingly.

The chances of advancing upward into senior levels of management can be improved measurably by developing a good ability to step back and understand the "big picture". You need to recognize how your job fits into your unit's operations—how the unit supports the company's goals—and how corporate goals and strategies give it a competitive advantage in your industry's marketplace.

Finally, it's very important that a young person decide on long term personal goals and then develop and maintain the inner discipline to keep focused on these multi-year objectives.

An overriding consideration in any young person's business pursuits should be a complete and total commitment to honesty and integrity. Being true to oneself and acting accordingly must be a given in a person's daily life. The ultimate test should be "can I look in the mirror every morning and feel comfortable with myself?" Although a short term advantage can sometimes be gained by acting otherwise, over the long run, such a person is almost certain to fall by the wayside.

ROBERT S. MacARTHUR
President
American Youth Foundation

Over the years Bob MacArthur has been employed as a steel worker, a minister, a farmer, a dean, an administrator, and an executive. He has climbed mountains, coached baseball, milked cows, composed music, and recorded a folk mass. He has been a classroom teacher, preacher, and a pastoral counselor. And, he is a cheerleader for his wife, Peggy, and their four children.

After graduation from Dartmouth College, Bob attended Berkeley Divinity School at Yale and served for two years in the parish ministry of the Episcopal Church. Exploring further his interest in intentional community life, he worked in the mountains of North Carolina on a farming cooperative patterned after Danish folk schools.

For 12 years he directed the Outward Bound Center at Dartmouth College, helping students relate the individual and team challenges of the wilderness to their formal and informal education. While at Dartmouth, he taught freshman writing courses and served as acting dean of the William Jewett Tucker Foundation, an endowment established to further the moral and spiritual growth of graduates.

Today, inspired by William H. Danforth's philosophy, Bob leads the American Youth Foundation in its efforts to motivate young people to achieve their best, live balanced lives, and serve others. Mr. Danforth's book, I Dare You, *is still available from the foundation.*

I Dare You

As a small boy, William H. Danforth was a sallow-cheeked and sickly student. One day in class his teacher looked Danforth straight in the eyes and said, "I dare you to be the healthiest boy in the class." That dare was enough to launch a lifetime of achievement and service.

Danforth changed his diet and began a regimen of physical exercise. He grew robust and healthy. As an adult with tireless energy and the talent to motivate others, he founded Ralston Purina, a company that has grown to worldwide prominence today. He never missed a day for sickness and outlived most of his classmates.

In 1931, Danforth shared the philosophy of his success in a book called, *I Dare You.*

The only reason you are not the person you should be is because you don't dare to be. Once you dare, new powers harness themselves for your service.

Danforth dared everyone to discover and harness the hidden powers of our mental, physical, social, and spiritual gifts. Living this four-fold life, he dares us to be "my own self, at my very best, all the time." And, he dares us to share ourselves in service to others.

From my work at the American Youth Foundation, I know that young people accept the dare today. They are taking control of their lives, motivating their peers, and inspiring younger students. By establishing these habits now, they are preparing for their roles as active citizens and community leaders in their adult years.

As an underclassman Tony was also an underachiever. After attending the AYF's National Leadership Conference he accepted the dare to seek his best and serve. Now in his senior year, he is president of the student council, captain of the football team, and a role model to seventh graders whom he is mentoring.

As part of the AYF Youth Leadership Compact team in her school, Michelle helped organize a Special Olympics Day for 250 disabled children. She and her team enlisted the help of 550 of their fellow students and teachers. The event was a great success, reminding us that the efforts of a few can achieve an impact many times their number.

Danforth concluded his book with a timeless dare:

> Never give up until you have released your unused capacities for service and shared your gifts with others. One enkindled spirit can set hundreds on fire.

(Continued on page 309)

MARY ROSE MAIN
National Executive Director
Girl Scouts of the U.S.A.

Mary Rose Main is national executive director of Girl Scouts of the U.S.A., the largest voluntary organization for girls in the world. She assumed the position in 1990.

Immediately prior to her appointment, Ms. Main served as assistant national executive director for 13 years. She played a leading role in increasing Girl Scout membership to its present total of 3.5 million, the highest in 19 years.

She was also responsible for implementing a corporate planning and management system for the Girl Scout organization, and for developing an acclaimed series of management monographs that are used by a number of outside organizations, including for-profit groups.

Ms. Main has a wide range of professional experience in Girl Scouting, holding key posts at the local and national levels. She has 14 years work experience in four different Girl Scout councils, including executive director, the top staff position on the local level.

In recognition of her commitment to meeting the needs and interests of American girls, Ms. Main has been awarded two honorary Doctorate of Humane Letters degrees—from her alma mater, Simpson College, in Indianola, Iowa, and from Lynn University in Boca Raton, Florida. She is the recipient of the distinguished alumni achievement award from Simpson College, serves as a member of the board of directors of the National Assembly and the National Collaboration for Youth. She is also a member of the national advisory board of America's Disability Channel.

A native of Moravia, Iowa, Ms. Main holds a Bachelor of Arts in Sociology and completed management programs at the Wharton School, University of Pennsylvania, and the Boston University Human Relations Center. She lives in New York City.

Give Yourself a Chance!

Being raised as I was, in a small town, had its advantages. I knew everyone in town by name and they all knew me. Living in such a friendly community environment is like having a large, close-knit family. Townspeople looked out for one another and took a personal interest in each other's children. When I began to play the piano at church, church members encouraged me, although I was still far from accomplished. As I grew and tried out new activities, older adult friends looked out for me. I was willing to take risks, to learn new skills because other people took an interest in what I was doing, and helped me develop new talents.

It was not until I moved away from my small town and met others who had not grown up in a protected and nurturing environment that I realized how lucky I had been. Those who had not been encouraged and supported as youngsters were more hesitant and shy as adults about trying new experiences. It was then that I realized that the closeness and sense of community of my home town had been important to my developing a sense of self-confidence and continued self-worth.

Not everyone has the advantage of growing up in a small town, with neighbors who take a personal interest in their welfare. Some of you may be growing up in large cities, where violence and drive-by shootings have become a terrifying but real part of everyday life. Trying to learn under these circumstances can be discouraging, and keep you from believing that your lives can be more rewarding.

It is difficult to envision a life beyond the compelling circumstances of the moment, but thinking big, stretching to reach a goal, making an effort to change is what the Girl Scouts of the U.S.A. is all about. Our outlook challenges each and every one of us to make the most of our circumstances, to rise above difficulties and to be the best that we can be every day. This approach can be useful to young men, as well.

I believe that each of us has been given qualities and abilities that make us special and unique, and that we are meant to use our lives to discover what these qualities are and how we can put them to use.

As you think about what you want to do with your life, you might be drawn in several directions, or, have several ideas that seem to contradict each other. That is wonderful! To be creative and interested in life is a wonderful gift. I encourage you to try each and every one of your ideas. Your talents might lead you in directions you never would have considered.

If someone had told me when I was young, that I would be travelling all around the world, representing the largest voluntary organization for girls in conferences for the World Association of Girl Guides and Girl Scouts in Tehran, Iran, Singapore and Denmark, I would not have

(Continued on page 310)

ABRAHAM LINCOLN MAROVITZ
Senior Federal Judge
Northern District of Illinois

The rich and colorful life of Senior Federal Judge Abraham Lincoln Marovitz is not only one but a multitude of Horatio Alger stories. His life is one of abiding faith and love for his parents and everyone around him. A man who rose from poverty to become one of Chicago's most respected citizens.

At birth he was named Abraham Lincoln because his mother had learned about the American president at a settlement house following her immigration from Czarist Russia. She made a promise to herself that someday she, too, would have an Abraham Lincoln of her own.

Little did she realize that her son would one day walk local, national and international corridors with such notables as the late prime ministers of Israel, David Ben Gurion and Golda Meir, Governor Adlai E. Stevenson, Senator Hubert Humphrey, and the late Mayor Richard J. Daley, among many others.

Judge Marovitz was the first professing member of the Jewish community to be elected to the Illinois State Senate. In 1942, at age 38, he joined the U.S. Marines. After the war, he returned to the State Senate, serving 11 years before becoming a Superior Court judge. He received an award as the "most outstanding legislator" for his courageous stand on civil rights. Later, he was elected chief justice of the Criminal Court.

In 1963, following his nomination by President Kennedy, he was sworn in as a United States district judge for the Northern Illinois District. Among his many honors is a Doctorate of Humane Letters from Lincoln College, the first annual Lincoln the Lawyer Award from the Abraham Lincoln Association, and the Spirit of Lincoln Award from the Anti-Defamation League of B'nai B'rith.

In observance of the great distance he has come from poverty to prominence, Judge Marovitz was presented the Horatio Alger Award in 1979. To his legion of friends he has remained "Abe."

Do the Right Thing

I believe that success and greatness is in the kindness, understanding, courage, faith, compassion, and desire to aid others that lie within a man's heart and in the way he uses those qualifications in all of his relations with other persons.

I was born in 1905, in very poor (monetary) circumstances. I was raised in a tough area of Chicago and was a mediocre student at best. In 1963 I was appointed to the U.S. District Court by the late President John F. Kennedy.

My chambers are filled with Lincolnia and memorabilia which prompts questions from the groups of children who visit me there. I tell them that I attribute what modest success I have achieved to first: the lessons I learned from my beloved parents who were uneducated, immigrant people possessed with native intelligence, common sense and high moral principle. My mother was the kindest person I have ever known and my father was the most honest man I have ever known.

I was also blessed with a lot of help during my lifetime; a little push from some, a big push from others. I have never met a self-made man or woman, everyone needs help. Helping people is my greatest concern. I find that I can't do any "big" things, but I can do a lot of "little" things. It is my practice to endeavor to do a "mitzvah" (good deed) every day and if I don't, I feel the day has been wasted and I try to make up for it the next day. I always encourage young people who visit me to follow the practice of doing something nice for someone each day.

Another thing I tell young people, perhaps the most important lesson I learned from my parents, is: "You must stand for something in this world and wherever you go, take along your self-respect—then be sure you leave with it."

There are many plaques on my chamber walls with sayings to which I give credence. One, written by Archer G. Jones, sums up my philosophy: "There is but one rule of conduct for a man—to do the right thing. The cost may be dear in money, in friends, in influence, in labor, in a prolonged and painful sacrifice, but the cost not to do right is far more dear; you pay in the integrity of your manhood, in honor, in truth, in character. You forfeit your soul's content, and for a timely gain, you barter the infinities."

Live by this rule and your life will be a success.

Abraham Lincoln Marovitz

N. LYNN MARTENSTEIN
Vice President/Communications
American Forest & Paper Assn.

Lynn Martenstein directs the public affairs, creative services and public information activities of the American Forest & Paper Association, the trade association of an industry, which accounts for 7 percent of all U.S. manufacturing output. She was hired to develop a comprehensive, long-term communications campaign to reposition the industry.

Previously, Martenstein oversaw worldwide communication for United Airlines, at a time when the airline was inaugurating services into Europe and Latin America. She also introduced the airline's new in-flight magazine, and directed disaster communications.

Prior to United, she headed external communications and advertising for the national American Red Cross. Her work during Hurricane Hugo and the San Francisco earthquake helped to contribute to disaster fundraising, unmatched in Red Cross history. She also served as liaison to the White House.

Earlier, the communications executive worked as director of publications for the American Automobile Association.

Martenstein's work in public relations and advertising has been recognized by the Television Academy Emmy Awards, Clio Awards, American Society for Association Executives, Public Relations Society of America, International Association of Business Communicators and the Outdoor Advertising Association.

Lynn is an honors graduate of Hollins College and holds a masters degree in business administration from American University. She is married to travel industry executive and publisher Richard F. Hebert.

Believe in Yourself

My parents had high expectations of me. If I expressed interest in becoming a nurse, they suggested I become a doctor. If I leaned toward office work, they encouraged me to become president of the company.

Predictably, perhaps, I played business as a child, at various times, selling seashells, original poems and drawings, rides around the block on a foot-pedaled surrey, even groceries back to my parents. My father was always my best customer.

Gradually, my parents' confidence in me took hold. And *I* came to believe I could achieve whatever I put my mind to. My advice to young people? Believe in yourself. And surround yourself with family and friends who also believe in you.

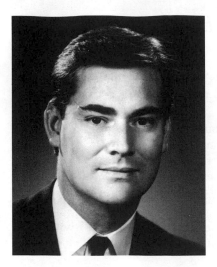

MICHAEL H. McCAIN
President & CEO
McCain USA Inc.

Michael McCain started at the bottom of his company's ladder and worked his way up through sales, marketing, information systems and management. At age 32, he now heads a major U.S. company.

The McCain heritage began with Michael's father and uncle, who were pioneers in the Canadian frozen food industry. In 1975, the company expanded into the U.S. market, and Michael earned the right to lead the company in 1990.

Building a team of experts in the organization, Michael encouraged his employees to put forth entrepreneurial efforts in response to emerging consumer opportunities. As a result, the company has developed new products that have established a solid base in the U.S. marketplace.

McCain is a graduate of Mount Allison University and the University of Western Ontario. An avid skier and tennis player, he most enjoys spending time with his wife, Chris, and their four children at their suburban Chicago home.

Age No Handicap

It's interesting how our culture looks at age. In a racehorse, three or four years is ideal. The careers of many fashion models peak at age 19 or 20. Professional athletes are usually considered "over the hill" by 35.

Coming out of college, I was anxious to make my mark. I was filled with the confidence and enthusiasm of youth that is ready and willing to change the world.

However, in the world of business where I've thrown my lot, age is viewed in an entirely different perspective. Our gymnastics are mental. We may have to be quick thinkers and fast talkers, but the race is not usually won by the speediest runner. Youth is sometimes viewed as an affliction which is best cured by time. "You have to put in your time" and "experience is the best teacher" are common themes. Champions of business traditionally are honed through years of practice. For the young graduate, it can be discouraging at times.

I've always been a little impatient about standing in line. I believe in serving my time, but I like to speed up the clock if I can. To make a faster turn on the learning curve of my career, I've tried to know my business from the inside out—better than my contemporaries and as well as anyone, regardless of their years in the industry. My goal: to compress my professional learning process and demonstrate that ability is not a matter of age, but a function of mental maturity and an accumulation of life experience.

Over the past 12 years, more than one person has been a "nay sayer" based on age or family connection. Fortunately, I have always accepted the challenge to prove them wrong where necessary. That's why I run a large business at age 32.

There are still people in the world who look at businessmen like bottles of wine—believing that our real potential won't be tapped until we're over 50. I have found that the best solution to this discrimination is to not be sensitive to it. Simply ignore it. Go on to be the best you can be at whatever age.

If my dozen years in business have taught me one valuable lesson, it's that what you think about yourself is most important. The key to success is, no matter what anyone thinks, that you know you can do it.

WARREN E. McCAIN
Chairman of Executive Committee
Albertson's, Inc.

Warren McCain was born in Logan, Kansas. He was raised in Payette, Idaho, where he graduated from high school before serving in the U.S. Navy during World War II.

While attending the Illinois Institute of Technology in Chicago, he worked at the National Tea Company to make ends meet. This piqued his interest in the grocery business. He next studied at Oregon State University from 1946 to 1950 before a second hitch in the Navy during the Korean War.

Upon returning home, he pursued a career in the grocery business at Mountain States Wholesale, where he spent eight years gaining broad experience in many facets of the food business. In 1959, he joined Albertson's, Inc. in Boise, Idaho, as general merchandise supervisor. He climbed the corporate ladder to the top, becoming president, chairman, and chief executive officer.

His outstanding success is reflected in some of the honors he's received:

University of Southern California Industry of the Year Award (1985).

The Wall Street Transcript selected him Best Chief Executive of Retail / Supermarkets & Food Chains (1987, 1988, and 1989)

First Place Award from Financial World as CEO of the Year / Grocery Industry (1990).

Named Retailer of the Year, Mass Marketing Retailing (1991).

In 1985, he received an honorary law doctorate from the College of Idaho. He was named Business Man of the Year by Alpha Kappa Psi Fraternity, Idaho State University, and was the recipient of the Leadership for Public Education Award from the Idaho Association of School Administrators.

(Continued on page 298)

Lessons to Follow

Back in 1945 I was aboard a Navy ship off the coast of Nagasaki, Japan, shortly after the atomic bomb had been dropped on that city. I was 20 years old, confused, and full of anxiety. I was thinking about what I was going to do with my life when I returned to the United States.

I was a small-town kid from Payette, Idaho, who didn't have a family that could afford to send me to college. I'd had enough exposure in the Navy to know I was capable of doing something beyond pumping gas in the local service station, and my high school education had given me a good base in mathematics and English.

During this time I read a book that made a big impression on me. I adopted some philosophy from that book, *Magnificent Obsession*, written by Lloyd C. Douglas, the world-famous novelist who also wrote *The Robe* and other bestselling books.

Two of the important lessons I learned from Mr. Douglas were to never try to run away from troubles, and to always repay your benefactors and mentors by doing the same for other people.

The first point he made was that you must face your troubles; overcome them, right where you are. Instead of trying to escape from frustrations, you need to triumph over them; otherwise, they'll be with you wherever you go.

I have been fortunate to be in a position to repay the 12 persons, not including my family, who had a significant impact on my life and career. I have attempted to repay each of these individuals in various ways. Three of them were high school teachers in whose honor I sponsor 16 four-year full-ride scholarships for students otherwise unable to attend college.

As for guidelines to success, I encourage young people to answer several basic questions before making decisions on their careers. Do you want to be with a small company or a large corporation? Do you want to travel, and where would you prefer to live? After you make those decisions and you begin working for a company, I think you have to be an extremely good listener. Then, you can't be too impatient for promotions and moving ahead. Worry about the job you're in today, then when the next job comes along, you'll be prepared for it. You have to be a good team player, set high goals for yourself, and you absolutely must practice great discipline in everything you do.

Warren E. McCain

CAROL PHILLIPS McELYEA
President
Proactive Financial Management

Carol Phillips McElyea is the daughter of a small town entrepreneur. Growing up in Bonne Terre, Missouri (population 3,000) she started working at age three stocking shelves in the family's grocery store.

In 1992, Carol fulfilled a lifelong dream of starting her own business and is now president of Proactive Financial Management, Inc., a registered investment adviser. The company provides comprehensive financial planning and implementation services for individuals, families and small businesses.

Carol's undergraduate degree is from Wheaton College in Norton, Massachusetts where she graduated cum laude with a Bachelor of Arts in Economics. She started her career achievements with Ford Motor Company in its highly selective Ford College Graduate Training Program. The first female Cost Analyst at Ford's Kansas City assembly plant, she simultaneously pursued her MBA from the University of Missouri graduating summa cum laude. She was the first woman to receive a promotional transfer to Ford's Automotive Assembly Division Headquarters in Michigan. She describes her years in Dearborn as "my Ph.D. from Ford Finance." In 1975, Carol joined Touche Ross Co. (now Deloitte & Touche) Chicago. She became the firm's first Woman Partner in 1981. Prior to starting her own company, she spent six years as a vice president at First Chicago's Commercial Bank.

Ms. McElyea is active in her community having served as Allocations Chair for the Oak Park River Forest Community Chest, President of the Wheaton College Alumnae Association, and a board member for West Suburban Hospital Medical Center Foundation and River Forest Helpmates, a Christian sponsored support group for single adults. Carol is also active in the River Forest Tennis Club, Riverside Golf Club, the First Presbyterian Church of River Forest and is the proud parent of a Roosevelt University student.

The Value of Money

I feel I have been twice blessed: first, to grow up inside the family business and second, to enter the business world in 1970. In my early life I learned the true value of money, both what it could and could not do. Many of my female peers did not enjoy the open environment of my early years where money management was a daily topic of conversation. Indeed, most women would rather discuss their intimate relationships than their financial situation. Some women view money matters as a distasteful topic and, more frighteningly, many women truly believe they are "not capable" of understanding financial matters, regardless of their intelligence and education.

One of my frequent messages is that money is a tool, a vehicle which can help you achieve your life goals. I encourage people to develop sound money management habits: To save before spending (if you can't pay for it, don't buy it); To establish an Emergency Fund (we all know they happen, why not provide for them); To save for a car (there is no law that "thou shalt make car payments"); To save for key life goals such as a home, college education, wedding, retirement, etc.; and To seek professional advice, but to ask questions and make their own decisions based on their individual financial goals and values.

Financial values are learned or taught at home, they're not taught in the schools or churches. Financial difficulties create numerous problems in our society, in our world, from being the number one cause of America, to being the major motive for serious crime. Each of us can and must take responsibility for our own financial affairs and realize that money should work for you, not vice-versa. If you take charge of money matters, career path, or your own individual growth, I know— You Can Do It!—I did.

Carol Phillips McElyea

DRAYTON McLANE
Chairman
McLane Group

Drayton McLane received a bachelor of business administration degree from Baylor University and a master of science degree from Michigan State University.

He is chairman of the McLane Group, which is a family owned holding company responsible for management of the Houston Astros Baseball Club, Astrodome USA, M-C International, and Classic Foods. He is also chairman of McLane Company, as well as vice chairman of Wal•Mart Stores, Inc.

McLane serves on the board of directors of Wal•Mart, Scott & White Hospital, and the greater Houston Partnership. He also is a trustee for Baylor University, South Texas College of Law, and the Cooper Institute for Aerobics Research. He is a former chairman of the National American Wholesale Grocers Association and the Texas Wholesale Grocers Association.

Currently chairman of the board of governors for the National Children's Miracle Network, he has served as president and campaign chairman for the United Way of Central Texas.

McLane was the recipient of the National American Wholesale Grocers Association's 1990 American Achiever Award. He also won the Arthur Young/Venture Magazine Entrepreneur of the Year Award in 1987. The Boy Scouts of America honored him in 1985 with the Silver Beaver Award and in 1989 he received their Distinguished Citizens Award. McLane received Baylor University's Herbert H. Reynolds Award and the 1991 Baylor Distinguished Alumni Award, and was inducted into the Texas Business Hall of Fame in 1992.

He and his wife, Elizabeth, have two sons, Drayton and Denton. They are members of Temple First Baptist Church, where McLane is a deacon and past chairman of the deacon board.

You Need a Goal

Youth is like an unwritten book and you are the author. What a marvelous opportunity! As the pages of life have unfolded day by day, year by year, I have discovered there are some very practical and applicable keys to success and happiness.

The primary key to success and happiness is to get a goal for your life. This includes both short range and long range goals. These will change periodically throughout one's life as goals are achieved, new opportunities arise, and we seek new directions. However, once you have identified and set your course, then charge forward. Be a leader, be courageous, believe in yourself, and be confident in your abilities.

Leadership requires one to set an example of high standards in both the quality of your performance and morally. Take the appropriate steps to accomplish your objectives with strong integrity, determination, commitment, and a winning attitude. You can make it happen through perseverance and keeping your mind set on achieving goals.

Courage is the inner strength one attains through his conviction and belief in what he is trying to accomplish. Leaders are also able to motivate others with enthusiasm and a well defined plan of action. Be a cheerleader and rally others around your cause.

Christopher Columbus was a great example of leadership, courage, conviction and determination. He developed an idea, turned it into a goal, defined a plan of action, pursued and motivated a group of teammates, rallied them around his cause, and set out to accomplish his objectives. Many historians have written volumes of books on his life, but he was the original author. You can do it, too!

Drayton McLane

GREG McMICHAEL
Relief Pitcher
Atlanta Braves

Greg McMichael was runner-up to the Dodgers' Mike Piazza in the 1993 Rookie-Of-The-Year balloting in the National League, voted on by the Baseball Writers Association of America.

Greg converted his first 15 save opportunities (19 overall) and ended up with the most saves by a rookie in the National League since Todd Worrell save 35 for the St. Louis Cardinals in 1986.

McMichael won the NL Rolaids Relief Man Award for August (9 saves/9 opportunities) and his 15 saves in as many chances, according to Rolaids statisticians, set a record for the start of a career, surpassing the Mets' Anthony Young's 12 consecutive in 1992.

He was elected by major league managers to the 1993 Topps Rookie All-Star Team.

Greg graduated from Webb (TN) High School and pitched three years at the University of Tennessee. He and his wife, Jennifer, are the parents of one daughter, Erin. His hobbies include fishing, golfing, and antiquing.

Give God a Chance

I would like to take you back nine years ago to the Little League district championships. I was on second base waiting for a teammate to drive me in. *Crack*, the ball hit the bat. I rounded third and headed for home. Out of the corner of my eye I saw the ball take one hop and into the catcher's mitt. I slid in hard with my feet up in the air. The umpire shouted "you're out and No. 10 you're out of the game." I had been thrown out and kicked out at the same time. I was crushed, because I had failed to succeed in the world's eyes. That day I felt unworthy of anyone's love. You see, I was controlled by my performance.

Some days I would come off the field and feel good about myself. At other times I didn't. This went on for many years until one day the doctor told me that there was a good possibility that I could never play sports again. I had developed a rare cartilage disease in both knees. I felt my life was over. All I was and ever wanted to be was gone. Now I was able to take a big step back and look at my life. You know what? I didn't like what I saw. I was a very selfish and insecure person. I only wanted what was best for me.

For the first time in my life, I saw the real me. I had put my trust in temporal things and now they were gone. Someone once said, "a man who finds no satisfaction in himself, seeks for it in vain elsewhere." I did just that for the next two and a half years. I tried to find satisfaction through drugs and the girls I dated. Spiritually, I knew who God was, but I wasn't ready to give Him control of my life. I went to church on Sunday's out of obedience to my parents. I sat in church physically, but mentally, I was thinking of the night before or the afternoon to come. I was afraid to give God my life, because I thought I would lose all the fun I was having.

I had this attitude until one night my parents shared with me four basic principles. They shared with me that God loved me and offered a wonderful plan for my life, but I couldn't experience his plan because I was separated from God. All I had to do was receive Him personally into my life, and He would come in. I thought "why not give God a chance since *I had tried* for sixteen years and was still miserable."

That night I decided to give my life to Jesus Christ. You're probably saying "now that's a miracle that you even listened to your parents." You're right, but if you had seen the events that had taken place before that you would have listened, too.

My parents were divorced and in three years I watched Christ transform their lives and they were remarried. God had changed a bitter relationship into one with love and obedience. I now wanted to be involved in people's lives. My desires changed. I no longer wanted to

(Continued on page 310)

HARRY A. MERLO
Chairman/President
Louisiana-Pacific Corporation

Harry Angelo Merlo was born March 5, 1925, in the little sawmill community of Stirling City, California. Those early years were filled with lessons of dedication, hard work and honesty, the foundation of his rise to success within the free enterprise system.

Since its formation in 1973, Harry Merlo has guided the growth of Louisiana-Pacific to become one of the foremost forest products companies in the world today.

Enjoy Serving Others

Personal excellence every day of our lives is what my loving Mother held out to her family as the goal worthy of our pursuit. She told us, "Because we are foreigners, we must work harder to be worthy of America. We must earn the right to be Americans."

As I grew up my Mother's teachings became for me the spirit of Yes, We can! The thinking is basic and timeless. To succeed, each of us must make a difference in everything we undertake. For ourselves, our families, our community and our country.

Everybody has his own formula, but for me life has always been rather simple because I am thrilled to serve people. My philosophy is this: "Alone we're nobody, but as a team we are important." You give your energy and ability unselfishly for your fellow worker and don't worry about yourself. If he does the same, your team will win and all will share in the victory. You know, the Good Book says: "He among you who shall lead will be a servant to all." If you enjoy serving others, I guarantee you will be a success.

Harry A Merlo

RAY MEYER
Legendary Basketball Coach

Perhaps the greatest compliment a person can receive is to be recognized in public. Ray Meyer is complimented often. More than seven years since he last coached DePaul University's Blue Demons basketball team, he is still recognized from coast to coast as "Coach."

After leaving the coaching ranks in 1984, Meyer turned his attention to a dual role as a special assistant to DePaul President Rev. John T. Richardson, C.M. and Athletic Director Bill Bradshaw working on fund raising and other special projects.

One of basketball's most respected authorities, he also serves as color commentator for DePaul broadcasts on WGN Radio. The Great Midwest Conference, formed in 1991, has named its Coach of the Year trophy the Ray Meyer Award.

Meyer knows basketball from all sides. An All-American player at Notre Dame, he served as team captain for two years and earned his bachelor's degree in sociology in 1938. He is only the fifth major college coach to record at least 700 career victories and remains among the all-time NCAA Division I leaders in wins. Meyer's record of 37 winning seasons in 42 years is testimony to his reputation as the consummate teacher. He fashioned a brilliant 180-30 (.857) record and guided the Blue Demons to seven consecutive post-season tournament appearances in his final seven years at the helm.

Meyer was elected to the Naismith Hall of Fame in 1979; earned four national coach of the year awards in a six-year span was named Man of the Year by the National Basketball Coaches Association in 1980, and is a member of the Illinois Sports Hall of Fame.

As decorated as Meyer is, his greatest honor comes regularly when he's recognized publicly by fans as simply "Coach."

Be Dedicated

If I had to pick a role model for young people my choice would be George Mikan, a great basketball player and a fine human being.

When George enrolled at DePaul he was 6'9" and about 230 pounds of raw talent. At a time when basketball featured small speedy guards and fast forwards, he was clumsy and lacked agility. The moment we met I told him he could become as good as he wanted to be. He readily accepted a rigid regimen I programmed for him. George spent hours jumping rope, doing vertical leaps, handling a medicine ball and doing drills to improve his foot work, in addition to the rigors of regular team practices.

Because of his dedication, he became an All-American and went on to an outstanding professional career culminated with his selection as basketball's "Player of the First Half of This Century." He also was an excellent student and today is a leading corporate lawyer. His success can be summed up in one word "dedicated."

I coached two years as an assistant at Notre Dame, my alma mater, and forty-two years at DePaul. I've seen countless players with natural ability waste their talent because of a lack of dedication. Whether you are an athlete or not, you must set high goals for yourself. Goals you need to stretch to reach and you must believe you can do it. Believing in yourself is half the battle. The harder you work to succeed—the harder it is for you to fail. You are never defeated unless you admit it. You are not going to be successful all the time. There will be setbacks and detours. The supreme test is not in your successes but in your failures. You must have the courage to overcome disappointments.

When things get difficult, in a game, or, in life, you must force yourself to do the things you have to do. One can't improve or succeed without desire, dedication, self-discipline and perseverance.

Don't always look for someone else to motivate you. Even a coach is limited in motivating. Sometimes a pep talk will work. Other times an old-fashioned chewing out will do it. Most often, it is the individual who ultimately is responsible for motivation. The successful person, on the basketball court, in business, or simply as a human being, is the one who makes a commitment to be the best he or she can be.

If it can be done, you can do it—if you dedicate yourself to the task.

Ray Meyer

THOMAS S. MONAGHAN
Founder/Chairman
Domino's Pizza, Inc.

Thomas S. Monaghan was born in 1937 in Ann Arbor, Michigan. His father died four years later, ushering in a childhood of foster homes and orphanages.

After graduating from St. Thomas High School in 1955 and enrolling at Ferris State College in Big Rapids, Michigan, Monaghan enlisted in the U.S. Marine Corps in 1956. Receiving an honorable discharge in 1959, he returned to Ann Arbor and enrolled at the University of Michigan.

While attending college, Monaghan and his brother James borrowed $900 and bought a small pizza store called DomiNick's in Ypsilanti. In less than a year Monaghan bought his brother's share of the business and formed another partnership, opening additional stores in Ann Arbor and Mt. Pleasant, Michigan.

The story behind Domino's Pizza, of the many obstacles Monaghan conquered throughout the years and the path he took to success, was compiled for the first time in his 1984 autobiography, Pizza Tiger, *coauthored by Robert Anderson.*

Monaghan pioneered several innovations in the pizza industry that have set standards among other operators. Monaghan is credited with developing dough trays, the corrugated pizza box, insulated bags to transport pizzas, the pizza screen, a conveyor oven and a unique franchise system.

As Domino's Pizza grew into the world's largest pizza delivery company, Monaghan's enterprising spirit allowed him to set his sights on other endeavors. As a boy, Tom always looked forward to the annual orphanage outing: a Detroit Tigers game. In 1983, he purchased his dream team for $53 million; in 1984 they won the World Series. He is now taking time to pursue philanthropic interests involving charitable organizations. Monaghan is married and has four daughters.

Priorities to Ponder

The management techniques I applied in building Domino's Pizza were developed mostly by trial and error. But all of them were based on homemade philosophy I call my five personal priorities. My five priorities are spiritual, social, mental, physical, and financial, in that order:

Spiritual

My background makes concern about spiritual matters as natural to me as breathing. My religious faith is strong. I know I would not have been able to build Domino's without the strength I gained from my religious faith. When it comes to secular matters of business, my spiritual priority is expressed in the Golden Rule: Do unto others as you would have others do unto you.

Social

A loving wife and family are to me, essential for a happy productive life. After family on my scale of social relationships come friends. Nobody can succeed in business without the help of friends.

Mental

The key factor in maintaining a healthy mind is a clear conscience. This means you have done your best to live up to your own expectations. A clear conscience fosters self-esteem, a positive attitude, and an optimistic outlook, all of which promote success in business.

Physical

It may sound corny but I subscribe to the idea that the body is the temple of the soul. If I lost my health, I'd give every penny I had to get it back, and I don't know anyone who wouldn't.

Financial

The financial priority is last on my list because it arises from the others. I know that if I attend to the first four properly, financial success will follow.

Another important principle I've stressed over the years is have fun in the work you do. I believe that if you've chosen the career that is right for you, it will give your life a feeling of purpose.

Thomas S. Monaghan

JEAN NIDETCH
Founder
Weight Watchers International, Inc.

Jean Nidetch has helped to change the shape of millions of overweight men and women throughout the world.

In 1961, after a lifelong struggle with overweight, she found a diet on which she shed 72 pounds. As she lost weight, Jean shared her success with friends. Little did she realize that a meeting with six overweight women in her Queens apartment was a prototype for a business.

At a time when support groups were non-existent and self-help was unknown, Nidetch's idea caught on. Within three months, 40 people were squeezing into her modest apartment for weekly meetings. Within a year, Weight Watchers expanded beyond her home and later became a public company. Nidetch knew she had succeeded beyond her dreams when 17,000 Weight Watcher members from around the world gathered in Madison Square Garden to celebrate the enterprises tenth anniversary.

Jean, with the help of a board of directors, took the company public in 1968. In 1978, after 15 years of phenomenal growth, they sold Weight Watchers to H.J. Heinz & Co. for $72 million.

She now serves as a consultant to Weight Watchers International, travelling as much as 10 months a year to spread the Weight Watchers message, including regular summer visits to camps for children. She encourages overweight youngsters to reach their weight loss goals and speaks about the emotional and behavioral changes that will take place when their goals are met.

Jean's commitment to both self-improvement and higher education is apparent. She has established the Jean Nidetch Foundation to benefit economically disadvantaged teenagers who wish to continue their education, and a UCLA scholarship has been established in her name to

Stay Healthy

Whenever I speak to a group of youngsters I tell them: "If you have a dream—go for it!"

Since I am usually talking to those with weight problems, I add what may be the most important suggestion for them to ever attain any kind of success—Stay Healthy!

Modern medicine, health clinics and spas can help keep us in shape, but there is little that can be done if we are not willing to personally commit ourselves to a responsible program of personal health care.

Let me caution you to learn early-on that you are what you eat. Make no mistake about that. Our most dreaded diseases including cancer, heart trouble, diabetes and kidney problems are all affected by faulty diet.

It is also well to remember that health care, like anything else, should be done in moderation. Too much exercise is as harmful as never exerting ourselves at all. The same goes for eating which calls for a balanced diet. Healthy persons carefully balance their physical, mental and spiritual well-being into a fully integrated way of living. The responsibility of healthy living rests with each of us.

An old proverb sums it up well: "He who has health has hope; and he who has hope has everything!"

Jean Nidetch

---

support postgraduate education in political science for deserving college students.

Nidetch has received hundreds of awards and accolades. The Ladies Home Journal honored her as one of "The Most Important Women in the U.S." She became the first woman to become a member of the New York Chapter of the Young President's Organization. In 1989, she received the prestigious Horatio Alger Award, and in 1991, she became a member of the Horatio Alger Association board of directors. Her autobiography, The Story of Weight Watchers, *sold over 2 million copies.*

Throughout her remarkable career, Jean Nidetch has realized her goals and potential and serves as a continuous source of inspiration for others in reaching theirs.

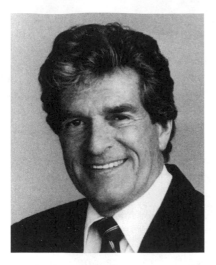

HUGH O'BRIAN
Founder
Hugh O'Brian
Youth Foundation (HOBY)

Motion picture and television star Hugh O'Brian mastered his craft across the entire spectrum of show business. His seven-year starring role as "Wyatt Earp" is a television classic and he appeared in scores of other stage, television and movie roles. But along with his success in his chosen field, he never lost sight of his civic and philanthropic responsibilities.

For the past 33 years, O'Brian has put his "guts, bucks and time" into the Hugh O'Brian Youth Foundation (HOBY). He walked away from a lucrative career in movies and television to devote his life to this effort. Its format is simple: bring a select group of high school sophomores with demonstrated leadership abilities together with leaders who are on the firing line in business, government, education and the professions— then let them interact.

Next spring, more than 13,000 high school sophomores selected for their leadership potential will attend 92 HOBY Leadership Seminars in all 50 states, the Bahamas, Mexico, Jamaica, and Canada. All seminars have the theme "America's Incentive System," and are all conducted by volunteers. Funding comes entirely from the private sector.

In recognition of the outstanding work he has done with youth, O'Brian has been awarded four honorary degrees and many awards. Most recently, in 1989, he received the 60th Annual American Education Award presented by the American Association of School Administrators. This award is the oldest and most prestigious award that the education profession bestows. In 1990, the Los Angeles Business Council awarded him its 6th Lifetime Achievement Award. The Freedom Through Knowledge Award, sponsored by the National Space Club in association with NASA, one of the nation's highest awards, is among the other honors he's received.

Freedom to Choose

In 1958, I was privileged to spend nine inspirational days in Africa with Dr. Albert Schweitzer which changed my life. Dr. Schweitzer's strong belief that "the most important thing in education is to teach young people to think for themselves" motivated me to form the Hugh O'Brian Youth Foundation (HOBY). The Foundation's goal is not to teach these future leaders what to think, but how to think. Hoby's purpose is to seek out, recognize and develop leadership potential in high school sophmores.

I do NOT believe we are all born equal. Physical and emotional differences, parental guidelines, varying environments, being in the right place at the right time, all play a role in enhancing or limiting an individual's development. But, I DO believe every man and woman, if given the opportunity and encouragement to recognize their potential, regardless of background, has the freedom to choose in our world. Will an individual be a taker or a giver in life? Will that person be satisfied merely to exist or seek a meaningful purpose? Will he or she dare to dream the impossible dream?

I believe every person is created as the steward of his or her own destiny with great power for a specific purpose, to share with others, through service, a reverence for life in the spirit of love.

You have the freedom to choose what you will do with your life.

Hugh O'Brian

PETER M. PALERMO
Vice President/General Manager
Consumer Imaging Division
Eastman Kodak Company

Peter Palermo began his career with Eastman Kodak Company in 1963 and held various management positions in Kodak's international operations as well as worldwide business units. In addition to his assignment as marketing manager for Kodak Caribbean operations, he has served as general manager for Kodak in the Philipines and Mexico.

In 1984, he was elected a corporate vice president and appointed general manager of Kodak's Health Sciences Division. In 1986, he was named general manager of Kodak's worldwide Consumer Products Division, and in 1989 became the head of the newly-formed worldwide Consumer Imaging Division.

Palermo holds a bachelor of arts degree in psychology and English from Bowling Green University, and an MBA degree in economics from the Graduate School of Management at the University of Rochester.

Palermo has been recognized as one of the "Outstanding Young Men of America" (1973), and is the recipient of the Catholic Archdiocese of the Philippines Award for Humanitarianism presented by Pope John Paul in 1981.

He has served as a director of the Photographic Society of the Philippines, the Association of Photographic Manufacturers of Mexico, and the Health Industry Manufacturers Association of the United States.

Active in community affairs, Palermo is currently on the board of trustees of National 4-H Council and is a member of the board of directors for the 1991 Special Olympics Games.

Education Is Essential

A fundamental factor in the definition of success lies in one's own evaluation of the quality of choices one has made. Without a quality education, there are no choices. Life simply "happens" and the consequences are, at best, painfully less than they could have been, and invariably, someone else's fault.

Understanding one's own value and capability is the wonderful by-product of a quality education. Understanding and believing that one can choose alternative roads to follow often separates those whose choices have been directed by a passion for life from those whose choices have been thrust upon them solely by ignorance and fear.

Education enables you to see, to understand, and to more fully appreciate just who and what you really are. It gives you a view of yourself independent of the reflections others provide suggesting who and what they would have you be. Education gives you the gift of yourself.

TOM PARKER
Educator/School Administrator

Tom Parker was born to be a teacher. He spent his entire life in the field of education, after deciding when he was a student at Taft High School in Chicago, that he wanted to be a teacher.

As an undergraduate student at Northwestern University, he used summer vacations to work for foreign steamship lines serving Chicago to finance his education. He earned bachelor's and master's degrees at Northwestern.

Tom began his career as an educator as a fourth grade teacher in the Highland Park (Ill.) School District, where he was to spend 31 years as a teacher and school administrator.

In 1960, he was granted a Fulbright Award to teach in a primary school in Nottingham, England, where he also was a guest lecturer at the University of Nottingham. During that year abroad, and in future years, he travelled extensively then used his first-hand experiences and photographic journals in his curriculum as a social studies teacher.

His interest in children led to his taking a two-year leave of absence to start a program for gifted children, in Bucks County, Pennsylvania. The program was recognized by his peers to be an outstanding contribution to education.

Returning to his home district in Highland Park, he joined the staff of the new John F. Kennedy School and later became principal. He taught at Utah State University during the summer of 1967 before beginning a doctoral program at Stanford University and completed his course work in 1972.

During the next 18 years, he held numerous administrative positions including those of curriculum director and district administrator. One

(Continued on page 299)

Travel and Read

If the following experienced-based suggestions benefit one young person planning his or her future, I will be grateful.

The more knowledge you acquire, the better you will be prepared to cope with the problems of our day. A college education will help you acquire that knowledge, but it is only the beginning, you must continue to study all your life, if you hope to achieve your goals.

The most rewarding personal educational experiences in my life came from my travels and in reading books. Not everyone can visit foreign lands and far-away places. But you can read about them and through your mind's eye learn to understand the life-styles and cultures of other people. In this electronic age, you can tour the world via audio-visual documentaries and travelogues, especially the quality programs found on public television stations. Nothing, however, is as rewarding as reading, whereby you use the greatest computer ever created—your mind.

The classroom, where you probably interacted with other people for the first time, is a reflection of the American society in which you will live. Everyone is different and unique. No two persons are alike. Some are gifted, some are not. What is important is that you learn to respect each individual for what he or she is. Always have a high regard for yourself and everyone you meet along life's highway.

My hobby is restoring antique furniture. It gives me an opportunity to work with my hands. I believe doing hands-on work is one of the best ways to relieve the stress we all experience in our fast-paced environment. If you select a creative activity as an avocation you will enjoy rewards that are most fulfilling and relaxing, too.

Also, stay in touch with nature. Revel in the beauty of mountains, oceans, birds, animals, wildlife and realize that "all the best things in life are free." Again, there are hundreds of books, with outstanding photography, that will take you into the world's greatest natural resources, should you not be able to visit them.

Two final suggestions, set a goal you have to stretch to reach, have high expectations that you'll be successfull, then follow through with determination. But, along the way, don't take yourself too seriously. Have some fun and smell the roses. You will only pass this way one time—make sure you don't miss anything you want to do.

Thomas M. Parker

JOE PATERNO
Head Football Coach
Penn State University

Joe Paterno, already No. 4 on the list of all-time winningest college foot-
ball coaches, tied Paul "Bear" Bryant for the top spot in postseason vic-
tories when his Nittany Lions defeated Tennessee in the 1994 Comp-
USA Florida Citrus Bowl.

Paterno is the figurehead of a program that shines with all the bril-
liance of a highly-polished precious metal. He has guided the Lion grid-
ders to 257 victories, 24 bowl appearances, two National Champi-
onships and a level of popularity that has produced routine sellouts of
93,967-seat Beaver Stadium and more than 100 appearances on televi-
sion.

Paterno's stature has been enhanced by the success of his football teams,
but is also a reflection of his reputation for integrity, for graduating the
athletes who enter his program and for facing the tough issues fairly
and honestly.

The role of teacher is one that Paterno finds most comfortable. "I would
prefer to be thought of as an educator rather than a coach," he has said.
Paterno's wishes notwithstanding, his reputation as a football coach is
difficult to shake. He entered the 1994 season with 257 career victories
(vs. 69 losses and three ties), which ranks him No. 4 on the list of life-
time major college coaching leaders. He heads all current Division 1-A
coaches in total victories.

Only the legendary Bear Bryant appeared in more bowl games (29 for
Bryant, 24 for Paterno) and Paterno matched Bryant's mark of 15 post-
season victories when the Nittany Lions beat Tennessee in the Citrus
Bowl last January. His teams have posted six undefeated regular sea-
sons and have won two National Championships (1982 and 1986).

Paterno has received a host of honors including the National Football

(Continued on page 299)

Striving for Success

A man's reach must exceed his grasp;
or what's a heaven for?

–Robert Browning

That Browning quotation has always been a favorite of mine. If everything worthwhile is within reach, what satisfaction is there in achievement?

Genuine satisfaction results from honest effort, often in the face of immense odds. Any athlete, indeed any ordinary citizen, gets a larger thrill from earning something than having it given to them. I've always told my players there is as much passion in the *pursuit* of excellence as there is in the *achievement* of excellence.

We establish exacting standards for ourselves on the athletic field. Eleven men must function as one. A player who operates independently can frustrate the goals of the team. Because football demands players act in harmony, I think success on the gridiron is especially satisfying.

Great individual efforts often turn the tide in college football but, acting alone, one athlete seldom produces victory. A great passer needs a receiver. A great kicker needs a holder and snapper. A gifted running back needs blockers. Even a respected coach needs assistants.

Football is a great game, most of all, for the lessons it teaches. Players must learn to be disciplined. They must conform to the team concept. They must become familiar with pain and deal with the limits of their own endurance. They learn to play within the rules. They face the disappointment of failure and the sweetness of success. These are all lessons which young people in the stands also need to learn as they move through life.

I've always preached to our players to have respect for their opponents. There is no victory so sweet as one over a formidable foe, an opponent who has tested our every resource before reluctantly bowing.

Most of all, football is about reaching—to become better as an individual, as a team, as a conference. And, as Browning said, the goals should require a healthy stretch. I always challenge our Penn State players to be the very best they can be. Twice that has been to the National Championship in 1982, and 1986. Future Penn State teams may come up short of the No. 1 ranking. But, I fervently hope, no one will be able to criticize us for not reaching!

Joe Paterno

JENO F. PAULUCCI
Chairman
Paulucci Enterprises

Jeno Paulucci is best described as an "incurable entrepreneur." His rags-to-riches success is legend. A fruit stand barker who started the Chun King Corporation with a $2,500 loan, he sold the company 20 years later for $63 million dollars cash, then became the first chairman of R.J. Reynolds Foods, now Nabisco-Reynolds. That accomplished, his Jeno's Inc., achieved phenomenal growth with unique and revolutionary products, packaging and merchandising symbolic of Jeno's creativity.

His spectacular achievements in business are but part of his story, for Jeno Paulucci is a crusader for the common man, a man of dedication to the responsibilities of life in our changing America, a man who cares and a man who makes things happen. He is a champion of the American system of free enterprise, and the social and economic responsibilities of all factions operating within that system.

The Paulucci Family Foundation, which he has endowed for worthwhile civic charitable work, is noted for its many acts of philanthropy. In 1982, he arranged for a contribution by Jeno's, Inc., of nearly $500,000 in foods to needy families in areas hard-hit by recession.

He has counseled Presidents Johnson, Nixon, Ford and the Carter-Mondale administration on economic problems in the U.S.; served as liaison between the White House and Rome to arrange economic conferences; and was presidential emissary to evaluate U.S. disaster relief efforts in Italy for President Ford in 1976 and President Carter in 1980.

Among accolades and honorary degrees too numerous to mention, Jeno has been acclaimed as the nation's Outstanding Italian American three times, was accorded the National Horatio Alger Award for business success, was the guest of President Johnson on Liberty Island at the signing of the Immigration Reform Law, and has received the highest civilian honors accorded by the Republic of Italy.

Be an Entrepreneur

You may remember a little jingle kids used to chant, mostly while skipping rope, to help decide what they would be when they grew up:

"Rich man, poor man, beggar man, thief,
Doctor, lawyer, merchant chief."

As kids, we didn't know the word "entrepreneur" existed. Yet you can be an entrepreneur in any field you choose. Just be prepared to commit everything—money, time, desire, dedication, and most of all—your personal life and all of your strength—to back your good ideas to the limit.

Whatever you plan to be, be sure to start with the right tools. Competition for the individual out there in the business jungle is intense, fierce. While corporations play monopoly to dominate their markets, the individual—you—must win his or her daily bread on your own performance, so you'd better be equipped to compete.

Take advantage of every opportunity to enrich your education. Your knowledge and especially your ability to communicate—the gifts of education—will be great assets throughout your life. Then, trust yourself. Learn to rely on your wits and instincts. When I started more than 50 years ago, I didn't have anything but a high school education, some street smarts, and damn little money. I trusted my judgement and took chances. But that, alone, won't cut it anymore. Today's business world is too sophisticated. You have to get the best education you can to survive.

Being an entrepreneur is not just long hours and hard work—it's guts. You have to go at it with sheer determination. Otherwise the pitfalls will put you off. That's why big companies have to go out and acquire smaller ones. There is a quality in starting a business that only an entrepreneur can provide.

The entrepreneur also must be like the farmer who puts back some of his harvest every year in order to deserve another harvest. Therefore, an entrepreneur must work constantly, tirelessly, stubbornly to make his area a better place to live and earn a living—for all. He must understand that making a profit is not his only responsibility.

The reward, of course, is a legacy of pride of achievement that stands as a challenge to the next generation. Be prepared when your turn comes.

Today he's leading the Paulucci family in development of Heathrow, an amazing self-sufficient "city of tomorrow" spanning ten square miles of Central Florida.

WALTER PAYTON
President
Walter Payton, Inc.

Walter Payton retired from professional football in 1987 leaving behind a substantially rewritten record book. During 13 seasons with the Chicago Bears he set ten NFL records; became the all-time leading rusher with 16,726 yards; broke 25 Bears records; had ten 1,000 yard seasons; one most valuable player award and nine Pro Bowl and one Super Bowl appearances. He was inducted into the Pro Football Hall of Fame in 1993.

As owner/president of Walter Payton, Inc., he's an energetic entrepreneur operating 21 entertainment clubs nationwide, serves as a spokesman for six large corporations, promotes his own line of nutritional products and dabbles in real estate.

His consuming interest is his campaign to bring an NFL expansion franchise to St. Louis. If Payton's dream comes true, he'll be the first black owner in NFL history.

Business isn't the only outlet for his competitive juices. He has his own auto racing "Team 34," and is also into speedboat racing, likes to fly helicopters, plays drums, and is a jazz music buff.

Despite his exhausting schedule, Payton manages to make time for charitable causes. He majored in special education at Jackson State and recently formed the George Halas-Walter Payton Foundation to help fund college scholarships for underprivileged youths. He works with 14 different charities including the Special Olympics, Society for the Prevention of Child Abuse, and the American Cancer Society. Walter has received numerous awards for his charitable work including the prestigious 1990 Personality of the Year Award.

Compete with Yourself

I have a secret I want to share with you. Before I tell you what it is, I want you to promise you'll put it to work in your life. If you do, you'll find it is a great game plan for successful living.

Competition is an intrinsic part of our daily lives. It encompasses schools, sports, business, even personal relationships. I have always been considered a fierce competitor. I still am in my business, motorsports and other ventures. Sure, I compete against other people, but, my main competition is MYSELF! I learned that from the Bible, when I was still in school. That's my secret.

"Do you know that those who run in the race all run, but one receives the prize? Run so that you may obtain it." That's found in 1 Corinthians 9:24, 25. Most people don't understand what it means. The race is not against other contenders, but against ourselves. The measure of success is not the margin of victory over our rivals, but how well we did compared to how well we could have done. St. Paul makes that clear when he tells us: "not to boast in another man's sphere of accomplishments."

To run life's race we need to be fit. Fitness of mind and body, over which you have a great deal of control, should be one of your lifelong top priorities. Health should always come ahead of wealth. When it does, you'll have the energy and drive to reach your goals—then financial security will follow.

Youth is a spendthrift of health and strength because there seems to be such a surplus. It isn't taken seriously nor appreciated. I want to put the thought into your head, and the urge into your heart, to be your best physically. There's no secret to good health other than just plain, good common sense. No need to be a fitness faddist—make a game of it. Eat right, exercise regularly and get plenty of rest—that's a simple regimen for good health.

Faith is the starting point for all accomplishments in life. The power of strong desire backed by faith is incredible. We conquer fear with faith. The absence of faith is a guarantee of failure. If you believe you can do it—you can!

CHARLIE PLUMB
"Top Gun" War Hero
Motivational Speaker

Charlie Plumb is a former P.O.W. and one of the most sought after achievement speakers in the United States.

A native of Gary, Indiana, he graduated from high school in Kansas and became a midshipman at the U.S. Naval Academy in Annapolis. He was graduated in 1964 with a bachelor of science degree and commission in the U.S. Navy.

From Annapolis, he went to flight training bases in Florida, Mississippi and Texas. He was one of the first in his class to receive wings of gold in the Navy jet aviation program. From flight training, he went to San Diego where he was trained to pilot the F4-B Phantom, the Navy's newest supersonic interceptor. There he helped start the "Top Gun" school before being sent to the South China Sea.

As flight officer for Fighter Squadron 114, Plumb was in charge of the air wing detachment. After 74 combat missions, he had received 3 Air Medals, 2 Navy Commendations, Combat Action, Navy Unit Citation, National Defense, Vietnam Service, Unit Citation, and Republic of Vietnam Campaign ribbons.

On May 19, 1967, he was shot down south of Hanoi while on a fighter cover mission. He was captured and taken to the Hanoi prison complex where he was tortured. He spent the next five years and nine months in captivity. During his imprisonment, he distinguished himself among his fellow prisoners as a professional in underground communication. He also served as chaplain of his prison unit for two years.

He was repatriated on February 28, 1973, underwent medical and security debriefings, and returned to Kansas City where he was awarded the Silver Star, two Purple Hearts, the Bronze Star, the Legion of Merit and the POW Medal.

(Continued on page 299)

Qualities of Survival

Several years ago I found myself a long way from home in a small prison cell. I had just made the violent transition from a "Top Gun" fighter pilot to the very scum of humanity: a Prisoner of War. I had been tortured, humiliated, starved, and left to languish in squalor for the next six years.

It's important that you get a vivid mental picture of this scene, because the most value I can be on this page is to invite you into my prison cell. I would like you to try your best to smell the stench of the bucket I called my toilet, and taste the salt in the corner of your mouth from your sweat, your tears, and your blood, and feel the baking tropical heat in a tin roofed prison cell. Not that you'll ever be a P.O.W.—but if I am effective in these few moments we spend together, you'll see that the same kinds of challenges you face as a teenager, as a student, a leader, a parent, are the same basic challenges I faced in a prison cell: those of fear and loneliness, feelings of failure and breakdown of communication. More importantly, your response to those challenges, if you're going to succeed, is the same menu of responses I had to have in a prison camp just to survive.

So, once you can vicariously put aside your comfort zone and assume the painful position of a prisoner of war, I would ask: "What qualities do you have within you that would allow your survival in a prison camp?"

Please pause here, think about this question, and write in the margin of this page at least five different qualities of survival.

Do it now!

(If you've written faith, commitment, dedication, etc., you've already broken the code.)

As I worked my way through the first several months and then years of imprisonment, I found I already had a foundation of survival factors learned early in life from my parents, preachers, youth leaders, and teachers. And that life saving techniques in that prison camp had more to do with my value system, my integrity and my religious belief than anything I had learned from a textbook.

Now here's the test (you were expecting a test weren't you?): the next time you have a huge problem facing you, turn back to this page and read not my writing but your writing in the margin. You'll find that the same factors you've written here, which would serve you well in a prison camp, will serve you even better in the challenge of every day life. Thumbs up!

Charlie Plumb

JERE RATCLIFFE
Chief Scout Executive
Boy Scouts of America

Jere Ratcliffe, Chief Scout Executive of the Boy Scouts of America, provides leadership to the nearly 4,000 Scouting professionals who serve in the fifty states, Puerto Rico, and at military installations around the world.

Through his leadership, the Boy Scouts of America is delivering the message that the development of strong character is necessary preparation for life in the 21st Century. His efforts throughout his adult life have been focused on the mission of Scouting—to serve others by helping install values in young people.

Mr. Ratcliffe has held a variety of positions during his years of service to Scouting. A Distinguished Eagle Scout, he began his professional career with the Boy Scouts of America as a district executive in Greenville, South Carolina. He then served as Scout executive in West Palm Beach, Florida; Clarksdale, Mississippi; and Birmingham, Alabama. After service at the national office as director of the Finance Division, he became Scout executive of the Heart of America Council in Kansas City, Missouri. He then was named regional director for the Central Region before becoming Chief Scout Executive in 1993. His office is at the national headquarters in Irving, Texas, but he travels extensively in support of Scouting.

Mr. Ratcliffe attended Wittenberg University and holds a bachelor's degree in business administration. He and his wife have a son and a daughter.

What Character Means

The most important message I could give to young people—or people of any age, for that matter—is this one: *character counts*. This message is now the national theme of the Boy Scouts of America, but, it was a personal belief I held long before we ever chose it as our theme.

My belief that character counts goes back far beyond my adult life as a professional Scouter. It goes back to my own youth when I learned and promised to follow the Scout oath:

> On my honor I will do my best
> To do my duty to God and my country and
> To obey the Scout Law;
> To help other people at all times;
> To keep myself physically strong, mentally
> awake, and morally straight.

Those words have helped to define for me what character means. My commitment to them has made a great difference in my life.

Sometimes it seems there may never have been a more difficult time for people, young and old, to live lives of genuine character. The difficulty does not lessen the importance of doing so, however.

You see, I'm convinced that nothing is needed more today than for each of us to be a person of genuine character, genuine integrity, whatever the price we may have to pay to do so. To be honest, I also must tell you that character may well cost you something—but only in the short run. In the long run, the benefits of being a person of genuine character are so great they cannot be calculated. With character you can face any challenges that come to you.

ORVILLE REDENBACHER
Entrepreneur

Undoubtedly one of the most successful and daring entrepreneurs of the past decade is popcorn king Orville Redenbacher. At the time he broke into the industry, there were 82 other popcorn brands competing with him. Within five years, Redenbacher, who advertised his product as "the world's most expensive popcorn," had become number one. In 1983, he came out with his microwave oven popcorn which became the top seller almost overnight.

Orville grew up in Brazil, Indiana, and as the son of a farmer he had an early interest in agriculture. He began his agricultural career by studying agronomy and genetics at Purdue University, where he earned his degree in agriculture.

Upon completing college, he taught briefly before becoming a county agricultural agent in Terre Haute. Later he managed a 12,000 acre farm which was partly owned by Tony Hulman, the late owner of the Indianapolis Motor Speedway. It was there he met Charles Bowman, manager of Purdue's Agricultural Alumni Seed Improvement Association, who became Orville's future partner.

They bought a hybrid seed business and developed it into the world's biggest producer of popcorn seed. But, when Redenbacher and Bowman developed a special line of seed, they had trouble selling it because of the high price. Instead they decided to market their own gourmet brand of popcorn in 1971, with Orville's face and name on the jar. Redenbacher's great down-home believability proved a natural, especially in TV advertising. He once spent six solid months on the road promoting popcorn while emphasizing it is a health food recommended by the AMA and the American Cancer Society.

The popcorn industry has grown very rapidly in the past 15 years and Orville Redenbacher is one of the biggest reasons why. From 1976 to

No Magic Formula

Education is one thing in life you can never get too much of (except perhaps popcorn). At any age, the things we learn shape our lives and the lives of those around us, for education is the tool with which we build an understanding of the world.

Education is the bridge that not only connects us to the ideas of the past but also provides us with a clearer path to the future.

I set off on my path as a young boy in rural Indiana, where I first learned about business by selling popcorn grown on our family farm for extra spending money. In 1924, I enrolled at Purdue University, where pioneering research in popcorn hybridization heated up my boyhood dream of developing a popcorn kernel that would consistently pop up lighter and fluffier.

Forty years later, after cross-breeding more than 30,000 popcorn hybrids, I introduced a gourmet popping corn.

If it hadn't been for the solid foundation of knowledge I gained on the farm and later formalized at Purdue, my name wouldn't be a household word today. Armed with a college degree and a lot of perseverance, I was able to realize my ambitions. So can you.

With good job opportunities for those with only a high school diploma growing scarce, post-secondary education is becoming increasingly necessary in finding a fulfilling and financially rewarding career. So, get all the education you can, formal or otherwise.

Beyond education, I simply followed some homespun principles: Never say die. Never be satisfied. Integrity is a must. Be stubborn and persistent in seeking your goals. Anything worth having is worth striving for with all your might. Does all this sound corny? Honestly, that's all there is to becoming a success—there is no magic formula.

Orville Redenbacher

1990, North American popcorn consumption has doubled. Total sales have reached 600 million pounds a year as popcorn has become a billion dollar industry.

NAOMI RHODE
President
National Speakers Association

Naomi Rhode is a business executive and professional speaker. She currently serves as president of the National Speakers Association, a 3,500 member organization of professional speakers. She is one of the first women to receive the coveted CPAE Award given by that organization in recognition of outstanding speaking skills and professionalism.

A graduate of the University of Minnesota, Naomi has had extensive private practice experience as a dental hygienist. She is the past president of the Arizona State Dental Hygienists Association. Known as an inspiring, dynamic speaker, she has spoken before thousands of dental professionals and their spouses, sharing her expertise in team building, interpersonal communication and motivation stimulating her audiences to achieve new levels of professional and personal growth.

*In addition to her speaking, she is the author of two inspirational books—*The Gift of Family/A Legacy of Love *and* More Beautiful Than Diamonds/The Gift of Friendship. *She has also produced a number of video tapes and cassettes.*

A proud mother of three grown children with eight grandchildren, Naomi and her husband, Jim, live in Phoenix, Arizona. Together they built and own SmartPractice, a successful company which markets practice building and infection control products to healthcare professionals throughout the U.S. and in many foreign countries.

Say "Yes" to Living!

One experience dramatically changed my life. The year: 1972. The event: a large dental convention in New York. The dentist I was working for was one of the prime speakers. In the middle of his speech, before 600 dentists, he received an emergency telephone call. I took the message to him.

After quickly reading it, he told the audience, "I need to answer an emergency call and therefore will turn the microphone over to my dental hygienist, who will spend half an hour sharing with you what it's like to work in a progressive preventative dental office. Help me welcome Naomi Rhode.

I was in total shock. I had never used a microphone. My mind raced back to speech classes in high school and college. I felt fearful and totally inadequate for this type of challenge. At that moment, I had several choices—to run from the room, faint, feign illness, or, to object in some other way.

There was another option. That was to say "yes" to the opportunity, taking to that speaking platform the passion and excitement I felt for the privilege of serving people in the profession I love! That "yes" was the beginning of an incredible journey into a professional career that has been fulfilling beyond my wildest expectations.

My challenge to you is to say "yes" to the opportunities you will be given during your lifetime. There will be times when you'll say to yourself, "I don't have enough experience," or "Jane is better at that than I am." Sometimes you'll be afraid that you'll fail. Other times you'll worry about looking foolish in front of your friends.

Don't ever let your life be controlled by fear! By doing the very thing you fear, you'll gain confidence, feel successful and be ready for the next challenge which comes your way. Who knows what wonderful opportunity is just around the bend for you!

Say "yes" to living and your life will be full of adventure!

Naomi Rhode

MICHAEL J. ROARTY
Executive Vice President of Corporate Marketing/Communications
Anheuser-Busch Companies, Inc.

Mike Roarty joined Anheuser-Busch while still attending the University of Detroit, and during his more than thirty-year career with the company, has served in virtually every sales and marketing position there, including field sales and brand management.

During his thirteen years as executive vice president and director of marketing for Anheuser-Busch, Inc., the world's largest brewing concern, Mike oversaw the introduction of 12 new beer brands into the American marketplace as the company's share of the U.S. beer market increased form 21 percent to more than 43 percent.

Success in the marketplace, however, has been only one facet of Mike's business career. He was instrumental in building the program through which Anheuser-Busch and its wholesalers have raised more than $44 million for the Muscular Dystrophy Association. While promoting Budweiser, the company has helped raise nearly $110 million since 1980 for the United Negro College Fund, and it is the largest contributor to the National Hispanic Scholarship Fund, which has provided more than 21,000 scholarships to deserving students. In addition, Mike has supervised Anheuser-Busch's efforts to fight alcohol abuse, drunk driving, and underage drinking and to promote personal responsibility among adults who choose to drink. Anheuser-Busch has invested more than $100 million in this industry-leading effort in the last 10 years.

Despite this success, Mike has never forgotten his roots. Irish-America magazine honored Mike as the Irish American of the Year in 1991, and in 1992, he was inducted into the Irish American Hall of Fame. One of the highlights of Mike's year is his annual trip to Ireland to host the Budweiser Irish Derby where he meets with the Irish Prime Minister and other government leaders involved in Irish-American business relations. In 1994, he was the first American to serve as grand marshal of the St. Patrick's Day parade in Dublin.

Treat Other People With Respect

There are a lot of factors that go into success. But I think one of the most important is treating other people with respect. Throughout my career I've found that the most successful business people are those that never forget that business is not just about the bottom line—it's about people.

I think, sometimes, those who lose in business (and in life) forget one very simple rule—the Golden Rule. Most people want the same things—to be treated with respect, to take responsibility for their actions, to provide for their family, and to work in a positive environment being able to use their talents to the fullest in a meaningful way.

Martin Mathews, who runs one of the most successful youth programs in America, the Mathews-Dickey Boys Club in St. Louis, says the three "R's" that young people really need to learn are respect, restraint, and responsibility. I agree.

Setting goals can be a great motivator in life and in business. Don't be afraid to set goals for yourself which others say are unachievable, but which you believe in.

In 1977 when I took over as director of marketing for Anheuser-Busch, the "conventional wisdom" was that Budweiser, our flagship, was a mature brand. The "experts" told us there was no point in marketing it. But we believed in the brand and instead of cutting back, we stepped up our marketing efforts. Over the next several years, Budweiser sales doubled and Bud became the dominant brew in America. One of every four beers sold is now a Budweiser.

In the past decade, we've directed our efforts to a new area—promoting responsible consumption of alcohol. We don't use scare tactics or preach at people. Instead, we respect our audience, reminding people of some basic values, urging them to act responsibly, to "Know When To Say When."

And as an extension of this effort we have such initiatives as "Talk to Your Kids About Drinking", "Stepping Into Adolescence", "Make the Right Call" and "Check Into a Winning Life", two programs with the NCAA and an extensive "Designated Driver" campaign.

Thanks to efforts like ours and the many others which address the issue of alcohol abuse we have seen dramatic reductions in drunk driving and underage drinking. If we talk to our young adults with respect for their own intelligence and their sense of responsibility they will accept the message in the spirit in which it is intended.

We can make a difference. We will make a difference.

SPENCER ROBINSON, JR.
General Secretary
Rotary International

Founded in 1905, Rotary International is an international association of more than one million service-minded business and professional leaders belonging to over 25,000 clubs in 172 countries and geographic regions around the world.

In 1968, Rotary founded Rotaract which has developed into a world-wide organization of more than 100,000 young men and women, ages 18 through 29, who believe they can make a difference. They are dedicated to improving themselves, their communities, and the world by actively carrying out community service projects, providing members with leadership training and professional development opportunities, and expanding international service and understanding.

The general secretary of Rotary International, Spencer Robinson, Jr., a certified public accountant, is also the general secretary of the Rotary Foundation, which provides funding for a wide range of humanitarian and scholastic programs.

Prior to joining the staff of Rotary International, Robinson was the executive vice president and chief operating officer of the University of Alabama Health Services Foundation. From 1963-85, he worked for Deloitte & Touche (formerly Deloitte, Haskins & Sells) and served as managing partner in Tokyo, Japan and New Orleans, Louisiana.

Robinson was educated at Georgia Institute of Technology, Jacksonville University, and the University of Alabama at Birmingham from which he received degrees in industrial management, accounting and health administration.

Service above Self

One of the most important needs in the world today is to gain a new perspective concerning success and failure. It is only by superficial standards that we have come to judge greatness in terms of being served rather than of rendering service. Jobs are often judged not in terms of what is accomplished or whether they are constructive, but in terms of hours, wages and ease. Even people are judged by ability to take from life, not give to life.

It is never too early or too late to come to the realization that greatness should be measured by contribution and service. Time and eternity stretch out before us all with all their possibilities. We each have one life to live, just one life. We shall not have unlimited opportunities to make our lives count the most—we must consciously decide how to spend our time and use our energies.

How can each individual make his greatest contribution? It is a wonderful day in a person's life when one makes up one's mind to be oneself—to do one's own work—to fill one's own special niche. Each of us has certain intuitive feelings about what we are capable of doing. These feelings are based upon those happy and satisfying moments when what we are about seems right for us. Time means nothing. Energy spent means nothing. We simply lose ourselves and are consumed.

We must listen to our inner selves. We must each discover and nurture our innate abilities and freely express our identities as unique persons. We owe this self-discovery to ourselves and we owe it to others. We will contribute the most when we are expressing our true nature and using our own special gifts.

What if this self-discovery seems elusive? Statistics show that 70% of Americans have already determined their life work by the age of 15. Perhaps this reveals how little attention this decision really gets—perhaps it is even made haphazardly, according to immediate opportunities or family background. We can do better. We can each actively seek our best self. We may consult family, friends or professionals at guidance centers. We may join a group of caring, service-minded individuals who will encourage and inspire us. It will be worth the time and effort because achieving personal awareness will free us to share ourselves with others.

True success then, seen in this new perspective, will be measured by what we give to life, not what we get; by what we put into life, not what we take from life. We can do it. Personal fulfillment and a higher quality of life await us all!

ROY ROGERS
King of the Cowboys

Roy Rogers, Hollywood's King of the Cowboys, is a full-blown American legend. He starred in 91 movies, singing in all of them, and also made 120 episodes of NBC's The Roy Rogers Show. Astride his palomino, Trigger, he was the hero in the white ten-gallon hat, who from 1943 to 1955, was America's leading cowboy star at the box office.

Over 2,000 Roy Rogers Fan Clubs dotted the United States and the London chapter had 50,000 members. A Life magazine survey asking children what person they would want most to be like found Roy sharing top billing with Franklin Roosevelt and Abraham Lincoln!

The legend has been kept alive by the ongoing success of his old movies and records. One of the highlights of the 1991 CMA Awards featured Roy and Clint Black, a current headliner, singing a duet on Hold on Partners, from Rogers' current album, Tribute, on which he performs with 20 top country artists, including his wife, Dale Evans, who joins him on Happy Trails, their signature song. Roy is the only person ever inducted into the Country Music Hall of Fame twice—in 1980, as a member of the Sons of the Pioneers and, in 1988, on his own.

Rogers' strong faith has helped him to withstand tragedies in his life, including the death of his first wife and three of his children. Now 80, he recovered from his second heart operation and a serious bout with pneumonia in 1991. He is now involved in numerous business ventures, including a chain of Roy Rogers Family Restaurants, owned by Hardees Corporation, real estate holdings, the Paramount-Roy Rogers Music Publishing firm and the Roy Rogers-Dale Evans Museum in Victorville, California, where he has his office.

Among the many honors he has received are Man of the Year and Father of the Year awards. He and Dale are members of the Cowboy Hall of Fame, as well as recipients of the National Film Society's Humani-

Happy Trails

True success includes a happy and enjoyable journey along the way. I like to call that Happy Trails.

But, whatever trail you ride, there will be ambushes and rough terrain to travel along the way. For me, faith in God and having a loving family got me through the difficult times.

Surely, at best, life was not intended to be easy. But, just as surely, Jesus came to show us safe passage. I've sung a lot of songs in my time, but the most beautiful verse ever written isn't found in a songbook. It's the 23rd Psalm, "The Lord is my shepherd; I shall not want." It assures us of the only success that is meaningful—our eternal salvation.

Family, the one you are born into, or, one you may help create in the future, is the most important relationship you'll have in your entire life. It is in the family setting we most often learn the real lessons of life—love, forgiveness, self-discipline and work.

Our memories of home are usually pleasant or unpleasant in direct proportion to the amount of love we experience there. In today's materialistic society, we've built thousands of houses but it takes love to make a house a home. So, if one of your goals is to have your own dream house some day make sure it is not just a material house. Fill it with love—the strongest foundation on which it can stand.

If you set out from such a home each day you'll find that most of your travel will be along "Happy Trails."

Roy Rogers

---

tarian Award, the USO Liberty Bell Award, the Kiwanis Decency Award, and citations from the Freedoms Foundation and The American Legion. Happy Trails, *the story of their lives, was published in 1977.*

KYLE ROTE, JR.
Owner
Athletic Resource Management, Inc.

- *Motivational speaker for such diverse clients as IBM, AT&T, Polaroid, Pillsbury and 3M, among many others. Has spoken at the White House for President Ford and in London for Prince Philip.*
- *In 1984, selected as one of the "Ten Outstanding Young Men in America."*
- *National television commentator on numerous occasions for CBS. Veteran "Game of the Week" announcer for USA Cable in football, track and soccer.*
- *Only American-born player to ever win a major professional soccer league scoring championship. Represented the United States in international competition from 1973-1976 and is the all-time leading scorer in Dallas Tornado history.*
- *One of only two people to win more than one of the popular, nationally televised Superstars competitions. He won three times (1974, 1976, 1977) over such greats as O.J. Simpson, Pete Rose, and hundreds of others including three Olympic Decathlon Gold Medalists.*
- *As a Christian, Kyle is dedicated to helping the youth of our nation develop their unique abilities and God-given potential. In addition, he took a one year leave from pro sports in 1980 to join the efforts of Mother Teresa and others in the battle against hunger—a cause he remains committed to.*
- *Kyle currently maintains an extensive speaking and broadcasting schedule in addition to being an active owner of Athletic Resource Management, Inc., a diverse financial services company and sports agency.*
- *Author of numerous articles and two books, Simon and Schuster's* Complete Book of Soccer *and* Beyond the Goal.
- *Kyle, his wife Mary Lynne, and their four children live in Memphis, Tennessee, where they are involved in many sports and civic activities.*

Success Formula

In the last few years, we have been reminded of many sports stars who were told at some point "You Can't Do It"!

The NBA Scoring Champion Michael Jordan was told at one point in high school he wasn't good enough.

World Series MVP Orel Herschiser was told he "wasn't a pitcher" both in high school and college.

Terry Bradshaw was told he was too dumb until he quarterbacked the Pittsburgh Steelers to four Super Bowl titles.

San Francisco's Joe Montana was told he was too small until his 49ers began their big string of Super Bowl victories.

And, oh yes, a promising 16-year-old football player named Kyle Rote, Jr., was told he was too old to start playing soccer and he could never succeed in a foreigner's game until he won Pro Soccer's scoring championship at age 22.

In each case, the athletes rejected "the rejection" and persevered—so can you. Now, that's not to say your life will have similar results as these men. In fact, God doesn't promise us Cy Young Awards, MVP Trophies, or Super Bowl victories—but he does promise us an abundant life if we will fully give ourselves to Him.

And frankly, overcoming our desire to "be in charge" is the biggest challenge any of us will ever face whether we love sports or dislike them. Who will win the next Super Bowl is of minor temporary consequence when compared with the eternal significance of who will win the battle for control of your life—you or God.

The Bible reminds us, in one of the good ironies of life, that "if you lose your life you will save it"—and therefore be in a position to overcome anything that life throws at you!

So what is the formula for you to follow when you face problems? What is the formula so YOU CAN DO IT? It has four parts, simple to understand but very hard to do:

1. Serve the Savior
2. Reject the Rejection
3. Decide to be Dedicated
4. Go for your Goal

May God Strengthen you in these pursuits!

Kyle Rote Jr.

DANIEL "RUDY" RUETTIGER
Football Folk Hero

The motion picture "Rudy" is the story of a working-class Catholic boy who refused to give up on his impossible dream of attending Notre Dame and playing on the football team. It is a classic underdog story based on the life of Daniel "Rudy" Ruettiger, the third of 14 children in a Joliet, Illinois family.

Rudy was a 165-pound starting guard on Joliet Catholic High's unbeaten 1965 football team with a grade point average of 1.77 out of 4. Neither qualified him to realize his dream.

After graduating from high school, he served in the Navy for two years, then returned home to work in a power plant. The sudden death of his best friend in a work accident galvanized his thinking, "I realized that life's too short not to pursue your dreams."

Rudy, then 23, moved to South Bend and enrolled at Holy Cross Junior College (his tuition was paid by the GI Bill), with the intent to transfer to Notre Dame. At Holy Cross, he was diagnosed for the first time as a dyslexic. He was given special tutoring and maintained a B average. In 1974, after two rejections, he was finally accepted at Notre Dame.

He went out for the football team and was relegated to practice play until the fateful day, with time running out on his collegiate career, Coach Ara Parsegian put him in for the last 27 seconds of his last game. It was the first time he ever came off the bench. He made a tackle as the game ended!

Rudy graduated with a degree in Sociology. He admits, "I like the chase," and was soon chasing another dream, to sell his life story to Hollywood. By happenstance, he met Angelo Pizzo, who directed the hit basketball movie Hoosiers, *and sent him a script, which was rejected. Unwilling as usual, to take no for an answer, he finally won over the director and that's how the movie "Rudy" was born.*

Persistence and Perseverance

We owe it to ourselves to try every day of our lives to make our dreams come true. But the dreams and hopes we all have in life will never be realized by just waiting and wishing they'll come true. Making a dream become a reality takes persistent effort.

When you have a dream, what may even seem like an impossible goal, you need to accept the challenge of searching, waiting, trying, maybe failing, and then trying again. You'll hear from a lot of naysayers. Criticism is often a form of jealousy and envy. Don't let the dream stealers take your dreams.

It is estimated that three out of four people sell themselves short by underestimating their abilities and potential. So, if you have a dream, write down your goals. Goals are the road maps to attaining your dreams. Review your goals at least twice a day. Focus on your goals. Obstacles are what we see when we take our eyes off our goals. It's an ageless human trait to fear the unknown. That's why you must believe in yourself to persevere.

Remember, you are unique, unlike any other person in the world. There is a place for you that no one else can fill in the same way that you can. Look for it until you find it.

Rudy

DONALD RUMSFELD
Former Secretary of Defense

Don Rumsfeld, who has more than 20 years of public service, has served as CEO to two major U.S. corporations. He headed General Instrument Corporation, the world's largest maker of broad-band equipment for cable television and satellite broadcasting, from 1990 to 1993. Prior to that, Rumsfeld was chief at G.D. Searle & Co., from 1977 to 1985, where he is credited with turning around the worldwide pharmaceutical company.

During his business career, he continued in public service in a variety of federal posts, including service as an adviser to the U.S. Departments of State and Defense.

A native of Chicago, he attended Princeton University and holds ten honorary degrees and the nation's highest civilian award, the Presidential Medal of Freedom.

After service as a naval aviator, Rumsfeld started his public life as a congressman from Illinois, serving four terms. He served in the Nixon, Ford, and Reagan administrations. His posts included service as ambassador to NATO in the Nixon years, as Ford's chief of staff and secretary of defense, and as Reagan's Middle East envoy.

After leaving Washington, D.C., he lectured at Princeton University's Woodrow Wilson School of International Affair and at Northwestern University's Kellogg Graduate School of Management, prior to entering business.

Rumsfeld serves on a number of corporate boards of directors and is involved in numerous civic activities, including the Eisenhower Exchange Fellowships.

Don and his wife, Joyce, have two daughters, a son, and three grandchildren.

Help Make America Better

When President Dwight Eisenhower left the White House, he was asked why he had bought a small, somewhat run-down farm in Gettysburg. He responded that he "always wanted to take a small piece of America and make it better, with my own hands."

That is the opportunity and challenge for each of us.

Whatever your next challenge may be, do it well! Do it with tolerance and understanding of others. But, do it with all of the drive, enthusiasm and joy of life you have in you.

Attack it, so that when you look in the mirror you'll know, with absolute certainty, that whatever God has given you, you've done the best with it that was humanly possible.

And, from time to time, look back. Look back and see if you are leaving footprints, and more, if you like where they are going. And, see if you too, "with your own hands," can help to make a small piece of America better.

Above all, don't be blown by the winds. A world of dramatic change, as our world surely is, is still underpinned by the timeless values of faith, family, honor and community.

CHARLES B. RUNNELS
Chancellor
Pepperdine University

Charles B. Runnels, chancellor since 1985 of Malibu-based Pepperdine University, has helped guide Pepperdine on a steady course toward academic excellence since joining its administration nearly a quarter century ago. Working closely with the University's president, he is actively involved in policy matters, strategic planning, and external activities for the 7,000 student school.

Recruited by Pepperdine in 1967, he left a senior corporate post at Houston-based Tenneco, Inc., to assist in laying the groundwork for a new campus. His service to the University includes membership on the Board of Regents and leadership of Pepperdine's 100-member University Board.

From humble beginnings in East Texas—where he picked cotton and cut wood to help with school expenses—Chancellor Runnels began his college studies at age 16 at Stephen F. Austin University, working as a bellboy and a hotel night clerk during his freshman year. He enlisted in the Navy Air Corps at 17, completed his midshipman school at Columbia University and flight training at Pensacola, Florida, and served one year with a seaplane squadron in the World War II Asia theatre. He returned to Stephen F. Austin to complete his bachelor's degree and earned a law degree at the University of Houston.

A member of the board of the Los Angeles Philanthropic League and the Americanism Educational League, Chancellor Runnels works tirelessly for higher education and Pepperdine. His dedication to young people is demonstrated in his annual leadership of the Southern California Youth Citizenship Seminar, which each year brings 250 outstanding high school students to Pepperdine to instill in them a greater understanding and enthusiasm for America and its pluralistic system.

Chancellor Runnels holds two honorary doctor of law degrees and in 1988 was named Alumnus of the Year by his undergraduate alma mater.

Read the Guideposts!

My advice to anyone traveling the road of life is: read the guideposts! People and events can serve as road signs, providing a vision of what lies beyond the horizon.

I was raised on a farm and my parents, though uneducated, were by first guideposts. They encouraged me to finish school and, thanks to them and others, I've succeeded in two different careers. For 15 years I worked in industry, then joined Pepperdine University's administration. I've tried to be a guidepost to youth, helping them see that the corporate world is more interested in your work ethic and character than with letters in sports or Phi Beta Kappa keys.

In naval flight school during World War II, my roommate Herb Kalmbach convinced me that we could become whatever we wanted if we focused on our goals and believed in ourselves. Dr. Norman Vincent Peale became our guidepost and later, our personal friend. Herb went on to become personal attorney for President Richard Nixon.

My own guidepost is: "Never greet the dawn without a map." Time management is crucial. My wife, Amy Jo, encouraged me to seek a law degree at night while working full time. And my spiritual mentor, LaGard May, convinced me that not only could I work and attend classes, but I could teach a Bible class as well. Teaching actually helped put my life in perspective.

Another guidepost has been George Page, who left school at age 15 to venture West from his native Nebraska. He hitchhiked to Los Angeles and arrived with nothing but pocket change. Working day and night, he saved enough to start his own gift fruit shipping company. He later sold his famous Mission Pak enterprise to invest in worthy causes, including Children's Hospital, the renowned George Page Museum, and Pepperdine University.

Finally, Mrs. Frank Roger Seaver, 100 years young, has been a tremendous guidepost as the single greatest motivating factor in the building of Pepperdine's beautiful Malibu campus. She has probably given more money to California higher education than any other person. "If you want to do something for our country," she enthuses, "do something for youth, for they are the future of our nation."

Se read the guideposts along the way. You are but one person, but you CAN make a difference.

Charles Runnels

DENNY RYDBERG
President
Young Life

Denny Rydberg is president of Young Life, an organization that helps adolescents understand what a relationship with Jesus Christ can mean for their lives now and later. Young Life has 1,300 employees, 16,000 volunteers and touches the lives of 200,000 young people each year through their club, camping and outreach programs.

Denny was born and raised in Anacortes, Washington. He graduated from Anacortes High School and Seattle Pacific University with a major in psychology.

Before becoming Young Life's fifth president in the organization's 53 year history, he served on three church staffs including the First Presbyterian Church, Tacoma, Washington; First Presbyterian Church, San Diego, and from 1984-93 as the director of University Ministries at University Presbyterian Church, Seattle, Washington, where he led one of the largest and most vital ministries to college students in the country.

He also was formerly owner of Youth Specialties, editor of the Wittenberg Door, Director of Operations for Inspirational Films, and a writer, speaker and consultant. Denny has authored 10 books including Beyond Graduation, How to Survive in College, Twentysomething, Building Community in Youth Groups *and* Run to Win.

Along with his wife, Marilyn, he helped start a ministry to women golfers on the LPGA Tour. Denny also served as chaplain for the University of Washington men's basketball team and for the Seattle Supersonics of the NBA.

The Rydbergs have four children, Heather, Joshua, Jeremy and Jonathan and one granddaughter, Monique. They reside in Colorado Springs, Colorado.

Take Along the Tartar Sauce

A couple of years ago, I came across H. Jackson Brown's book, *Life's Little Instruction Book*, 511 suggestions, observations and reminders on how to live a happy and rewarding life.

Jackson had written this booklet as a gift for his son, Adam, on his departure for college. Many of the observations were personally helpful but there's one of "life's little instructions" that grabbed me and would not let me go. Number 271—"When facing a difficult task, act as though it's impossible to fail. If you're going after Moby Dick, take along the tartar sauce."

I'd like to pass on that advice. In all of life, bring along the tartar sauce. I believe in the 80-20 rule of life. Eighty percent of life is difficult, hard, challenging, exasperating—20 percent is easy. Anyone can live the 20 percent, it's the 80 percent where we show who and what we really are.

That means that during 80 percent of our lives, we will be facing difficult tasks. Because of that reality, we'd better have a strategy for facing challenges that's effective or we will spend most of our lives overwhelmed.

My strategy: in all that you face, bring along the tartar sauce. Bring some zest to what you do. Don't be overwhelmed by the challenge. And how do you have a good chance of success. I'd suggest that first you pray and ask God to help you. Then think through the problem. What are the issues involved? What additional information do you need to succeed? What similarities does this problem have with others you've faced? It there anyone who can help you or give you advice?

Then remind yourself that enthusiasm does make a difference and that in the past you've met challenges and difficulties and succeeded.

Straighten your back, thrust your chest out, put a smile on your face and go after the whale!

DR. ROBERT H. SCHULLER
Founding Pastor
Crystal Cathedral Ministries

Dr. Schuller reaches millions weekly around the world with his "Hour of Power" televised ministry which was first broadcast in 1970. Today it is the highest rated religious program in the country.

In 1989, Dr. Schuller became the first non-Soviet pastor ever to be invited to speak on Soviet television. In 1990, he was asked by the Soviet government to begin a monthly televised program there called "From Heart to Heart."

Dr. Schuller came to Garden Grove, California in 1955 to found the Reformed Church of America's congregation there. With his wife, Arvella, as organist and $500 in assets, he rented the Orange Drive-In Theatre and conducted Sunday services from the roof of the snack bar.

The congregation's growth over the years dictated the decision to build the internationally acclaimed Crystal Cathedral, which was dedicated in 1980 to "the glory of man for the greater glory of God." Today the congregation numbers about 10,000.

Born in Alton, Iowa in 1926, Robert Harold Schuller knew all his life that he wanted to be a minister. He fulfilled that dream in 1950 when he was ordained by the Reformed Church of America after receiving his bachelor of arts degree from Hope College and a bachelor of divinity degree from Western Theological Seminary, both in Holland, Michigan. After ordination, he became minister of the Ivanhoe Reformed Church in Chicago, where he remained five years before establishing his ministry in Garden Grove.

Dr. Schuller is the author of more than 28 hard cover books, including four which appeared on the New York Times best seller list. His latest, Believe In The God Who Believes In You *is based on the Ten Commandments. In 1970, he founded the Robert H. Schuller Institute for Successful Church Leadership, which has more than 20,000 graduates.*

Believe and Succeed

Your success in life depends upon the degree of belief you have in yourself and in God.

That's a very profound statement. But, as you read the messages written to you by successful people in this book, you will find ample evidence that it is true.

I recently wrote a book called *Believe In The God Who Believes In You,* which is based on the Ten Commandments. The Lord's commandments were given to us to help us find our way through life.

I'm reminded of the story about the little girl who misquoted the first line of the 23rd Psalm saying, "The Lord is my shepherd, that's all I want!"

Talk about a blueprint for success. We should all be so firm in our decision as to where we're going, who we are following, and where we will end up.

Surely, at best, life is difficult—it was never meant to be easy. So, we've been given the commandments for our own good, our own peace and comfort.

If you will live by these God-given rules, I guarantee you'll be successful—not only spiritually, but, in an earthly sense as well. That's because God believes in you and, in His own time, will give you the hope and help you need to reach your goals.

All you need to do is Believe In The God Who Believes In You.

Robert Schuller

He has received numerous awards and serves on various boards. He has honorary doctorate degrees from Azusa Pacific College, Hope College, Pepperdine University and Barrington College in Rhode Island.

Dr. Schuller and Arvella have five children. His only son, Robert A., also is an ordained minister of the Reformed Church of America, the oldest Protestant denomination in the U.S., with a continuous ministry since 1628.

CHARLES "RED" SCOTT
President & CEO
Fuqua Industries, Inc.

Red Scott became president and chief executive officer of Fuqua Industries, Inc., in February, 1991. Prior to joining Fuqua, Scott was president and chief executive officer of Intermark, Inc., a California based operating/holding company.

An Horatio Alger Award winner, he is chairman of the Horatio Alger Association of Distinguished Americans, an organization which provides scholarships and a "mentor" program for aspiring high school students. He frequently speaks to students and business leaders on his principles of success and achievement.

Scott is founding director and vice chairman of the American Business Conference, past president of the Greater San Diego Sports Association, and former chairman of the Special Feasibility Committee that staged the first Holiday Bowl game.

He has served on the boards of numerous civic, charitable and industrial organizations, and was honored in 1988 by San Diego Mayor Maureen O'Connor with the State of the City "Seahorse Award." In 1990, Scott was named by California Business as one of the "Top 25 CEOs of the Decade" in California.

In 1986, he was honored by the Boy Scouts as "Distinguished Citizen" of San Diego, was one of five honorees of the California Museum of Science and Industry in 1973, and in 1968 was a national recipient of the Sales Masters Oscar Award.

A native Texan and 1949 graduate of the University of Texas, early in his career he was selected as one of the Outstanding Young Men of Dallas. Scott and his wife, Katherine, live in Atlanta. They have two grown sons.

Six Secrets of Success

These secrets to success hold true whether you're seeking success in business, athletics, art, politics or just in your personal life. They need to be "top of mind" and referred to every day as guiding principles.

First, you must believe you are lucky. Consider the fact that there are 5 billion people on the face of the earth, and only 250 million, or one in 20 people, were lucky enough to be Americans and to enjoy the gifts of freedom and opportunity.

Second, you have to be a dreamer, and dream bold dreams. You can do and be anything you dream. Remember, all great achievements in life are the result of someone dreaming. You too can dream and achieve, if you choose to.

Third, you must be enthusiastic. "I will" is more important in life than "IQ". You must have the energy and spirit to achieve, and when you mix enthusiasm with your dreams, you're on your way to being successful. It's like pouring lighter fluid on a fire!

Fourth, don't be afraid to fail. Remember, you fell down the first time you walked. Even the great success stories started with failures. Babe Ruth struck out 1,330 times. Thomas Edison failed 548 times before inventing the light bulb. Don't give up, and don't fear failure. It's better to try and fail than to not try at all. You can't learn without failing.

Fifth, you must believe in yourself. A high level of self-esteem is critical to personal success. Don't confuse this with egotism. To succeed you must think you can succeed and have self-confidence. Accept yourself as you are, improve where you think necessary, and make the most of your God-given talents.

Finally, believe that a supreme being loves you and believes in you, just as you believe in yourself. Remember, you never walk alone. This is not a religious issue, but an issue of success versus failure. I've made a life's work of studying success and I have never yet met a successful person who didn't accept the love of a higher being. It was from that basic belief that they drew their strength, their courage and wisdom.

Cecil R. Scott

JOHN M. SEGAL
President
North American Products
Corporation

John Segal received a Bachelor of Science Degree in Business from Indiana University in 1988. He was a member of Phi Kappa Psi Fraternity and Chairman of Indiana University Great Issues Senate. In 1971, Mr. Segal received a Juris Doctorate from Indiana University School of Law, in Bloomington, Indiana.

From 1971-1973, Mr. Segal served as a 1st Lieutenant in the United States Army, as Executive Officer of C461 Air Defense Company; and as DISCOM Brigade Legal Officer.

John Segal joined North American Products in 1974 in sales and marketing. He was promoted to Vice President of Operations in 1982 and President in 1989. The Company is the largest manufacturer and servicer of carbide tipped cutting tools in the United States, and operates three manufacturing plants and fourteen tool service centers throughout the eastern, central and southern states. The company also has two subsidiaries, Precision Disc Corporation, a manufacturer of steel cores for the diamond saw industry and S&J Manufacturing, a currer body manufacturer. Mr. Segal is also managing partner of two commercial real estate partnerships.

John has been active in various community activities. He is a former board member and active supporter of Big Brothers/Big Sisters, and is active in the Southwest Indiana Walk to Emmaus. In 1987, he founded ERFINDEN, a community-based professional organization for the continuation of adult learning and community improvement. Mr. Segal is a member of the Board of Southern Hills Mental Health Association, a chapter officer of the Young President's Organization, and is a member of Trinity United Church of Christ, where he teaches an adult Sunday School class.

244

Be a Lifelong Learner

Yes, YOU CAN DO IT! You can do anything you conceive of, if you will commit yourself to being a learner. It takes courage to be a lifelong learner, because it always places you in the position of being a student. Most people quit learning before they complete their formal education. But truly successful people—those who develop personal power and balance in their lives—discover that the challenge and joy in life comes from being a lifelong learner. Here are some areas where I have found learning to be particularly helpful.

1. Be learning to work hard. Whether it's schoolwork, athletics, building a business, cleaning the garage, or serving your community, be learning that going the extra mile, doing the job better than it has to be done, will take the drudgery out of work. When you set your standards a notch above others, it puts you in charge and makes hard work a joy.

2. Be learning to take responsibility. My dad always told my brother and me, "Take things from where they are, not from where you would like them to be." You may not have caused your circumstances, but if you take full responsibility for them, you gain the power to change them. Ultimately, if you decide to take responsibility for everything that ever happened in your life, you gain control over all of it.

3. Be learning to write down goals and achieve them. Very few people set any goals in life, and fewer yet write them down. Setting goals eliminates irrelevant options and focuses resources. Writing your goals allows their regular review and development. The fifth chapter of "How To Get Control Of Your Time and Your Life," by Alan Laikan, shows you how to do this in 20 minutes.

4. Be learning to read good books. As my friend, Charlie Jones says, "You are the same today as you will be in five years, except for two things; the people you meet and the books you read." Getting to know great people is terrific; unfortunately, you can't take them home with you, they won't always return your phone calls, and some of the best ones are dead. But the wisdom of the greatest minds, on every subject, is available in books.

5. Be learning to know God. I once thought that education, goals, and hard work would insure success and happiness in life—they won't. There is a learning that is beyond mere human understanding. Only

(Continued on page 311)

John and his wife, Sara, live in Jasper, Indiana, with their two sons, Jason and Michael. Family activities include snow skiing, camping and Cub Scouts.

WILLIAM S. SESSIONS
Former Director
Federal Bureau of Investigation

William S. Sessions was born May 27, 1930, in Fort Smith, Arkansas. He graduated from Northeast High School in Kansas City, Missouri, in 1948. He enlisted in the United States Air Force in 1951, received his wings and commission, then served two years active duty. In 1956, he was awarded a Bachelor of Arts degree from Baylor University, and in 1958 received his LL.B degree from Baylor University School of Law.

Sessions was a private practitioner of law in Waco, Texas, from 1958 until 1969, when he left his firm, Hale, Fulbright, Winniford, Sessions and Bice, to join the Department of Justice, in Washington, D.C., as chief of the Government Operations Section, Criminal Division. In 1971, he served on the board of Federal Judicial Center in Washington, D.C., and on committees of the State Bar of Texas and Judicial Conference of the United States.

On November 1, 1987, Sessions resigned his position as United States District Judge to become Director of the Federal Bureau of Investigation.

Sessions has received the Baylor University Distinguished Alumni Award and has been awarded honorary degrees from John C. Marshall Law School, St. Mary's University School of Law, and the Dickinson School of Law. In 1988, he was honored as Baylor Law School's "Lawyer of the Year"; was named "Father of the Year" for public service by the National Fathers' Day Committee; and received the Golden Plate Award from the American Academy of Achievement. In 1989, he received the Law Enforcement Leadership Award from the Association of Federal Investigators.

Repay What You've Been Given

(Adapted from remarks by William S. Sessions, Director,
Federal Bureau of Investigation, before the American
Academy of Achievement, Nashville, Tennessee.)

I want you to know that when I was asked to come here it caused me to reflect back over the years and go over briefly those things that were going through my head when I had reached the ripe old age of eighteen.

I was born in 1930, and as the older folks here remember, we were in the midst of the Great Depression. So, I was a child who understood that things were very dear and times were very tough. As I began to grow, I began to worry about those things that were happening all around me over which I seemed to have no control. It was very personal to me, because I truly, at that time, did not have any idea at all what would happen to me.

When I was sixteen I had polio. Suddenly my world was shattered because I had thought I would probably be the world's greatest 6'1" basketball player, yet I realized that my dream was not going to work for me. And I realized that life did not necessarily deal with you fairly. I learned that, in life, you did not necessarily succeed at what you originally wanted to do.

I have talked to so many of you and I find that you have some very definite goals. Yet, all of you seem to be searching; all of you seem to be looking. I want to talk about some of those things which helped me in my search.

The thought that gave me the determination to enter public service was the realization that we have so much to give and so much to repay. All of us here are privileged—we are privileged to have education; we are privileged to have people who care about us deeply, love us sincerely, and want us to succeed. So, we are compelled to try to pay back, to try and see the truth for what it is, and to try to express it and be a part of it.

I believe you have an absolute obligation to repay what has been given to you. The fact that you are 16, 17, or 18 does not take away from that at all. And, if you forget your obligation, then God help you, because it is yours whether you want it or not.

My father had a great effect on me and upon my spirit. He told me years ago, and he repeated it a number of times, that he was not concerned about what I was going to do. He was concerned about what I was going to be! That is our concern for you, the kind of men and women you are going to be, the kind of character you will portray, the strength you will have, the kind of determination you will display.

(Continued on page 311)

DAL SHEALY
President/CEO
Fellowship of Christian Athletes

Dal Shealy was named president of the Fellowship of Christian Athletes in 1992. FCA is the oldest and largest athletic and sports outreach movement in America. FCA serves junior highs, senior highs, and college campuses throughout the United States.

The mission is: "to present to athletes and coaches, and all whom they influence, the challenge and adventure of receiving Jesus Christ as Savior and Lord, and serving Him in their relationships and in the fellowship of the church."

FCA carries out its mission through summer camp programs consisting of leadership camps, specific sports camps, and coaches and volunteer family camps. During the school year, Huddles (small groups) usually meet weekly at school or in individual's homes, giving athletes and coaches an opportunity to share their faith, and discuss topics and concerns based on Biblical principals. FCA adult chapters are formed for adults who have an interest in young people, and identify them with the FCA movement. They meet weekly for accountability, covenant prayer time, Bible study, and to support the FCA Huddle coach and the local Huddles.

FCA's drug and alcohol program, One Way to Play Drug Free, has been a very effective program. Students pledge to abstain from using drugs, alcohol and steroids and hold their teammates accountable. FCA has various other events that involve working with various denominations and mega events to use the catalyst of sports as a means to share testimonies and bring people to Christ.

A native of South Carolina, Shealy played three sports at Batesburg-Leesville High School, played football at Carson-Newman College in Tennessee, as well as with the Quantico Marines, who were National Service Champions in 1960. He coached for 27 years and joined the Fel-

Soar Like Eagles

A friend of mine, Loren Young, was on a hunting trip in Wyoming. As he climbed a mountain, he saw an eagle only a few yards away with a great wing span soaring through the sky. Continuing to climb he kept watching the eagle soar back and forth going higher and higher. After about 10 minutes, the eagle was about out of sight. Loren could barely see him and asked his Indian guide, if he could see the eagle. He said, "Yes I've been watching the eagle soar majestically with a great wing span helping him soar so high I almost can't see him." How do you explain that? The guide replied, "It's the set of his wings. It's how he holds his wings with the wind under the wings lifting him higher and higher."

We are born and created in God's image. He wants us to succeed and not fail in whatever we do. So, it is the set of our heart and the set of our mind in tune with the Holy Spirit dwelling in us that enables us to soar like an eagle. Isaiah 40:31 says that they that hope (or trust) in the Lord, shall renew their strength. They shall run and not grow weary and shall walk and not faint. If we are to run the race of faith, the Lord will empower us to run and not grow weary and He will give us the stamina to walk and not faint for the long haul in serving Him.

Jesus Christ came to give us the example of how we should walk each day. He shared with his disciples that He was going to leave and send another who would replace Him, who would dwell within us and enable us to great and mighty things. This would be the Holy Spirit.

As we strive to make a difference in the world today, for the glory of Jesus Christ. We should set our heart with the character of Jesus Christ, then let the Holy Spirit have control over us as we set our minds on good things to make a difference.

I believe that the Fellowship of Christian Athletes can impact the athletes and coaches of America and make a difference by helping eliminate the problems of drug abuse, physical and mental abuse, sexual promiscuity, abortion and gambling, while turning America back to God.

Let's commit ourselves to soar like eagles as we are empowered by hope in the Lord that created us in His image.

Dal Shealy

---

lowship of Christian Athletes in 1989 as Executive Vice President before being named president.

Dal and his wife, Barbara, have three children (all involved in FCA) and make their home in Liberty, Missouri serving out of the FCA home office in Kansas City.

JOHN SILBER
President
Boston University

John Silber was born in San Antonio in 1926. He took his B.A. summa cum laude in philosophy at Trinity University and his Ph.D. at Yale. After teaching at Yale he returned to Texas, where he joined the department of philosophy at the University of Texas at Austin. After serving as chairman of his department he became dean of the College of Arts and Sciences. He was the first chairman of the Texas Society to Abolish Capital Punishment and a leader in the integration of the University of Texas. He was also instrumental in founding Operation Head Start.

In January, 1971, John Silber became the seventh president of Boston University. At Boston University President Silber has emphasized the attainment of financial stability and academic excellence. Under his leadership the University has balanced its budget every year since 1972, sponsored research has quintupled, its net worth has sextupled, and its endowment has increased tenfold. Going against a national trend of declining SAT scores, Boston University's increased steadily. Boston University's standards for appointment and tenure of faculty were, in Silber's words, raised to an easily understood standard: the highest.

President Silber's innovative program under which Boston University has contracted to operate the schools of Chelsea, Massachusetts, has attracted international attention.

Silber has written widely on philosophy (especially on Immanuel Kant, on whom he is a leading authority), education, and social and foreign policy. His work has appeared in the philosophical journals, the Atlantic, Harper's, New Republic, New York Times, Wall Street Journal *and elsewhere. His book* Straight Shooting *was published by Harpers in 1989. a German edition,* Ist Amerika zu retten?, *will be published this spring by Verlag Ullstein.*

In 1983, President Reagan appointed Silber to the national bipartisan

Be a Great Boy!

When I was growing up in San Antonio, Texas, there was a sign posted on the wall of the YMCA: "Don't wait to be a great man; be a great boy!" I think back to that sign as I try to put myself in the place and point of view of a young person today thinking about the future.

Being young is different for every person. I wish we were all born healthy and loved. We aren't. I wish we had all the time we need to fulfill our dreams and be with the people we love. We don't. I'm not the first one to tell you these things, and I think you know more about life and death than many grown-ups give you credit for.

Recently I watched a television program about a house in Portland, Oregon, where children who have lost relatives and friends—often violently—come and talk with each other about their loss. I was deeply moved and impressed by the maturity and courage with which these children faced devastating loss and helped each other to face it. Many of them could have taught adults how to deal with tragedy and grief.

This program was an example of television at its best. Television at its worst is another challenge imposed on young people today. I want to give you credit for trying to get your bearings amid the relentless flow of stimulation and false expectations that comes out of the television set. That is a challenge that children in my generation didn't have to face. Before television, we were forced to find ways to pass the time, ways that challenged our abilities to create rather than to consume. I think we were lucky in that.

When I think back to the injunction "Be a great boy!" I wish for you the kind of freedom that was provided to me as a child—not the freedom to do as I pleased or freedom from the consequences of my actions, but freedom from the cares and expectations of adulthood.

The protection my family gave me allowed me the freedom to develop my awareness of myself and the world. Now we seem less and less able to nurture the young in safety. But "Be a great boy!" remains an important message for me because it taught me that hard work and achievement shouldn't be put off to the future. They are possible right now. Not that easy rewards are there for the taking,

(Continued on page 312)

---

commission on Central America. President Silber has been decorated by the governments of France, Germany, and Israel.
John and Kathryn Silber are parents of seven children.

DEAN SMITH
Head Basketball Coach
University of North Carolina

The head basketball coach at the University of North Carolina is Dean Smith, a man who has accomplished almost everything imaginable in his sport.

Smith, who has completed 32 seasons as Carolina's head coach, has won 774 games in Chapel Hill and lost only 223. That's a winning percentage of .776, the best mark of any active coach and the fifth best in history.

Teams coached by Smith have won an NCAA Championship, a National Invitation Tournament title and an Olympic Gold Medal. The only other coaches ever to accomplish that have been Pete Newell and Bob Knight.

Carolina's second NCAA title under Smith came in 1993. The Tar Heels completed a 34-4 season with a 77-71 win over Michigan in the national championship game.

Smith's other NCAA crown came in 1982 with a 63-62 victory over Georgetown. His 1971 Carolina team won the NIT and he guided the United States to a sweep of the 1976 Summer Olympic Games in Montreal.

Smith, who played for Phog Allen at Kansas, is also one of only two men to play on an NCAA championship team and then coach one. Knight is the other.

In the last 27 years Smith's Tar Heel teams have been among the most dominant in the game. His teams have a record of 708-179 during that stretch, a percentage of .798 and an average record of 26-7.

Carolina has been to a national post-season tournament every season in that 27-year period. The Tar Heels have reached the NCAA Tournament's Final Four nine times in that stretch. Only UCLA has been there more often in that period. Smith has won 55 games in NCAA Tourna-

Success in Perspective

Each basketball season colleges from across the nation begin a quest to win the NCAA championship. Being the national champion means your team is number one. That's a worthwhile goal.

It's also a harbinger of failure because 63 entries in the 64-team tournament fall short. Some will lose early in the tournament, some will lose late. But, 63 of the 64 will eventually lose one game and not be declared champion. Are they a failure? Of course not.

To help our players understand that genuine success is not just climbing to the top and staying there, each year I have them read an article "How To Be A Failure." It was written by Dr. Ernest A. Fitzgerald, North Carolina Methodist bishop and a regular contributor to the old Piedmont Airline magazine, *Pace*.

As Dr. Fitzgerald sees it, and I agree, "Success is doing what you can, with what you have, where you are." I suggest you write that down and read it every day. It will help you keep things in perspective.

A contemporary of mine, former UCLA Coach John Wooden, expressed the same philosophy another way: "Things turn out best for those who make the best out of the way things turn out."

Failure can often be the beginning of success. Let me share a personal experience with you. After a loss at Wake Forest, one of our biggest rivals at the time, our team returned to campus to find some disgruntled fans had hung me in effigy. That might be considered first-class failure. In reality, it motivated the players and myself to do better.

In basketball, as in life, everyone will not and cannot make it to the top. Each of us has unfulfilled dreams, incompleted plans and unrealized hopes. For some this spells failure, while others see opportunities. Throughout this book you will read about people who turned failure into success. These are people who realized that adversity was a circumstance which enabled them to make their greatest leap forward.

The Special Olympians are great examples of Dr. Fitzgerald's beliefs. Who better than they do what they can, with what they have, where they are?

Dean S. Smith

---

ment play, more than any coach in history. His nine trips to the Final Four have been topped only by John Wooden's 12.

A native of Emporia, Kansas, Smith attended the University of Kansas on an academic scholarship. He played freshman football and varsity

(Continued on page 300)

RAY R. SODEN
Past Commander-in-Chief
Veterans of Foreign Wars

Ray Soden's dedication to serving the nation's veterans resulted from his service in the Navy during World War II. He served aboard the USS Claxon in the European and Pacific theatres. After surviving the North Africa, Okinawa, Leyte Gulf, Guadacanal and Iwo Jima invasions, he pledged himself to serving his fellow-man upon his return home. He holds European and Asiatic theatre ribbons with seven battle stars and shared in two Presidential Unit citations.

Following the war, he joined Illinois Bell Telephone Company which enabled him to become active in a variety of community service and philanthropic programs in which the company was involved. Concurrently he began a progressive personal program in the Veterans of Foreign Wars. From commander of his home Post 2149, in Bensenville, Illinois, he worked his way through the ranks to become Commander-in-Chief of the national organization in 1973.

During his tenure, he became a tireless champion of veterans' rights and has been working on their behalf ever since. His VFW activities include service on a score of committees. He served as chairman of the National Voice of Democracy Committee which today directs a program serving 700,000 young Americans.

Soden served as chairman of the Illinois Veterans Commission and was the first president of the National Combined Veterans Association. He received the Freedom Foundation's Americanism Award in 1961.

Upon retiring from Illinois Bell, he was elected a commissioner on the DuPage County Board and the Forest Preserve Commission. He is also former president of the DuPage County Forest Preserve District.

As a youngster, Soden gained fame as a singer on the National Barn Dance, a network radio program. He worked with future greats George Gobel, Homer and Jethro, Red Foley, Bob Atcher and the Williams

Treasure Freedom

Freedom did not come to America on a silver platter. Over 1,000,000 men and women have died to gain and preserve the freedoms we enjoy today. I don't know that I gave much thought to that as a youngster. So, I doubt that today's youth does either—except in a time of crisis like Operation Desert Storm.

The greatest freedom we enjoy is not freedom from want. It is the freedom to choose, to try, to compete, even the freedom to fail. But, most of all, we have the freedom to succeed and go as far as our initiative and talent will take us.

You are living in a fabulous age, in the greatest country in the world, filled with opportunities, where you can accomplish any carefully planned objective.

Each human being is unique; there will never be a carbon-copy of you. Discover what is unique about yourself. Then seek employment which will make best use of those talents uniquely your own. That's a sure road to success and happiness. Keep in mind that happiness comes not from having much to live on, but much to live for.

When you become a success, as you will if you make an all-out effort and sacrifices, don't forget to give something back. Practice good citizenship through service to your family, church, school, community and country.

Volunteerism has always played a role in American progress. Working together, helping one another and getting involved is the only way we can overcome the mounting human and social problems which beset our nation.

Make your life meaningful and productive. You're never too young, so start here and now! Make today the stepping stone to tomorrow. There is no challenge that you cannot meet—You Can Do It!

Jay R. Soden

Brothers, *a singing act which featured a youngster named Andy Williams.*

Soden resides in Wood Dale, Illinois, with his wife, Shirley. They have three grown children and six grandchildren.

LOUIS SPORTELLI, D.C.
Doctor of Chiropractic/Author

Louis Sportelli has served his profession in many capacities for more than 30 years. He finds that choosing the profession of chiropractic has provided him an opportunity to demonstrate that one person can make a difference.

The son of Italian immigrants, his early childhood did not provide him with many role models. After graduating from Easton High School, in Easton, Pennsylvania, with no focus on what he wanted to do for a career, he recalls being influenced by an "old time" practitioner who believed that everybody should become a chiropractor. Without realizing it at the time, Dr. Sportelli remembers it was the PASSION of that field practitioner which had the impact on his decision. How could anyone be that happy with what they are doing?

Entering a very controversial field, Dr. Sportelli quickly recognized that there were many areas of his newly found profession which needed to be advanced. He entered his state association, then became Chairman of the Board of the American Chiropractic Association, and now holds a position with the World Federation of Chiropractic.

Feeling that patient education was important early in his career he wrote a book titled Introduction to Chiropractic, *which is now in its 10th printing, published in three languages, and several million more have been utilized by patients throughout the world.*

He attributes his drive, ambition and determination to this good fortune in having many mentors during his career. "One mentor can change a life, and I've had many," says this chiropractic advocate. Dr. Sportelli continues to fight for health care reform and to advance the science and research in the areas of alternative health care.

Commitment Versus Interest

One of the most under-rated words today is the word *passion*. Without a burning desire to do whatever is necessary to achieve your goals, nothing will be accomplished. Opportunities come to each of us, in one form or another. Some seize the moment while others show an interest in opportunities.

The big difference is simply this: Commitment is making the time to do what is necessary—interest is doing what is necessary if you have the time. A vast difference is the end result.

Therefore, the *passion* of achievement is not only defining your goals, identifying the talents necessary to reach that goal, but also determining what you are willing to give up to achieve your goal. That willingness to give up something, such as free time, television, or other pleasures, must be replaced by the *passion* for achievement.

Too often, attitudes about work and achievement are reflected in this anonymous story:

> This is a story about four people named EVERYBODY, SOMEBODY, ANYBODY and NOBODY. There was an important job to be done and EVERYBODY was sure SOMEBODY would do it. ANYBODY could have done it, but NOBODY did it. SOMEBODY got angry about that, because it was EVERYBODY'S job. EVERYBODY thought ANYBODY could do it, BUT NOBODY realized EVERYBODY blamed SOMEBODY when NOBODY did what ANYBODY could have done.

Attitudes determine if situations are viewed as problems or opportunities. *Passion* is the vital difference between mediocrity and success. I encourage each of you to find that *passion*, pursue your dreams and remember to take a few moments for reflection—it's the window of the soul and the fuel which keeps the *passion* burning.

Louis Sportelli, D.C.

BART STARR
Football Great
Business Executive

Bart Starr was born in 1934 in Montgomery, Alabama, where he was to begin his athletic achievements.

Bart was an All American high school football player before becoming a four-letterman at the University of Alabama. He was named to the Dean's List for academic excellence in his junior and senior years, before graduating in 1956 with a B.S. degree in education.

Drafted by the Green Bay Packers, he played 17 years with the legendary National Football League team. He was the NFL's Most Valuable Player in 1966 and MVP in the 1967 and 1968 Super Bowls. NFL Man of the Year in 1969, he is a member of the Pro Football Hall of Fame and the Green Bay Packer Hall of Fame. The Columbus Touchdown Club named him Professional Player of the Decade in 1970.

After retiring as a player, Starr served as coach of the Green Bay team from 1974 to 1983. He also was a game analyst for CBS.

Recognized not only for his athletic achievements, he was the first recipient of the Byron White Award (NFL honor for citizenship and exemplary conduct as a professional athlete); named as one of the Jaycees' 10 Outstanding Young Men in America in 1968; member of the President's Council on Physical Fitness and President's Advisory Committee for Environmental Protection, just to name a few of his honors.

Besides his chairman duties with Starr Sanders Properties, he's a general partner in RAL Asset Management Group; and director of Sentry Insurance Company and Barry, Huey, Bullock & Cook.

Make the Effort

"For when the One Great Scorer comes to mark against your name. He writes—not that you won or lost—but how you played the game."

That maxim, written by the late, great sportswriter Grantland Rice, could be a blueprint for living. It is applicable not only to sports, but to business and every aspect of life as well.

Winning is not the most important statistic, but making the effort is. Therefore, whatever the task, at work or play, always seek to excel, but do so honestly and within the rules. In the real world, everyone seeks to gain a competitive edge. There's nothing wrong with that, as long as you do so with integrity.

There will be tough times along the way. All of us suffer failures of some kind. Vince Lombardi, whom I had the privilege of playing for with the Green Bay Packers, had this to say: "Failure isn't getting knocked down. Failure is not getting up after you've been knocked down."

The one common denominator in the lives of successful men and women is a superb attitude—they got up when they were knocked down!

Bart Starr

MARK STASIULIS D.D.S.
Speaker/Consultant

Dr. Mark Stasiulis is a dentist, business executive and professional speaker. A graduate of Illinois Benedictine College (B.S. Biology), he received his Doctorate of Dental Surgery from the Loyola School of Dentistry. A Chicago native, he established his private practice in suburban Bensenville, Illinois in 1981.

It was while helping a fellow dentist, whose practice was floundering, that he decided to undertake studies to become a practice management consultant.

Today he is Vice President of Summit Healthcare Management, which helps doctors set personal and professional goals enabling them to tap into the hidden potential in their practice.

A stimulating speaker, he has conducted seminars and given speeches to thousands of dental professionals and their staffs in the U.S. and Canada. He shares his practice building techniques, helps evaluate practice administration functions, aids with financial analysis, operation streamlining and long-range planning.

Dr. Mark is a regular visitor to schools in the Elmhurst (Ill.) Grade School System. He counsels elementary students about nutrition with one of his goals being to keep them out of the dentist's chair. Active in the Cub Scouts, he serves as Committee Chairman for the local troop.

He and his wife, Donna, have three children, Peter, Andrew and Cydney. His hobbies are reading and cooking. He's earned a reputation as a gourmet chef as a result of his culinary creativity.

Look Into the Mirror

"You can't be a success in business without being a success in life."

Look at your life as if it were a reflection in a mirror. First, view your physical appearance. Pay attention to your hair, teeth, hands, clothes, even your smile and posture. That's how other people see you. Remember, too, you can go no farther in life than your physical body will carry you. So, develop your body with care. Get enough sleep, eat right and get adequate exercise.

Take another look in the mirror. This time look beyond the reflection into your inner-self. Someone once said: "There are mirrors for the face but none for the mind. Let careful thought about yourself serve as a substitute."

Your inner-self is where you'll find your conscience and where your ethics, morals and values are developed. These qualities rule the decisions and judgements you'll make in everyday living. They are the building blocks of your character and the measure by which others will judge you.

Conscience is the small voice that tells us which precepts are right and which course to follow. A clear conscience will give you two of your most precious possessions—confidence and peace of mind.

The great English writer Aldous Huxley pointed out: "There's only one corner of the Universe you can be certain of improving; that's your own self." Cultivating our inner-self should be a key priority in life for each of us—it is essential to any success we might achieve.

We are untrue to ourselves and others if we pretend to be something we are not. If change is required, then change is what we should do—inside and out—for our best side should be our only side.

The path to success begins with a trip to the mirror. You must like what you see. If not, change it, because if you believe in the person you see, others will, too!

JERRE STEAD
President
AT&T Business Communications
Systems

In August 1991, Jerre (pronounced like Jerry) Stead was named president of Business Communications Systems at AT&T, Bridgewater, New Jersey. He accepted the post because he wanted the challenge of turning around a troubled business of one of the world's premier companies.

It was a challenge to make a difference that had brought him to Square D Company in Palatine, Illinois, in 1987. He was appointed president and chief operating officer just a week short of his 44th birthday. Stead went on to become chairman, president, and chief executive officer as he directed the company to world leadership in industrial control and electrical distribution products, achieving record sales and earnings.

Stead graduated from the University of Iowa with a BA in business administration in 1965. He participated in the Harvard University Advanced Management Program in Switzerland in 1982. Prior to joining Square D, he had 21 years of management experience in international and domestic marketing, sales, production, finance, and general management with Honeywell, Inc.

Jerre was born and reared in the small town of Maquoketa (population 6,500) in Northeastern Iowa, where his parents still live. He was an outstanding athlete, captaining the football, baseball and basketball teams at Maquoketa High School. He was also elected president of the Student Council and of his senior class. Stead was brought up in a Christian heritage with a strong positive, upbeat influence from his father, Victor (an independent insurance agent), his mother, Anna, and his grandparents.

Jerre is a member of the boards of directors of Square D Company, Ameritech, USG Corporation, and Eljer Industries. He is a member of the board of visitors of the University of Iowa, the board of trustees of Coe College, and the advisory board of the Kellogg Graduate School of Management of Northwestern University.

People Power

All my life, from my youngest days, thanks to my parents and grand-parents, I've believed in "You Can Do It"—that you have the power to make the decisions to do what needs to be done to reach your life goals and objectives—that you can do whatever you set out to do if you have the right positive mental attitude.

That was basically the philosophy of Don Scholfeldt, our high school basketball coach. Don had only one arm (he lost his lower left arm in an accident while a freshman in high school) yet he always said, "No matter how far down you are, you can do it!"

In business, "You Can Do It" translates into "People Power"—the power of our people to make decisions, to take educated risks, even to make mistakes in pursuit of ways to do a job better and more effi-ciently.

Take educated risks? Make mistakes? Yes, indeed. I've always be-lieved that the best work culture rewards risk taking. It's a culture in which people have the right to be wrong and it's okay to make a mis-take. But when you make a mistake, make sure you can identify it to someone else, talk to them about it, and put the appropriate resources into correcting it. Secondly, learn from your experience and don't make the same mistake again.

I believe in rewarding and recognizing people who meet or exceed their own increasingly stringent job requirements—and our work envi-ronment is designed for people to have fun striving for new levels of excellence.

This same self-managing "people power" ability applies to achieving personal life objectives. Set forth what you want to accomplish. Don't be afraid to set goals that appear unreachable, that even may appear risky. Determine the best ways to reach your goals. Follow through on every detail that needs to be done. Keep moving forward. Always think positively.

You'll find that no matter what you want to accomplish, with good planning and the right positive mental attitude and determination, You CAN do it —You CAN make it happen!

JUDITH M. SWEET
President
National Collegiate Athletic
Association

Judy Sweet was elected president of the NCAA in January, 1991. She was secretary-treasurer from 1989 to 1991, becoming the first woman to serve in each of these positions.

Judy has been director of athletics at the University of California, San Diego, since 1975, when she became one of the first women in the nation selected to direct a combined men's and women's intercollegiate athletics program. The UCSD athletics program involves 23 varsity teams, with an even distribution of men's and women's teams. Prior to her faculty appointment at UCSD in 1973, she taught at the University of Arizona, Tucson, and Tulane University.

A native of Milwaukee, Judy is a graduate of the University of Wisconsin, Madison, where she majored in physical education and mathematics. She earned a master's of science degree from the University of Arizona, Tucson, and a master's of business administraton degree from National University, San Diego.

Judy's presidential duties for the NCAA include presiding over the NCAA administrative committee, council, and executive committee, as well as the NCAA Convention. She also serves on numerous other committees.

She has served on various local, state, and national committees including the board of trustees of the United States Sports Academy, the board of directors of the Council of Collegiate Women Athletic Administrators, and the board of directors of the National Association of College Directors of Athletics.

In 1984, Judy was selected as an Outstanding Young Woman of America and, in 1990, the Los Angeles Times selected her as the Top College Sports Executive of the '80s.

Academics and Athletics

Education is both the primary challenge and the primary opportunity facing American youth today. It is essential that students learn to read and write in the early grades. The computer age has greatly accelerated the learning time-frame and the need for early development of basic learning skills. Colleges and universities are institutions of higher learning, yet in many cases these schools have had to provide remedial reading and math programs for a number of incoming students. It has been reported that some college athletes have earned a college degree without the ability to even read what appears on their diploma.

One of my responsibilities as president of the NCAA is to help enforce the rules governing collegiate athletics. As a teacher and administrator at a major university, I must also abide by those rules. I have a sincere appreciation of how important it is to play by the rules. Part of playing by the rules means that an athlete must perform well academically. A "student-athlete" must be a student first and foremost. Student-athletes must put the same energy into being successful in the classroom as goes into pumping iron, shooting baskets, or spiking a volleyball.

As a teacher and athletics administrator, it is my obligation to see that our athletes are held as accountable in the classroom as every other student on campus. Some of the lessons learned on the playing field need to be brought into the classroom also. Discipline, the desire to learn, an aggressive pursuit of classroom studies, the commitment to do one's best, and the realization of the value of proper academic training are most important to a successful future.

Academics and athletics provide excellent preparation for the future. Achievements in athletics may be important in your career plans, but academic tools are essential to a productive career. Very few athletes have the opportunity to become college and/or professional athletes, and even those who do need to be well skilled in other areas in anticipation of when their playing days have ended. It is not enough to just be a successful athlete. The best combination is a healthy mind and a healthy body.

I urge you to maximize your educational opportunities. Academics are the tools for life.

Judith M. Sweet

RICK TELANDER
Senior Writer
Sports Illustrated

Rick Telander was born and raised in Peoria, Illinois, where he spent his time playing sports, reading books, running in the woods and cornfields around his home, all the while trying to figure out what he was going to do with his life. In a manner of speaking, Telander, now 42 and a senior writer for Sports Illustrated, who lives in Chicago with his wife and four children, is still trying to answer that question.

He was an All Big 10 football player at Northwestern and a two-time Academic All Big 10 selection, but, his concern over the meaning and integrity of the college game led him to write a book called The Hundred Yard Lie, *revealing the corruption he saw spreading from high level entertainment-driven collegiate sport to the educational system itself. The book, published in 1990, won him few friends among college football coaches, athletic directors, and some college presidents, but it thrust Telander into the limelight as a crusader for fairness and integrity in the ivy towers as well as on the gridiron.*

Telander has written two other books, one of which, Heaven is a Playground, *about inner-city kids playing basketball, was recently made into a feature movie. He has taught English and journalism at Northwestern University. In 1987, he was awarded the Arch Ward-Warren Brown Award for Excellence in Sports Journalism by the Notre Dame Club of Chicago.*

His love of play, generally, and his ability to continue playing at the things he loved as a kid—and write about those things to make his living—has led him to believe it is possible to never quite grow up. It also has made him aware that the things a child intuitively knows often far outstrip the knowledge of experts and adults.

Hang in There

Giving someone advice on how to be successful always has the ring of fraud to it, if you ask me. There is smugness rooted in the message, whether the giver means it or not. Hey kid, the advice-giver is saying, I'm the big shot and you're not; that's why I'm up here polishing my apple and you're down there looking for an errant seed or stem.

Okay, that's a cynical way of looking at the passing on of knowledge, but I think you all know what I mean.

I'll never forget a coach I had during my ever-so-brief career with the Kansas City Chiefs. "Men," he told us players, "you've got to be winners in everything you do. I surround myself with winners. All the people I associate with are winners. Whether it's a doctor or a businessman, he's successful. He's made it to the top. I don't want anyone but winners around me."

I thought of my own friends, mostly guys like me, just out of college. What a crew. None of them had any power or money. A lot of them didn't know what they wanted to be. Waiters, cab-drivers, one guy who volunteered for psych experiments to pick up extra cash, one guy who sold firewood. Jeez, I was surrounded by losers. I felt terrible. I'd never be a winner like the coach.

Then a few weeks later, long after I'd been released from the NFL, the coach himself was fired. The winner had lost. I didn't feel good about that, but I did come to a realization: winning is a relative thing.

Nobody wins all the time. Indeed, nobody SHOULD win all the time. That's not the way life works. A lot of apparent success is simply the result of good fortune, whimsy, or good timing. A lot of successful people are in positions of power because they're just older then the people under them. In time, the younger people will replace them. My vagabond friends are now getting into positions of power, because, well, because they've hung in there.

And that might be the truest lesson any successful person can give someone eager for direction. Hang in there. You must try hard, and it's nice—sometimes essential—that you have talent. But if you don't hang in there, you'll never be in position to capitalize on such things as whimsy, timing, or the inexorable march of time when they affect your own life.

You also have to be realistic. For me to hang in there at football would have been pretty dumb. A cornerback with a 4.6 40 time is like a birdwatcher with bad eyes. You're just setting yourself up for trouble.

So try a lot of things. Don't be terrified of quitting when you know you're in too deep. But never let quitting be the easy way out. It should always hurt—quitting. Still, quitting under the right condition can be the smartest thing a person can do.

(Continued on page 312)

WILLIAM G. THEBUS
President
Logan House, Ltd.

Bill Thebus and his late associate, John Hurst, founded Logan House to work together in the fields of literacy, language, and basic employability skills. Each had spent nearly 30 years as an educator and trainer in those areas. They chose to pool their resources for the benefit of the American work force, many members of which now find themselves unable to compete in an increasingly technological society.

Thebus began his career as a writer, editor, and journalist in San Antonio, Texas. He joined the Navy to see the world, but never was assigned outside of the Pentagon in Washington. After his military service he became an English language teacher and worked in Syria, Turkey, Thailand, and Iran over a period of 15 years, and finally satisfied his desire for international travel and intercultural experiences.

His language teaching career expanded into other areas of education and training, and he spent more than ten years as a designer and developer of language, basic skills, and technical training programs, both in the U.S. and abroad. This work has taken him throughout the U.S., Europe, the Middle East, and Southeast Asia, to countries as diverse as Saudi Arabia, the United Arab Emirates, Egypt, Indonesia, Brunei, Taiwan, and the Peoples' Republic of China.

Thebus now continues the operation of Logan House, specializing in promoting literacy training for American workers, developing basic level technical training curricula, and advising on the readability and usability of such material.

He was educated at St. Mary's University in San Antonio and the University of Southern California. He holds a B.A. degree in English and an M.S. in education.

"I Have Made It!"

I know that "you can do it." I know because for many years my partner, John Hurst, and I worked with people who did it—people who moved from "hopeless" to "successful." These were people who, for a variety of reasons, were unemployable in our society. No job meant no money. No money meant no future. They appeared to be headed for hopeless lives.

We've seen many such people reach "success." You won't read about them, or see them on TV. They're not rich and famous. Then how are they successful? One definition of success is "the gaining of wealth, fame, rank, etc." But, another is "a favorable or satisfactory outcome or result." That's what these people achieved. They set a modest goal, and they reached it.

Like some breakfast cereals, success comes in bite-size portions. John and I could tell you of many people who bit off only a very small piece of success—but enough to change their lives. A favorite example is a story that John told me many times, the story of Cleveland Davis.

As a young man, Davis had a job as a stock clerk in a warehouse. He also had a problem—he couldn't read. He got by, though. Using memory and other tricks, he hid his problem. Then his company got bigger, and the number of parts he had to memorize grew too large. His mental computer finally crashed. His illiteracy was exposed and he was fired.

He couldn't find another job. He had a wife, a baby, and a hopeless looking future. But life offered him one small chance. He joined a program to teach employability skills.

Davis worked at it. John was proud to say that he was there to help Davis when he needed it. John found him in class one day with his infant child on his lap, almost hidden beneath the desk. "Kind of young for a trainee, Cleveland," John said. Davis scowled, and said: "I couldn't get anybody to stay with her." Then he added, "And I *had* to come to class."

Davis' vision of success was to be an auto mechanic. He didn't aspire to wealth or fame. He had a modest goal, and he took advantage of an opportunity that, with his own hard work, got him to that goal.

John's last contact with Davis was an audio tape, sent by Davis as a Christmas greeting. John played the tape for me several times. On the tape, Davis told about his success. He was able to read, was employed, and looked forward to a better future. He prefaced his story

(Continued on page 313)

R. DAVID THOMAS
Senior Chairman/Founder
Wendy's International, Inc.

R. David Thomas was born on July 2, 1932, in Atlantic City, New Jersey. Adopted at six weeks, he never knew his birth parents. His adoptive mother died when he was five. His early years included moving from state to state as his adoptive father sought work.

As they traveled, Thomas was fascinated with the restaurant business. When he was 12, he lied about his age and landed a job at the lunch counter at Regas Restaurant in Knoxville, Tennessee.

At 15, in Fort Wayne, Indiana, he made the decision to remain in town with his restaurant job rather than continue traveling with his family. Later while in the Army and trained in the cook and baker school, Thomas became one of the youngest soldiers ever to manage an enlisted men's club.

It was back in Fort Wayne, in 1954, he met and began to work with a Kentucky entrepreneur named Harlan Sanders. In 1962, Thomas took over four failing Kentucky Fried Chicken carryouts in Columbus, made them successful and built four more outlets. The deal he had made in making the franchise profitable and the cash sale of the restaurants back to KFC in 1968 made him a millionaire at age 35.

But Thomas was always drawn back to one of his favorite foods—hamburgers. Using fresh beef and making hamburgers to order, he opened the first Wendy's Old Fashioned Hamburger Restaurant in November, 1969, in Columbus.

Wendy's and its franchisees operate about 3,800 restaurants throughout the U.S. and in 23 countries worldwide, providing employment for 130,000 people.

Citing his commitment to "return something to the communities" which make Wendy's prosper, Thomas favorite charities include St. Jude

(Continued on page 300)

Opportunity Doesn't Knock

There's an old saying that opportunity only knocks once.

That's not true. Opportunities don't knock at all. They don't have to, they're already all around us. It's up to us to see where they are and take advantage of them.

A lot of times when the news media interview me, they want to know about my early years. Things like the fact I had my first job when I was 12, and was pretty much on my own when I was 15. Some writers have even called my life a rags-to-riches story. It never seemed that way to me.

It's true I didn't have a lot of material things when growing up, but I was fortunate to realize there were opportunities all around me. It created a drive in me, but it wasn't just to make money. There also was the pride of accomplishment, of doing the best I could even on the smallest jobs.

This is a wonderful country filled with opportunities, but you have to be ready to take advantage of them. You have to work and learn all the time.

Effort brings success. Whatever career you choose, your best efforts to gain knowledge and experience will give you an advantage that others will lack. The simple truth is success is earned.

Doing a job right—no matter what it is, no matter how small it seems—is education that isn't going to be forgotten.

There always will be leaders and followers, but leaders don't start at the top, they learn and work their way there. They see opportunities, do their jobs, and are rewarded with promotions.

That's important to remember: Leadership is learned. It begins by doing small jobs well, so that the individual is ready for the next step— to learn a new job, to take on more responsibilities, to be promoted, and to grow as a person.

When I started Wendy's, I saw the opportunity of having a few restaurants. When they were built, we saw other possibilities, and the company grew, and still more opportunities opened up.

None of them knocked, but they were all around us.

Look, and you'll see them, too.

Dave Thomas

BRIAN TRACY
President
Brian Tracy Learning Systems

Brian Tracy is one of America's foremost authorities on the development of human potential. He is the author/narrator of many best-selling audio and video programs on success, sales, business, and personal achievement. His programs have been translated into 14 languages, and are used in 26 countries. He speaks to thousands of people each year throughout the U.S. and other countries.

Brian has an M.A. and C.P.A.E. and is president of Brian Tracy Learning Systems, Inc., a human resource company based in San Diego, California. As a consultant, he has trained key executives of more than 1,000 corporations in the U.S., Canada, Mexico, the Far East, Australia, and Europe.

Role Models Help

Its been said that great men and women spend their formative years studying the lives and stories of great men and women who have gone before them. Many of today's most successful people have patterned their lives after just one famous person, Napoleon or Churchill, Schweitzer or Mother Teresa.

Great men and women then spend their working years striving to emulate the characteristics and qualities of those they admire. We all have a tendency to identify with and emulate people we read about, our heroes and heroines from history or literature. The more we immerse ourselves in their lives, the more we internalize and demonstrate the qualities that made them great!

A famous book, a runaway best seller many years ago, told of a town in which everyone agreed to ask the simple question, "What would Jesus do?", prior to every decision. The story told how dramatically the lives of every person in town improved as the example of Jesus became the guiding principle for each person.

I worked with Dr. Albert Schweitzer in Lambarene, Africa, before his death, and quite honestly, I've never been the same person. From that day to this, I still strive to practice his "reverence for life" and his gentle practical approach to living the spiritual life. Many people have had similar experiences as a result of being exposed to Mother Teresa, or to some other positive and uplifting person.

Finally, great men and women spend their later years helping and guiding others up the rungs of the ladder of life, and helping them ascertain that the ladder is leaning against the right building.

The wonderful help that comes from studying biographies and autobiographies is the realization we have that it is mostly ordinary people who do extraordinary things. And what they have done, we can also aspire to.

You can do it! Choose great role models and pattern your life after them. Decide right now to become a great man or woman, a person of courage and character and deep, abiding faith. Select your heroes and heroines with care and commit yourself to being as admirable as they were, or are.

Remember, you were born for personal greatness, and anything anyone else has done, you can do too, if you really want to, long enough and hard enough. You CAN do it!

JIM TUNNEY
President
Jim Tunney Associates

Jim Tunney is a recognized professional speaker and corporate consultant, specializing in leadership, team building and peak performance. He has received the National Speaker's Association's highest award, the CPAE (Council of Peers Award of Excellence).

Tunney gained national recognition during his 31 years as an official for the National Football League. Regarded by many as the "Dean of Referees," Tunney distinguished himself by officiating three Super Bowl games and ten Championship games, along with many divisional and Pro Bowl games.

As an educator, Tunney served 27 years as a teacher, coach, high school principal and superintendent of schools in southern California. During this time, he earned his doctorate in education from the University of Southern California. His undergraduate degree is from Occidental College.

Tunney devotes time to a number of community and professional organizations, serving on the boards of the California State Special Olympics, the Los Angeles Boys and Girls Club, and the National Football Foundation and Hall of Fame.

Tunney has appeared on numerous network and cable television and radio shows, including "CBS This Morning," "Sports Talk" with Roy Firestone, and "The Larry King Show." He is a member of the Screen Actors Guild and AFTRA.

His book Impartial Judgement *(Franklin Watts, 1988) expands on the ways that athletic discipline is beneficial in everyday life: Goal-setting, commitment, and preparation to develop the winner in you.*

Making the Cuts

Yes, you can do it, but what is "it?"

Without a goal, confidence, energy, and the willingness to strive won't get "it" done. You have no route, no destination.

General uncertainty gets the blame for much of this type of indecision. Chaos is a hot new buzzword, but making uncertainty trendy and using it as an easy cop-out doesn't speed you toward accomplishment. It makes no sense to wait for all the quandaries to get solved, or, for uncertainty to disappear from daily life.

So, what is "it?" Recently a poll gave us the news, startling to some, that more than 60% of the undergraduates at a major university said they "didn't know themselves" well enough to decide what they wanted to do after graduation.

I wasn't surprised. Twenty-seven years in public education taught me something about the difficulties encountered in acquiring self-understanding. These undergraduates join psychologists, humanists and virtually everyone in search for a sure path to self-understanding. Still, we've learned more about what doesn't work than what does. There is no set formula. Gaining self-understanding is an individual progression, developed ultimately by one person seeking an authentic, distinct identity.

The idea of being a "winner" persists on everyone's mind, even if you haven't named "it" yet. To help, consider the word W-I-N. It contains a clue on how to make the necessary distinctions—What's Important Now?

The process of lining up your options, putting the most important at the top, the less important at the bottom, appears to be an intimidating task for the undergraduates who were polled just as it is for many.

Here's where being a good coach to yourself comes in. Not everyone who shows up to play makes the team. You have to make the cuts. You have to be straight with yourself. You have to declare what's important to you.

When you learn to cull the options (which requires naming what's important to you), commitment and focus result. Your confidence, energy, and willingness to strive then have a destination.

Once "it" is known, the goal is set. The next step is reassuringly inevitable: Do it yourself, and do it now.

Jim Turner

#32

R.J. VENTRES
Former Chairman & CEO
Borden, Inc.

R.J. Ventres was the first of his Italian immigrant parents' six children to be born in the United States, and the first to attend college. His father was a blue collar worker who often worked two jobs to make ends meet.

Ventres grew up in Worcester, Massachusetts, and worked his way through Worcester Polytechnic Institute, earning a bachelor's degree in chemical engineering in 1948. He served in the Navy in World War II.

After graduation, he became an oil-industry engineer for Atlantic Refining (now ARCO), then spent two years in the Middle East training Iraqis to operate oil refineries. He joined Borden in 1957 as assistant chief engineer at the company's PVC operation in Leominster, Massachusetts.

He rose steadily through management ranks, becoming a vice president of the Borden chemical division in 1968, and group vice president four years later. He became president of the chemical division and an executive vice president in 1983.

In 1985, Ventres was elected Borden's president and chief operating officer, and a director of the company. He became chief executive officer in 1986, and chairman in 1987.

Ventres led a transformation of the 134-year-old company, moving Borden out of commodity chemicals and focusing it on six business areas, and used selective acquisitions to grow these businesses rapidly.

Ventres is a director of Banc One Corporation, Marsh & McLennan Companies, Inc., Schering-Plough Corporation, and a trustee of St. Clare's Hospital and Health Center, New York.

Success Is Open to Anyone

The most important life lesson I can share with others is this: *Success is open to anyone—if you really want it, you can have it.*

Success and achievement are two different things.

Achievement depends on more than your own individual talents and preparedness. It also depends heavily on timing and opportunity.

For opportunity we have to rely on *others* to give us a chance to work on even bigger canvases in our chosen fields.

Throughout my life, the Lord has taken care of the timing—and other people have been generous in giving me the opportunities.

Success on the other hand is entirely under your own control.

Successful people have a purpose in life and hunger to live a meaningful life.

Successful people are able to distinguish the difference between what they have and what they are.

I've met successful people at every level of achievement, from the humblest occupations to positions of power and importance.

Their success was the product of how they lived: doing the very best with what life presented them, working hard, always learning, never losing faith or integrity.

Each successful person glowed with the courage, confidence and inner peace that follow when you do your best with what you're given.

A wise man said: "Some men and women make the world better *just by being the kind of people they are.*"

To me, *that's* success—the *only* success that really counts. It is open to everyone of us.

REGGIE WHITE
Green Bay Packers/Minister

Reggie White, defensive end for the Green Bay Packers, was the most sought-after player to become available when free agency came to the National Football League in 1993. Upon signing White, Green Bay Coach Mike Holmgren said the Tennessean "may be the finest player to ever play his position."

White enjoyed such a legendary career at the University of Tennessee that, during the school's centennial football season in 1991, he was named to the Volunteers' all-time team. Nicknamed "Minister of Defense," he was a consensus All-American and Southeastern Conference Player of the Year as a senior.

With the Philadelphia Eagles, White was the cornerstone of one of the finest defensive units to ever play in the NFL. A seven-time Pro Bowl selection, he is the only defensive lineman in NFL history to have more sacks (124) than games played (121).

During the 1991-92 seasons, White, an ordained Baptist minister, spent after-practice Friday afternoons on Philadelphia street corners trying to educate area youngsters about the perils of drugs and alcohol, as well as the importance of staying in school.

In 1991, he and his wife established the Reggie and Sara White Maternity Home (a second home on their property in Knoxville, Tennessee) for the purpose of aiding unwed mothers. Making a strong financial commitment to the home, the Whites have funded $600,000 of the operating costs to date.

Known as well for his work in the community as for his football skills, in 1992, he was the recipient of the prestigious Byron "Whizzer" White Humanitarian Award in honor of his "service to team, community, and country in the spirit of Supreme Court Justice Byron White.

Reggie White's Testimony

Let me tell you about the real Reggie White, the one under the pads and helmet. I was playing in a controlled scrimmage against the Detroit Lions one hot, muggy summer day. I had outmaneuvered a frustrated Detroit rookie for most of the day from my left defensive end position. Then our helmets accidentally locked together on a play.

This guy used foul language that I would not let my dog hear. I can take losing a game, but I cannot tolerate being cussed out to my face. I looked him right in the eye and announced, "Jesus is coming back soon, and I hope you're ready." But he just tossed more choice words into my face and returned to his huddle. I was angry. My teammates were urging me back to our defensive huddle. Instead, I eyeballed this rookie and shouted to my teammates, "Jesus is coming back soon, and I hope he's ready."

The next play, I lined up in front of him and said, "Jesus is coming back soon, and I *don't think you're ready.*" The ball snapped, and I announced, "Here comes Jesus!" as I thrust my 6' 6", two-hundred-eighty-five-pound body right into his chest and drove him back about five yards. He plopped to the turf just in time to see me sack his quarterback. My teammates and coach often asked me after that if Jesus was coming back on the next play!

I'm still not sure why I said what I did on that steamy day in Detroit. Maybe it was the heat. Maybe it was his language. Maybe it was just that I desire to live my life glorifying Jesus Christ.

Talking about my relationship with Jesus Christ is as natural as breathing to me. I say *relationship* because it's a day-to-day, night-by-night, ongoing communication between Jesus and me. The wonderful thing about this relationship with Jesus is that you can have it too! How? Let me explain. A coach usually prepares a game plan ahead of time. God also designed a plan for our lives before the world began. He created us to love Him, glorify Him, and enjoy Him forever. But why don't we?

We are sinful, and our sin separates us from God. What is sin? Sin means missing the mark, falling short of God's standard. We all are sinners not only when we do wrong, but also in our human nature. And worst of all, the penalty for our sin is death. We face God's judgement because of our sin. But God loved us so much that He sent His Son Jesus Christ as the holy and perfect substitute to die in our place. Three days after Jesus died for us, He rose from the dead to defeat death.

But knowing a lot about a sport and "talking the game" doesn't make you a member of a team. The same is true about becoming a Christian. It takes more than knowing about Jesus; it requires faith in Him.

(Continued on page 313)

HAROLD R. WILDE
President
North Central College

At age 29, Hal Wilde was the youngest state insurance commissioner in the country, achieving national recognition in dealing with challenges such as the "medical malpractice insurance crisis" and "insurance redlining." But, four years later, when his term of office ended, Wilde decided he wanted to be a college president. In 1991, he got his wish, becoming only the ninth president in North Central College's 130-year history.

Harold R. Wilde, Jr., was born in 1945 in Milwaukee, Wisconsin. Valedictorian of his high school class in nearby Wauwatosa, he also graduated with high honors from Amherst College in 1967. He received his doctorate in government from Harvard University in 1973.

His academic path was less conventional than it might appear. Along the way, he quit school and spent time in a variety of jobs (lemon picker, field hand, construction and factory worker) across the country; worked six months on a presidential campaign and three months on a civil rights project. He wrote his undergraduate thesis on the Reverend Martin Luther King, Jr., and his doctoral dissertation on the Detroit Police Department.

Following his term as Wisconsin's Insurance Commissioner, Wilde became an aide to the President of the University of Wisconsin System. In 1981, he was named Vice President of Beloit College, Wisconsin's oldest private college before he assumed the presidency at North Central. In his first years at the distinguished comprehensive liberal arts college of 2,500 students in Naperville, Illinois, he has increased the endowment by 150 percent and inaugurated a strategic plan to take the school into the 21st Century.

The father of three children, two in college and one in high school, Wilde has been married for 24 years to Benna Brecher Wilde.

There's So Much to Learn

Every year at North Central's commencement I tell this story. When I was in junior high, our family had a neighbor, a gentleman in his late seventies. Every day he left first thing in the morning and went to the library. He came back eight or ten hours later ... smiling. Every day.

I couldn't understand it. With the attention span of about 15 minutes, all I had on my mind were the Green Bay Packers and the Milwaukee Braves. Why, I wondered, would a retired person read and study all day with no job to point to? And why was he always so happy?

One day I asked him. He smiled and said: "There's so much to learn." And then he repeated those words: "There's so much to learn." It would be many years before I understood what he meant ... and why he was so happy.

What distinguishes human beings from all other species is our capacity to learn. It is a gift from God. Learning is not something that stops when we graduate from school or retire from our jobs.

A great college education is one that teaches us both to learn and how much we still have to learn. When we stop learning, we stop living.

My friend had it right. There's so much to learn. And it is one of the great joys of life.

Harold R. Wild

ROGER WILLIAMS
Entertainer

A child prodigy from Des Moines, Iowa, Roger Williams played 13 different instruments by the time he was eight years old. He was his church's organist at age 12.

His schooling was interrupted when he left Drake University to join the U.S. Navy. Despite his accomplishments in the field of music, to this day Williams claims his proudest achievement was being voted "Man of Warsmen" by the men of his entire company at the end of military training. His hitch included being a boxing champ, imperiling the hands which have since made him a piano virtuoso and an electrifying performer. Billboard calls him the largest selling pop pianist in history.

At his home in Encino, California, in addition to 18 gold albums and presidential mementos, the walls are lined with keys to cities, citations for humanitarian acts, honorary doctorates, and memories of a career that began when he was three years old. At that age, he literally walked up to the piano and started to play!

Called the "pianist of the presidents," Williams has played for Truman, Eisenhower, Kennedy, Johnson, Nixon, Ford, and Reagan. Shortly after Kennedy's death, they found Roger's recording of "Yellow Bird" on the turntable of JFK's portable record player. It was the last music the president ever heard.

Today, still touring the globe nine months a year, he may be on his way to Japan, to a concert date in Hollywood, a symphony performance in New York, or headlining in Las Vegas. Annually he kicks off the summer season at Disney World's EPCOT Center as pianist-conductor of the All-American College Orchestra, a Disney talent search for the brightest young musicians in America.

His hobby is mountain climbing! Just show him a high hill or rugged terrain and he's off to see if he can get up—or down, as the case may be.

How to Be a Winner

Winners do things that losers don't like to do. Read that sentence again because it is sage advice.

Like most young people, I found things that I did not like to do—and still don't particularly enjoy doing to this day—but I do them. The five things I've made myself do have each contributed to my success.

First, I hated to practice. Practicing exercises on the piano for hours is a tedious, tiresome task. But it pays off. Whenever I get a standing ovation I remember those practice sessions. By the way, I still practice up to eight hours a day. Practice may not make perfect, but it comes as close as we'll ever get.

To be mentally alert you must be physically fit. Exercise is essential to maintaining good health. I still jog three miles a day, five days a week. I hate every step of it—except the last one! I've traveled as much as 30,000 miles in one month, and been on stage 24 out of 30 days. That's when my exercise regimen proves its worth.

Vegetables have always been distasteful to me. But, I realize that a balanced diet, including vegetables, is necessary for me with my grueling schedule. So, each morning I toss a mixture of produce into my blender, hold my nose, and down my vegetable cocktail—then I don't worry about salads for the rest of the day.

Worrying and agonizing over decisions is something most people don't like to do. It's tough to sit and hope you get an idea. I remember my first recording. I was asked to come up with a special arrangement and given just three days to do it. I sat up two nights searching for the right sound. I was ready on the third day and recorded Autumn Leaves, my first recording which became a big hit. When you've got something important to consider, give yourself some quiet time. It will prove worthwhile.

Cooperation was not always one of my strong suits. In fact, there was a time when I was a loner. I liked to conceive an idea, then carry it out from start to finish, taking all the credit or blame as the case might be. I've since learned the importance of listening to and working with others. I have the privilege of conducting some of the

(Continued on page 313)

His wife, Louise, is his inspiration and, coupled with his music, his fountain of youth, which he says "may keep me young forever."

BOB WOOLF
Former President
Bob Woolf Associates
(In memorium 1928-1993)

Ever since former Red Sox pitcher Earl Wilson chose Bob Woolf to represent him in 1964, more than 500 other athletes have followed suit, thus establishing Woolf as both the first and the top sports attorney in the country.

He has been nationally and internationally recognized for negotiating over 2,000 contracts in the fields of sports and entertainment in a manner respected by players, owners, and fans. Author of two widely acclaimed books about his experiences, Behind Closed Doors *and* Friendly Persuasion. *Woolf has been lauded by the media for his expertise and philosophy of fair play, as well as his reputation for honesty and integrity.*

Carl Yastrzemski, Joe Montana, Doug Flutie, Larry Bird, Al and Florence Joyner are just a few of the sports figures he has represented, while entertainment clients have included Larry King, Gene Shalit, and New Kids on the Block.

A native of Maine, Woolf attended Boston College on an athletic scholarship prior to receiving his LL.B Degree from the Boston University School of Law, where he was president of the senior class. He established a successful criminal law practice in Boston prior to pioneering the field of sports law that is now being taught at law schools throughout the United States.

Woolf has been selected as one of the 100 Most Powerful People in Sports. Massachusetts Governor Michael A. Dukakis proclaimed December 28, 1990, Bob Woolf Day in State House ceremonies.

Widely recognized in his field, Woolf has appeared frequently on the To-day Show, Johnny Carson's Tonight Show, Good Morning America, Lifestyles of the Rich and Famous, CBS' Sports Illustrated, and has been interviewed in a wide variety of newspapers and periodicals, including Time, People, *and* Fortune.

World's Most Important Rule

You can do it, and do it well, whatever you set out to do, by trying harder and by following a simple philosophy of friendly persuasion.

One of the oldest and most revered guidelines to treating people fairly is the Golden Rule. Philosophers of all persuasions have preached it over the millennium. Zoroaster taught it to his followers in Persia 2,500 years ago. Confuscius preached it in China 24 centuries ago. Lao-Tzu, the founder of Taoism, taught it to his disciples in the Valley of the Han. Buddha preached on the banks of the Holy Ganges 500 years before Christ. Jesus taught it in Judea 19 centuries ago. He summed it up in one thought—probably the most important rule in the world—"Do unto others as you would have others do unto you."

In reviewing my experiences over the years, I've followed a three-part philosophy for dealing with people from all walks of life. It's been a constant through every one of my negotiations, professionally and personally:

Number one: You don't have to be disagreeable to disagree.

Number two: The Golden Rule, which is timeless.

Number three: Be true to your convictions.

Stick to what you believe in: your convictions, values and standards. For your own self-esteem and for the respect you hope to earn from others, you can't change your beliefs to fit each new situation and fashion.

Following this philosophy makes things easier and produces successful results. Taken together, the philosophy adds up to a method of treating people with fairness and respect.

You CAN do unto others as you would have others do unto you.

Bob Woolf

A Dedication

Indiana Pacer guard Byron Scott dedicated his season to the memory of Bob Woolf.

"My contract with the Pacers was the last one he negotiated before he passed away, and I feel very honored in that respect," Scott said. "So I want to do something to pay tribute. Each time I put on a new pair of gym shoes, I write the name "Woolf" on the heel. He was not only one of the greatest agents who ever lived, but a beautiful human being as well."

KAY YOW
Women's Basketball Coach
North Carolina State University

Kay Yow is a winner on and off the basketball court. She rates as one of the all-time great women coaches with an overall record (high school and college) of 532 wins, 182 losses (.754 winning percentage).

In 17 years at North Carolina State, she has posted a 386-136 record, including four Atlantic Coast Conference Championships. Her teams have won five ACC regular season championships. Equally impressive, she has achieved a graduation rate of over 97 percent among four year players.

Her athletic achievements are what legends are made of and the honors she has received too numerous to list. Highlights include leading the USA women to the gold medal in the 1988 Olympics. She was head coach of the USA National Squad which won gold medals at the 1986 FIBA World Championships and Goodwill Games, beating the Soviet Union in the finals of both events in Moscow, marking the first time in 29 years that an American women's team had beaten the Russians in major tournament competition.

Kay is a member of the Women's Sport Hall of Fame and the fifth woman ever inducted into the North Carolina Sport Hall of Fame. In 1990, she was named Converse/WBCA Coach of the Year and District III Coach of the Year. The Fellowship of Christian Athletes named her Coach of the Year in 1989.

Off the court, she is involved in numerous associations. She's been a tireless cancer crusader since undergoing a mastectomy and is the recipient of the Outstanding Volunteer Award from the Lineburger Cancer Research Center.

She holds a bachelor's degree in English from East Carolina University, and a master's degree in physical education from the University of North Carolina at Greensboro.

Attitude Quotient

"We can't change the direction of the wind, but we can adjust our sails." Attitude is the key to success. Though there are many things in life which we have little or no control over, we have 100 percent control over the way we will decide to respond to our situations or circumstances. One hundred percent control—it is our choice! Thus, in essence we *choose* to succeed or fail.

To enjoy success we *must* have the ability to overcome obstacles and adversity. It is our choice to be negative or to be positive! We choose whether to make the circumstance one in which we learn or one in which we complain. We become a better person or a bitter person depending on the way we choose to respond to our situation. "When life kicks you, let it kick you forward!"

We are always faced with circumstance control versus attitude control. Do our circumstances control our attitude or does our attitude control our circumstances. Herein lies the difference between winners and losers—between ChAmps and chumps. The A (Attitude) is the key!

Be a winner. Winning is choosing to have a positive attitude no matter what the circumstance. A positive response will transform each setback into a step forward. Winning as a person is most important! Choose the response that will help you to find the winning way in any circumstance. When you are a winner as a person, you will have your best shot at being a winner in sport or any other area. A positive attitude enables you to give your best and be determined in your effort.

I have always believed that AQ (attitude quotient) is much more important than IQ (intelligence quotient). Always remember that attitude will determine your altitude!

Kay Yow

JEFFREY ZASLOW
Chicago Sun-Times
Syndicated Columnist

Jeffrey Zaslow has been a syndicated advice columnist based at the Chicago Sun-Times since 1987. He won the job over 12,000 other applicants in a nationwide search to replace Ann Landers at the newspaper.

Zaslow, then 28, took the job promising to be "off the wall" and "on the mark." His column, "All That Zazz," is a fresh departure from traditional advice columns.

He makes housecalls, visiting readers' homes to talk over their problems. Oft-times he skips the question-and-answer format to write essays about his readers' hopes, struggles and triumphs. And for common sense advice, he consults his Regular Joes Advisory Board—a cabbie, a hairdresser, a nurse, teacher, etc.—all named Joe, Joseph or Josephine.

Through stories told in his column, Zaslow has raised tens of thousands of dollars for a host of local charities. He also sponsors an annual singles party in Chicago that most recently drew more than 3,000 readers. Seven couples who've met at a Zazz Bash have already gotten married.

Zaslow joined the Sun-Times after four years as one of the Wall Street Journal's livelier feature writers. His offbeat, whimsical stories often attracted national attention. In fact, Zaslow entered the Landers competition to get a fresh angle for a Journal story he was writing. Before signing on at the Journal, he spent three years at the Orlando Sentinel.

Jeff was twice nominated by his editors for the Pulitzer Prize for feature writing, and has won many other journalism awards, including the 1992 Peter Lisagor Award for column writing.

A Philadelphia native, he is a 1980 honors graduate of Pittsburgh's Carnegie-Mellon University, where he majored in creative writing.

He commutes between Chicago and Detroit, where his wife, Sherry Margolis, is a TV news anchor with WJBK, the CBS affiliate. The couple married on July 4, 1987. They have two daughters, Jordan and Alexandria.

Resist Coasting

From the moment I learned how to scrawl my name, I always wanted to be a writer. No other occupation ever appealed to me. I was so enthusiastic about writing that I had articles published in local newspapers starting at age ten. I even won a $500 prize in a poetry contest when I was 14. It was the most exciting moment of my childhood.

And yet, like most kids, I wasn't disciplined enough. I liked writing more than reading. My mother, a gifted writer herself, would tell me that you improve your skills and broaden your world by reading the works of great authors. I didn't take her message to heart. I was too often satisfied reading Cliff Notes, or, skimming the classics. Still, my teachers were impressed with my writing. But, I was getting by on raw talent, rather than on hard work.

In eleventh grade, I announced that I wanted to major in creative writing in college. My parents were supportive, even though they feared I'd have trouble earning a living with such a degree. Then, one day, I brought home a report card showing that for the third straight marking period, I'd received a B in English. My mother was not pleased.

She told me she didn't care if I didn't get A's in math and science. But here I was, planning to make writing my life's work, and having the talent to do so. Yet, I was not willing to work hard enough to get A's in English. If I wanted to succeed as a writer, she said, I'd better start applying myself in English class. Of course, she was right. I'd been coasting. You don't make it to the top by coasting.

By the time I got to Carnegie-Mellon University, I'd vowed that I wouldn't be satisfied with anything lower than an A in any English class. My work ethic in those courses carried over to my other subjects. I got A's in almost every course.

I've come to realize that my mother's advice had great value. You don't have to be a scholar in every subject. But, if you dream of being a doctor, you'd better get high marks in science. If you want to someday run for office, apply yourself in social studies classes. Know your strengths and interests and work hard in those areas.

It might be easy to coast, but, you'll have a tough time getting where you want to go if you do. Thanks, Mom, for setting me straight.

PETER ZOLLO
President
Teenage Research Unlimited

Peter Zollo co-founded Teenage Research Unlimited (TRU) in 1982 as the first market research firm specializing in teenagers.

Since then, TRU has become the country's leader in youth research, providing services to more companies than any other firm. In 1993, Zollo launched Kids Research Unlimited, the firm's youngest division.

Peter has appeared before countless industry and corporate groups in his role as teen expert. He is also widely sought after as a research moderator for focus groups and to conduct in-depth interviews for clients.

Widely published, he has appeared on numerous network news programs, including "The CBS Evening News With Dan Rather," "Real Life With Jane Pauley," "Good Morning America" and "The CNN Morning News."

TRU's clients account for about one-quarter of the Fortune 500. Companies like Pepsi-Cola, Coca-Cola, Frito-Lay, Levi Strauss, MTV, Helene Curtis, Procter & Gamble, Rolling Stone Magazine, AT&T, M&M Mars, just to name a few, rely on Peter's research in creating advertising and products for young people.

Zollo was recently named the first chairperson of the Advertising Research Foundation's new teen subcommittee and is currently writing a book on the teen market due out next winter.

Peter took a hiatus from TRU for a three-year period in the mid-80's, during which time he and a college friend, Jay Silverman, created one of the country's fastest-growing board game companies—despite having no inside knowledge of the toy business. In fact, their Trivia-Sense Cards was the hottest selling game in many of the nation's top retailers for a short period of time.

The Present Is the Greatest

I may be unique among the contributors to this book in that my work is entirely devoted to finding out what teenagers think and sharing this knowledge with others (who happen to be adults). This book gives me the rare opportunity, then, to share a little of what I've learned with teenagers themselves.

Much of what I discover about people your age is encouraging, but much is also troubling. One finding which my clients find particularly important is that three-fourths of teenagers agree with the statement: "I always try to have as much fun as I possibly can—I don't know what the future holds and I don't care what others think.

Thinking back on my older teen years, I can really relate to this attitude. I felt that these were life's greatest years—lots of independence and no adult responsibilities. So, these were the years to enjoy full out, with little regard for the future. As an adult, I now understand that as important as it is for each individual to fully enjoy her or his teen years, this enjoyment can't come at the expense of future health or happiness.

Too many teenagers I talk with feel they're invincible and, therefore, they become involved in high-risk behavior which threaten their future. For example, for the past three years teens we've surveyed have named AIDS as the social issue about which they're personally most concerned. On the surface, this sounds like teens understand the seriousness of this disease. Other research we conduct, however, uncovered that—depending upon the situation—most teens will *not* use safe-sex practices. So, as much as teenagers intellectually understand that AIDS is a disease from which they're personally at risk, they still believe it won't happen to *them*.

Because of my work, I often think back to my own teen years and am interested to find how my perspective as an adult has changed. Just as when I was 17 and believed that the high-school years had to be the best life could offer, I've continued to believe the same about whatever happens to be my current age. I remember believing nothing could be better than being in college ... that nothing could be better than first being out of college and being on your own ... that nothing could be better than being young and married ... that nothing could be better than having young children.

Now, my kids are aged 6, 8 and 10, and, again, I can't imagine life ever being more enjoyable or more precious. I hope as my family and I continue to age, my perspective continues to remain the same; the present is the greatest.

What I ask you to consider, then, is that your adult years can offer you incredible excitement and fulfillment. But first, to even have a

(Continued on Page 314)

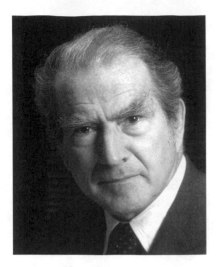

E.R. ZUMWALT, JR.
Admiral, U.S. Navy (Ret.)

Admiral Elmo Russell Zumwalt, Jr., was Chief of Naval Operations and a member of the Joint Chiefs of Staff from 1970 to 1974. He is currently president of Admiral Zumwalt and Consultants, Inc., a consulting firm in the fields of management, energy, health care, overseas business operations, foreign and defense policy, and strategic planning.

A cum laude graduate of the United States Naval Academy, at age 44 he became the youngest officer ever promoted to rear admiral. At 49, he became the youngest four-star admiral in U.S. history. He was promoted over 35 senior admirals to become the youngest man ever to serve as Chief of Naval Operations.

Admiral Zumwalt initiated wide-ranging reforms and is credited with revitalizing the Navy and making service careers much more attractive. As the Navy's senior officer, he increased the fighting capabilities of the dwindling United States fleet by outfitting remaining ships with more sophisticated and efficient weapons.

Admiral Zumwalt was commander of the United States Naval Forces in Vietnam from 1968 to 1970.

Currently he is co-author of "Zumwalt's Report," a weekly column on vital current issues published in newspapers around the country. He has also authored two books. On Watch *recounts his Naval career and warns Americans about the Soviet naval threat.* My Father, My Son, *which he wrote with his late son, Elmo Russell Zumwalt III, is an account of their Vietnam experiences.*

Admiral Zumwalt has received honorary degrees from Villanova University, the University of North Carolina, United States International University, National University, Central Michigan University, and Michigan Technological University. He has been a visiting professor

Keep Trying

The essence of what I have learned in 70 years of life and adventure is that perseverance and drive are far more important than one's physical or mental capabilities when it comes to both happiness and success in life.

To me, the most important model with which to guide one's life is "if at first you don't succeed, try, try, again."

and guest lecturer at Stanford University, the University of Pennsylvania, Vanderbilt University, the University of Nebraska, and Whittier College.

He serves as a director on numerous corporate boards, as well as charitable organizations and not-for-profit foundations.

Admiral Zumwalt is married to the former Mouza Coutelais-du-Roche of Harbin, Manchuria, and has one son and two daughters.

FROM THE AUTHOR

I may sound self-serving, but, I encourage everyone who reads this book to read more books. That's a tall order in this fast-paced electronic age when tele-viewing, faxes, and proposed information highway, influence what we see and read these days. I assure you that reading good books will be of benefit throughout your life. Young people especially should cultivate this habit early-on.

Until my retirement, like most people, I was caught up in the busyness of life. While I've always loved to read, circumstances found me minimizing the time I spent with books. Once out of the workplace, the first goal I set was to read the entire Bible. I found it's easy to do. Most Bibles now include a systematic division of the books, so, by spending 10 minutes in the morning and a like amount of time in the evening, you will have read the complete Bible over a 12-month period.

Numerous people have told me they have trouble understanding the Bible. I refer them to a great book, My Utmost for His Highest, by Oswald Chambers (Executive Books). This book is not only a joy to read, it also gives one a better understanding of the Bible and will stir your faith, as well.

A little 62 page volume, *As a Man Thinketh*, by James Allen, has most influenced my life. Had I read this book as a youth I would undoubtedly have lived a better life. Fortunately, it came my way in time to influence my later years.

Allen, who remains almost unknown today, wrote the book in the early 1900's. It is still timely today and can be found in most book stores. He writes about the power of thought. His writing is suggestive rather than exploratory. Its object is to stimulate men and women to understand they are makers of themselves because: "Every thought seed sown or allowed to fall in the mind, and to take root, produces its own. Good thoughts bear good fruit and bad thoughts bad fruit." You cannot read this book without it having a profound effect on your life.

As my good friend, Charlie Jones, notes in the introduction to *You Can Do It!*, "You are the same today as you'll be in five years except for the people you meet and the books you read." He's right—have you read a good book lately?

Bob Budler

Tomorrow

If you have been putting off doing a good deed, or, in some way showing that you love your neighbor, now's the time to do it:

> He was going to be all that mortals should
>   be—Tomorrow;
> No one should be kinder nor braver than
>   he—Tomorrow!
> A friend who was troubled and weary
>   he knew,
> Who'd be glad of a life and who needed
>   it, too
> On whom he would call and see what he
>   could do—Tomorrow!
> Each morning he stacked up the letters
>   he'd write—Tomorrow!
> And thought of the folks he'd fill with
>   delight—Tomorrow!
> It was too bad, indeed, he was busy
>   today,
> And hadn't a minute to stop on the
>   way;
> More time he'd have to give others
>   he'd say—Tomorrow!
> But the fact is he died and faded from
>   view,
> And all that he left here when living
>   was through
> Was a mountain of things he intended
>   to do—Tomorrow!
>
>   Anonymous

Foreward (Pat Williams from p. 4)

What motivated the Williams to undertake this herculean child-rearing effort? Pat told World Magazine: "We simply responded to the need. Each person has his own hot button, his own cause, and adoption is ours." He quotes D.L. Moody, whom he came to admire during his early years in Chicago. Moody said: "This one thing I do, not these many things I dabble with."

"I think Moody was saying to Christians," Pat noted, "rather than just slither around and have your hands in many things and not be very effective in any of them, find out what your real desire is, what your calling is, what really turns you on, and then go for it—and really make a difference.

Nancy Lieberman-Cline (from p. 64)

NBC, ESPN and Sports Channel America. Her credits include the NCAA Women's Final Four in 1986 and 1989, as well as the 1988 Olympics in Seoul, Korea.

Nancy is currently vice president of ProMotion Events, Inc., a sports-marketing firm based in Omaha, Nebraska. She resides in Dallas with her husband, Tim Cline, a teammate when she played with the Washington Generals team.

Denton A. Cooley, M.D. (from p. 70)

societies around the world and a dozen fraternities and clubs. He is the author or coauthor of more than 1,000 scientific articles and several texts. Among his 45 honors are the Medal of Freedom, the nation's highest civilian award, and the Rene Leriche Prize, the highest honor of the International Surgical Society.

Paul Fullmer (from p. 102)

Active in civic and charitable organizations, Fullmer has served as chairman of the Junior Board of the National Conference of Christians and Jews in Chicago, president of the Notre Dame Club of Chicago, treasurer of its Scholarship Foundation for 20 years, board chairman of St. Mary's Academy in Nauvoo, IL, and founding member and chairman of Amate House (a young adult volunteer organization in Chicago). He is married to the former Sandra Clifford, an amateur golf champion. They have two children Monica and David.

Monty Hall (from p. 126)

chairman. In 1983, he received the prestigious Variety Clubs International Humanitarian Award.

In 1988, the Government of Canada bestowed on him the highest award that Canada can offer—the prestigious Order of Canada—for his humanitarian works in Canada and other nations of the world. Monty is married to Marilyn, a writer-producer, and winner of an Emmy Award as co-executive producer of "Do You Remember Love," a drama concerning Alzheimer's disease. The Halls have three children—Joanna Gleason, a star on the Broadway stage, who won the Drama Desk Award and 1988 Tony Award for the best actress in Stephen Sondheim's "Into the Woods;" Richard, a television producer in San Francisco; and Sharon, who is manager of development for BBD&O in New York.

Paul Harvey (from p. 130)

Freedoms Foundation Awards. He's been elected to the National Association of Broadcasters Radio Hall of Fame, and the Hall of Fame in his home state of Oklahoma. One hundred eleven of his broadcasts have been reprinted in the Congressional Record, more than those of any other commentator.

Congressman Henry J. Hyde (from p. 140)

Service Award, American Legion; Alumni Medal of Excellence, Loyola University School of Law; and Alumni Achievement Award, Georgetown University, just to mention a few.

Bo Jackson (from p. 142)

rehabilitation program to rebuild strength is his left hip. Bo returned to baseball with the Chicago White Sox and played an important role in their winning a division championship. He now plays for the California Angels.

Jackson and his wife, Linda, have three children. He neither smokes nor drinks, and lists hunting, fishing and archery as his hobbies. He's become a worldwide celebrity, not only for his feats on the baseball and football fields, but also through his equally lucrative career as a commercial spokesman. Bo appeared in an episode of Lois and Clark on television and has completed negotiations with the Fox Network for a movie based on his life.

Henry (Hank) Ketcham (from p. 156)

Playground in Monterey, California, brings enjoyment to children in the area all year round and has served as a model for similar parks across the country.

With a constant flow of new projects and the demands of a daily newspaper panel, Ketcham arrives at his Pebble Beach, California studio every morning at 8:30. He puts in eight-hour days on thepanel, working at least 10 weeks in advance of the publication schedule. Today he is aided by a secretary and two artists who work on the panel.

Ketcham's autobiography, The Merchant of Dennis (1990) provided a look back over the invention of his slingshot-toting tyke. Dennis the Menace: His First 40 Years is a paperback compilation of cartoon strips tracing the evolution of the five-year old mighty mite.

Richard E. Lapchick (from p. 166)

Lapchick, the famous original Celtic center, who became a legendary coach for St. John's and the New York Knicks. The elder Lapchick helped integrate the NBA when he brought Nat Clifton to the Knicks. Inspired by his father, Richard decided to devote much of his adult life to civil rights issues. Many of those issues have been in the area of sports.

The recipient of numerous awards, Lapchick recently received an honorary Doctor of Public Service degree from Bridgewater State University, where he also was the commencement speaker. The University of Nevada and Northeastern University will also present him honorary degrees in 1994. In 1993, he was named outstanding alumnus by the University of Denver, where he received his Ph.D. in International Race Relations in 1973. He received his B.A. from St. John's University in 1967.

Lapchick is married and has three children.

Warren E. McCain (from p. 188)

Warren was inducted into the Horatio Alger Association of Distinguished Americans in 1991.

He serves as a director of Albertson's, Inc., Portland General Corporation, and Pope & Tolbot, Inc., and is a member of the Board of Trustees, College of Idaho.

Tom Parker (from p. 208)

of his major contributions, prior to his early retirement in 1990, was his development of a resource center for his colleagues. He also created a staff development program that became a model for other Illinois school districts.

Tom Parker, age 56, died on August 22, 1991, a victim of cancer. In honor of his memory and contributions to education, the facility he started has been rededicated and is now the Tom Parker Teacher's Resource Center.

Joe Paterno (from p. 210)

Foundation and Hall of Fame's 1991 Distinguished American Award. He was selected as the 1994 recipient of the Ernie Davis Award, presented by the Leukemia Society of America. He also is the only four-time winner of the American Football Coaches Association coveted "Coach-of-the-Year" award.

Fifty of his players earned first team All-American rankings and he has sent more than 100 players to the National Football League. Two of this products, linebacker Jack Ham and fullback Franco Harris, have been elected to the Pro Football Hall of Fame. Ham, defensive tackle Mike Reid, tight end Ted Kwalick and running back John Cappelletti are Paterno pupils in the National Football Foundation College Hall of Fame.

Born in Brooklyn, N.Y. on Dec. 21, 1926, Paterno attended Brooklyn Prep and Brown University. The late sportswriter Stanely Woodward, described him as an athlete who "can't run and can't pass. All he can do is think and win." He's still doing it today.

Charlie Plumb (from p. 216)

A captain in the Naval Reserve, he was seen on television as an analyst during Operation Desert Storm. He lives in Santa Barbara, California, with his wife, Cathy, and their two children. Charlie is author of two books, I'm No Hero and The Last Domino, as well as audio and video tapes.

Dean Smith (from p. 253)

baseball and basketball there. He was a member of the Jayhawk basketball teams which won the NCAA championship in 1952 and finished second in 1953.

Smith was assistant basketball coach and golf coach at the Air Force Academy in 1958 when he was brought to Carolina by Frank McGuire. When McGuire left to coach in the NBA in 1961, Smith was named the head coach.

After taking Carolina to the NCAA title game in 1977, Smith was named National Coach of the Year by the National Association of Basketball Coaches. In 1979 he was selected the country's top coach by the U.S. Basketball Writers Association and Basketball Weekly. Medalist named him the nation's coach of the year in 1982. He won the Naismith Award this season as the top coach in the country.

Smith was inducted into the Naismith Basketball Hall of Fame in 1983. He is also a member of North Carolina's Sports Hall of Fame.

Smith has five children. Daughters Sandy and Mrs. Sharon Kepley are Carolina graduates as is son Scott. He also has two young daughters, Kristen Carolina and Kelly Marie. Smith's wife, Linnea, is a physician.

R. David Thomas (from p. 270)

Research Hospital in Memphis, Children's Hospital in Columbus, Recreation Unlimited, the Ohio State University Cancer Research Institute, and the Children's Home Society of Florida.

Thomas is a national spokesman for the White House adoption initiative called "Adoption Works—For Everyone." Profits from his autobiography, Dave's Way, *will go to the cause of adoption.*

The Eagle in Your Mind: James H. Amos, Jr. (from p. 27)

The first step in this process is becoming a person of "eagle vision". The eagle, with visual cells eight times denser than a human's, can see a dime in six inches of grass from a height of 600 feet. The person with eagle vision can see the goal far off in the distance.

Eagle vision people see what others would miss. Eagle vision people have faith and positive attitudes, refusing to sink into cynicism and doubt. They have faith and believe in the long haul. They soar, because they are people of dreams. Dreams—not desperation—move people and organizations to the highest level of performance.

This is the hope and power and challenge of renewal. It is also one of the lesser known attributes of the eagle. When the eagle's mighty wing feathers become heavy with dirt and oil and its beak becomes calcified and brittle, he retires to a cave or rock and, out of reach of predators, experiences a time of renewal. With its great beak the mighty wing feathers are plucked one by one and then each claw is extracted. Finally, the beak itself is smashed against a rock until it too is gone. Defenseless for a time, this magnificent metaphor patiently mends until beak, talons and feathers have reemerged—larger, stronger, renewed, restored to climb to even greater heights than before.

Embracing the eagle in your mind means setting priorities and pursuing them with conviction and determination. It is understanding that choices determine how high you soar, and knowing that you are accountable for your actions. Embracing the eagle in your mind means separating the lasting from the temporary, the short term from the eternal; it is the quality that produces greatness.

Keep looking up! Be an EAGLE.

There Is No Magic Formula: Gregory J. Butler (from p. 57)

Build Relationships—In business, as well as on the football field, you cannot be successful without teamwork. Working together toward a common goal is based not only on individual effort, but, just as important, on how well that effort is harnessed with the efforts of others. The schools we serve rely on the teamwork of their parents, teachers, principals, students, and Market Day associates to make their programs a success. Our company has been built on relationships, working closely with and for people.

Think Creatively—Think about what you're doing every day. Develop new ideas and act on them. Making something work better is a natural extension of creativity. Innovation and filling a need, are at the heart of creativity. Whether making schools available for community use in the evenings and on weekends or providing high quality nutritious food as a means to raise money for education, the initiative and achievement orientation that grow out of creativity are powerful assets in whatever you choose to do.

One closing thought: You can achieve anything you want to achieve, provided you set your mind to it. Set your goals, and then muster the determination and persistence to reach those goals.

You Can Do It!

Guy Butler

You Must Have Goals: Marva Collins (from p. 67)

"good" student "superior". I believe that like Pygmalion, I, the teacher, have the unique ability to make my students whatever I would like them to be. I believe that when my students fail, that I, too, have failed. I, in other words, am selfish in my teaching.

I consistently create the kind of student that I would like to have as my surgeon in a life-threatening situation, the kind of attorney that I would like to have if my life depended upon it, the kind of neighbor that I would like to have if my very safety depended on it, and the kind of citizen I would like to have if my freedom depended upon it. With this kind of attitude, there is no room for failure, and there is no room for mediocrity and excuses.

We tell our students that not to reach your goal is no sin, but to have no goal to reach is a sin. We tell our students when they give us a mediocre paper that if they could not give that paper to God, or, drop the paper anywhere in the world and be proud to say that it is their paper, that we, too, will not accept mediocre work.

Marva N. Collins

Use Your Ability to Reason: Michael W. Copps (from p. 75)

if it's combined with poor performance the complaint will never be listened to. Poor performance will over-shadow everything. He/she will not be promoted because of the fear that the poor performance will be repeated.

Do yourself a favor, perform well.

Michael W. Copps

Have a Role Model: William E. C. Dearden (from p. 79)

and girls, ages 4 through 18, and has over 6,500 graduates. It is still privately funded through the original trust.

What's the point of the story?

1. If Milton Hershey would have listened to his detractors in 1886 and abandoned his dream there would not be a story of success to relate.

2. He had the courage of his convictions, and believed in himself when everyone else gave up on him.

3. Early on in his business success he decided to share his wealth so that others could get a better start in life than he had.

4. Only in America under our competitive free enterprise system can success stories like this happen then and now.

Have a plan for your life—a dream—which you will not compromise, even when the going gets tough. Then, work hard to make it happen! It works!

Dearden

Principles for Productive Living: Dr. Arthur DeKruyter (from p. 83)

and discover that by trying again and again things can be accomplished that I thought were impossible. Never give up when you know that what you are working on is in keeping with your best instincts. If you succeed, you will be contributing something to make this world a better place in which to live.

Finally, I want to share a very rudimentary bit of philosophy. When I was young, I learned from my older brother one very simple bit of wisdom. He would often say to me, "If something is not going to matter two months from now, it isn't worth worrying about." I thought about that often. It helped me set priorities in my life. I learned to make moral judgements and to form work habits. I learned to discipline myself.

Ask yourself the question, "Will it matter two months from now?" If not, dismiss it. It is not worth your time, and it certainly should not soak up your energies for thought and for worry.

These five things I offer to you as simple principles for productive living. They will help you in life and give you a hold on some of the essentials which will make you a productive and happy person.

Find a Firm Foundation: Dick DeVos (from p. 85)

These are the guiding principles of Amway Corporation and its distributors, I would urge all young people to find a firm foundation in the principles of people who have succeeded in building lives truly worthy of respect.

The POSITIVE THINKING Balance: Eric J. Fellman (from p. 97)

Upon hearing my name, the second woman grabbed back her pen and said disgustedly, "Oh, I see you really aren't anybody!" Whereupon several onlookers began to laugh at me.

I didn't ask to be made foolish in front of a bunch of strangers, but, sometimes life does that to us. We must believe in ourselves, yet that belief must be balanced with deep concern for other people.

Once I was trying to get ready for a speech in front of a large audience and became filled with stage fright. I went to Dr. Peale for some advice on how to make a good speech and to lay out my fears. Two minutes into the conversation he held up his hand and said, "Stop right there; all I hear is you saying "*I* am worried, and *I* don't think, and *I* can't. *I, I, I,* you are so focused on yourself you won't be any good at all.

"Now, just get out there and look into the faces of those people and think about their needs. Then say a little prayer that something will come into your mind that will help them with their problems and forget about yourself. You can never make a good speech thinking about how you are doing. You have to think about that poor person on the back row who slipped in hoping to hear something to help them with how they are doing."

That is the magic balance of Positive Thinking, believe in yourself and in your ability to overcome problems and then take that belief and put others first.

Eric D. Fellman

"Ud' en Ud' en" Attitude: Bill Glass (from p.113)

It's the same way with God. You've got to get an "ud'en ud'en" attitude with Him. To humble yourself and say, "God I botched it ... I haven't done right ... I've sinned ... I need your forgiveness and your eternal life. I need the blessing of God the Heavenly Father through Jesus Christ the Son."

It's not enough to say I'm going to do better to an offended son or daughter. You've got to say directly to the hurt child, "I've been wrong, will you forgive me? I've really fouled up. I've been trying to teach you so much, I failed to bless you ... I need you to forgive me. Will you forgive me? I want to start all over and give you my unconditional love."

It's the same way with God. You have to confess that you've been wrong and haven't really trusted Him as Lord and Savior or haven't repented and asked Jesus to come into your heart. You need an "ud'en ud'en attitude."

The epitome of what life is all about is to get the blessing from God the Father through Jesus Christ the Son and then give the blessing to your spouse, children, grandchildren, other loved ones, fellow church members, and those outside the church. Everyone needs to constantly be getting and giving blessings!

Bill Glass
Phil 1:3

Something Greater than Self: Fred Grandy (from p. 117)

I plunged into my speech, took a few questions from the crowd, then feeling utterly defeated, headed for my car. I was approached by an 18-year old youth who thanked me for coming. He explained his father was fearful of losing his farm and if that happened his own ambition to someday be a farmer wouldn't happen. "It means something to us that you gave up what you were doing to come and get involved in our problem," he said, "I just wanted to say thanks."

That young man, whoever he was, taught me a lesson that night and I resolved to stay in the race regardless of what seemed like impossible odds.

My epiphany, my discovery, was that I knew I had to serve something greater than myself. Each of us, at some point in our lives, will have a similar epiphany—somehow, some way, you will be called to serve something greater than yourself. It may be your church, your community, or your country. But when you decide that you want to measure your life, not by what you've gotten but by what you can give, I hope you will work to leave this world a better place than you found it.

Try and Don't Quit: Lt. Gen. Howard D. Graves (from p. 121)

to great achievements: "Even youths grow tired and weary, and young men stumble and fall; but those who hope in the Lord will renew their strength. They will soar on wings like eagles; they will run and not grow weary, they will walk and not be faint."

Lovers and Leaders: John Haggai (from p. 123)

years after His death and resurrection, He has a far larger following than any mere political leader. So when He says, "Greater love has no one than this, to lay down his life for his friends," I, for one, take Him seriously.

Never Stop Learning: T. Marshall Hahn, Jr. (from p. 125)

Our future leaders can not afford to breathe a sigh of relief upon graduation and figure that their learning days are over. Tomorrow's leaders are the ones who never stop learning. The people who succeed will be the ones who keep challenging themselves, exploring the world and their role in it. Education is a life-long process.

You can do it. Learn to question conventional wisdom, trust your own intellect, and recognize and appreciate the abilities of others.

T. ̃ ̃ ̃ Hall, Jr.

You Can Make a Difference: Theodore M. Hesburgh (from p. 137)

improved as they did it. Many of them continue to serve, here at home and abroad. One man had the idea, one man made it happen.

One could make a long list of single persons, men and women, who have changed the world for the better. It is still happening. *You can do it.!*

C.m. Hesburgh

Ten Commandments for Failure: Bonnie McElveen-Hunter (from p. 139)

Commandment 5: Thou Shalt Seek Easy Street. Seeking Easy Street is seeking a dead-end street. Work is a privilege. Through work and struggle we find challenge and personal growth. Celebrate the struggle!

Commandment 6: Thou Shalt Do It Alone. Never underestimate the value of teamwork. Lefty Gomez, a great New York Yankee pitcher, was once asked about the secret of his success. The secret, he said, was a fast outfield. Give others credit, no one succeeds alone. I've had a superbly fast outfield!

Commandment 7: Thou Shalt Not Be Accountable. Accountability often stands between success and failure. The ability to stand up when you are wrong, admit it, and accept responsibility marks you a winner, and distinguishes you from the people who fail.

Commandment 8: Thou Shalt Have No Sense of Humor. Many business situations in which I have been involved have been successfully resolved by the inclusion of some levity. We need more laughter in our lives. Learn to laugh, especially at yourself!

Commandment 9: Thou Shalt Give Nothing Back. Companies and individuals who focus on nothing but material and bottom-line success reap only those rewards and miss the reality that ultimately in life all we keep is what we give away.

Commandment 10: Thou Shalt Believe that Failure Is Final. Failure is never final. Failure is an opportunity for success in disguise. How we respond to failure determines what is final.

Daily we have opportunities through our choices to succeed or fail. What commandments will govern your life? What standards will you adhere to? What principles will you embrace? What values will you instill?

Ernest Fitzgerald, a Methodist bishop, asked these questions in an article written for Pace Magazine several years ago, in which he reminded us that we will all stand in a higher court than one where we are judged by our fellow man. It's a splendid thing to hear the shouts of acclamation coming from the grandstand, but it's even greater to feel the applause from within. The person who feels this inner applause, even if he has failed, provided he has given his all and played his very best, is a winner. Winners are not necessarily those at the top, but those who have come the farthest over the roughest road. Your personal victory may never make headlines, but you know it and that's what counts.

Bonnie McElveen-Hunter

Character Counts: Michael S. Josephson (from p. 153)

and I cannot do everything. But I am one, and I can do something. That I cannot do everything will not prevent me from doing what I can do." Don't let anyone ever tell you that you cannot do something of importance. A few hours working with people in need of help (and no matter how bad you think you have it, there are always those who have it worse) or for a political or environmental cause you believe in—anything that makes the world a better place is important.

It's like the young boy who while walking on the beach discovered that there were thousands of starfish lying helplessly in the sand. He knew they would die before the tide came back in so he began to pick them up and throw them into the ocean so they could live. An old guy laughed at him and said, "There are so many starfish out here it doesn't matter what you do." The boy held up a starfish and said, "It does to this starfish."

Start saving starfish now and make for yourself a more rewarding life than you ever imagined.

Michael S. Josephson

Let the World Come to Life: W. Daniel A. Lamey (from p. 165)

The skills needed to succeed in understanding the world and its impact on life are not that special, although the ability to learn and speak a foreign language is not something you should ignore. The same natural inquisitiveness that helped you explore a new house, a new school or a new town, will work for you just as well when it comes to another country or even simply an encounter with a person from another country.

I have always felt that empathy—the ability to deeply understand the thinking or situation of another person—is an especially important skill in my life. The ability to walk in another's shoes and really understand another person's point of view, can prove invaluable in daily life. The same is true in learning and appreciating the customs and traditions of people from other countries, with whom you may one day do business or with whom you may simply "do lunch".

It is a surprise for some to learn that many Japanese young people feel that they are not that "international" in their outlook and knowledge. They don't mean "international" in terms of naming world capitals or calculating the time half way around the world; what they mean is understanding what makes an American, Canadian, or French business person tick or react in a particular way. How do they approach a problem? How would they go about finding a solution?

To you, the world may be important only as a headline that flashes by on CNN or as a vacation destination featured in a travel brochure; but it is much more important than that. You may think that travel by itself will make you knowledgeable of the world. Without the right attitude, however, you might just as well stay home; with it, you may not even need to leave home.

What I urge you to find is the state of mind in which you will be open to the world outside; that you anticipate how it will affect your life; that you learn from the people from other countries whom you may meet from day to day; and that you will be ready to act on the opportunities which come to you as the world comes to your life.

I Dare You: Robert S. MacArthur (from p. 179)

Tony and Michelle are but two examples of hundreds of young people with "enkindled spirits" who are making a difference. Regardless of our accomplishments, each of us can do better to achieve our best. And each of us can do more to make a positive difference in the lives of others.

I dare you, reader, to seek the best that is in you and never be satisfied with less than your best. "I dare you, reader, to burn with a vision for a better world, and to become a spark for others. I dare you to become My own self, at my very best, all the time." You Can Do It!

Give Yourself a Chance: Mary Rose Main (from p. 181)

believed them. At that time, my thoughts couldn't stretch that far. Today, I believe anything is possible, and so can you.

What interests you? What intrigues you? What secret dreams lie hidden in your heart? Life makes many demands on us, and time passes quickly. Reach for your dreams, work for your goals, no matter what problems throw themselves in your path. Give yourself a chance!

Give God a Chance: Greg McMichael (from p. 195)

alter my state of consciousness. I got involved in my church and surrounded myself with fellowship and God's people. Finally, church became a time of worship as I had seen God's power work in my parents' relationship, as well as my own life.

2nd Timothy 1:7   "For God did not give us a spirit of timidity, but, a spirit of power, of love, and of self-discipline."

Be a Lifelong Learner: John M. Segal (from p. 245)

after I asked Jesus Christ to come into my life, did I find a way to sustain happiness and balance in life. The Bible is the greatest single source of learning I can recommend. Proverbs is the best business and personal success book ever written.

6. Be learning to love others. Loving another person makes us vulnerable. There will inevitably be times when love hurts, because there are no perfect people. But the potential rewards are enormous, and the alternatives—hate and apathy—aren't too hot. Start, if you can, by telling your parents how much you love them, regardless of their faults and imperfections; it will open your heart for greater love.

7. Be learning to pray and listen. Prayer is simply talking to God like you would talk to your best friend. When you have a problem, pray about it first, then think about it and listen for the answer. Norman Vincent Peale called this the "Pray-Think Formula." It is incredibly effective.

8. Be learning to have joy in your life. Always have something to look forward to; some small or large reward for doing your best, achieving your goal, or just getting through a tough day.

Learning never has to end. You can always grow your heart and mind. Choose to be a lifelong learner. YOU CAN DO IT!

John M Segal

Repay What You've Been Given: William S. Sessions (from p. 247)

We're deeply concerned about your willingness to serve this country and to give back part of what was given to you. I foresee great days ahead for America because of what you are and will be.

You'll recall that Winston Churchill was a man whose hour came during the great Battle of Britain. He was a man who knew more about defeat than victory; who had been out more than he had been in; who had been down more than he'd been up; who had been accepted only on an occasional basis; who was picked for his character to lead that great nation from the depths of despair to victory.

The following quote from Churchill exemplifies part of what I believe about character traits that you must have and you must continue to stress: "Never give in; never give in; never, never, never—in nothing great or small, large or petty—never give in except to convictions of honor and good sense." These are things of which great Americans are made.

So, conscience, determination and a strong sense of responsibility are things I think should guide your life. I have tried to let them guide mine. You will be called upon to undertake unusual endeavors. You will be called upon to do things that you do not want to do, but feel compelled to do. Yield to those compulsions. Decide where you will walk and decide that you will do so with honor and that your conscience will always be your guide.

William F. Sessions

Be a Great Boy!: John Silber (from p. 251)

but the search for fulfillment can begin at any time, and the rewards of the search are great.

I took many steps as a young man that might now be seen as wrong turns: I studied art, music, law, and theology before I settled into the study of philosophy. I did not see these studies as side trips or failures, but as means to discover who I really am. When I found that I lacked the talent to be a professional musician, I learned the hard lesson of when to let go of one dream and search for another.

The search for true fulfillment is tiring and difficult, and it is rarely down the road that leads to pleasure. But the search does follow the road that leads to happiness. If you listen to those whom you most admire and love, and try always to hear the voice of your best self, your contributions to the world will give meaning to the lives of others and thereby to your own.

John Silber

Hang In There: Rick Telanderl (from p. 267)

But hanging in there might really be the key. Through thick and thin. And when your time does come, grab everything you can. I don't mean money and power. I mean happiness. Happiness is the only success there is.

Rick Telander

"I Have Made It!": William G. Thebus (from p. 269)

with a personal greeting, one the embodies all the pride and glorious sense of achievement that bubbles over in those who have conquered hopelessness, the final words shouted exuberantly: "Merry Christmas, Mr. Hurst. This is Cleveland Davis, and *I have made it!*"

[signature: William G. Thebus]

Reggie White's Testimony: Reggie White (from p. 279)

Are you willing to admit your sinfulness to God and trust in Jesus Christ alone as the payment for your sin? If you are, express your heart to God. You know, someday Jesus *will* come back. I'm ready. Are you? You can be sure if right now you will trust in Christ alone as your Savior.

[signature: Reggie White]

How to Be a Winner: Roger Williams (from p. 283)

major symphonies from time to time. Symphony means sounding together. It epitomizes what teamwork is all about—together we can make beautiful music.

You'll find that life's not always fair, but, if you will do the things that loser's don't like to do—you'll be a winner, too!

[signature: Roger Williams]

The Present Is the Greatest: Peter Zollo (from p. 291)

future, you need to recognize that—no matter how you feel right now—you're not invincible. Nobody is. So, to make your teenage years truly memorable, you need to be around to look back on them. Second, try to understand that by working hard now—by dedicating yourself to fulfilling your potential—you can put yourself in the position of continuing to have "fun" your whole life.

There's no reason not to fully enjoy your teen years. But there's also no reason why your adult years can't be as much or even more fun. The harder you work now, the harder you can play your whole life!